FAT DOGS AND WELSH ESTATES
Fat Dogs series - Prequel

BETH HASLAM

Ant Press
Large Print
Edition

Paperback ISBN: 978-1-915024-20-6

Hardback ISBN: 978-1-915024-21-3

Large Print Paperback ISBN: 978-1-915024-22-0

Large Print Hardback ISBN: 978-1-915024-23-7

Copyright © Text, Beth Haslam, 2023

Formatted and published by AntPress.org, 2023

All rights reserved.

No part of this book may be reproduced in any form or by any electronic or mechanical means, including information storage and retrieval systems, without written permission from the author, except for the use of brief quotations in a book review.

Contents

Author's Note	1
Preface	3
Chapters 1 to 33	7
Traditional Welsh Recipes	477
A Request	485
References	487
Acknowledgements	503
About the Author	507
Ant Press Books	509
Publish with Ant Press	515

Author's Note

At the outset, I decided to change the names of nearly all the characters in this book. Why? Inevitably, because the events described took place long ago, I have lost touch with several of the folks concerned, and many have passed away. I felt it was courteous to use a different name to honour their privacy.

While the events I describe are true, I can't be certain in every case who was involved. I have given my best guess and ask forgiveness of those involved who recognise themselves but were not part of the scene in question. For the same reasons, my school stories are broadly based on similar characters I studied with.

A key aim was to offer fleeting glimpses of the rich Welsh tapestry of myths and legends. To do this, I have often used Pa's voice. He was a great raconteur anyway, so it made sense to use him as one of my storytellers.

Preface

L ooking back on my childhood has been an interesting experience.

Lots of memories are so vivid they could have happened yesterday. Others are like gently evaporating mists that leave a suggestion of their existence, though little else.

I touch on subjects that may not rest easily with you. They might engender strong emotions, wrath, even, but they formed part of the fabric of Wales and my life, so they must stay. There are no political or social messages in this book. I ask you to accept that this is the story of a little girl growing up. Just that. A youngster who, in her early years, assumes that her environment is entirely normal, and why not? Life is pretty straightforward when you're tiny.

It's a funny thing, being Welsh. Feelings run deep; we're a fiercely proud lot. Passions are expressed through song, poetry and prose, as well as actions. I'll tell you stories of battles and sporting heroes, myths and swashbuckling disasters, and I'll describe the undulations, seascapes and mountain crags of Wales. The colourful kaleidoscope that shapes my homeland. And I'll share how I grew up with animals.

For as long as I can remember, my life has revolved around animals, big ones, little ones, bitey ones and cuties. It didn't take me long to realise that I was destined to live with them forever.

Fat Dogs and Welsh Estates

MAP OF NORTH WALES (ARTIST'S IMPRESSION)

Chapters 1 to 33

Chapter One

'To be born Welsh is to be born privileged. Not with a silver spoon in your mouth, but music in your blood and poetry in your soul.'

Brian Harris

A sunny afternoon. In North Wales? It's less rare than you might think.

Ankle-deep paddock grass tickled my ankles as I stuck to the task.

"*Ouch*, that hurt."

"It will. You're not holding her correctly."

"I'm trying, Ma, but the rein keeps slipping out of my hand."

"Try again and hold it tighter."

"*Owww*, see? She bashed me on the nose!"

"That's because you're standing too close. You know how crotchety Kitty can be."

Ma was grooming our Shetland pony, Kitty.

Curry combs might be a handy tool for removing dirt from a pony's coat, but our mini woolly mammoth thought otherwise. Kitty disliked being brushed. To my cost, I already knew that some of life's smallest creatures come in the feistiest packages.

True to their name, Shetland ponies really do originate from the Shetland Isles off Scotland's northeast coast. The weather gets wild up there. Screaming winds scour the headlands, challenging nature's very existence. Some say that's why there are so few trees. The ones that survive are a hardy lot. So it stands to reason that the indigenous ponies will be sturdy critters.

Kitty stood at around 42 inches (106 cm) at the

shoulder. Small but determined. Actually, she was a bit like our father, although slightly less forbidding.

Shetlands may look super sweet, but it's a cunning disguise. Behind that cuddly façade dwells a crafty beastie with special powers. Let's start with attitude. They've got bags of it, intelligence too. Tack on a level of stubbornness unmatched by most equines, and they can be a challenge for any youngster to manage.

I was aged five-ish, and my job was to hold Kitty's rein for Ma. I can't remember how old our pony was; somewhere in her twenties. She was the matriarch who taught my big sister, Di, how to ride and mind her horsey manners. Now it was my turn.

A stickler for doing things properly, Ma said Kitty must have a thorough grooming before we could go riding. Our mother was English and exacting about everything. It wasn't until I was older that I understood why she was so, well, prim.

Ma had a Victorian young lady's upbringing and was educated by a live-in governess. 'Strict' was ingrained from an early age. Her youth involved helping to manage the family household and included running a kennel and nurturing various prized pedigree dogs and cats. Her natural affinity with animals extended to horses, and she quickly became an accomplished rider. Nonetheless, she was never soppy. There was no messing about with Ma.

With Kitty tidy, the next job was to tack her up. She stood stoically while I fumbled around, trying to hoist the felt saddle. Frustratingly, I was too short. Ma assisted and passed the girth under Kitty's belly.

"Take the strap, Beth, and try to attach it to the saddle buckle."

I yanked and hauled and heaved and stretched. I swear Kitty was sticking her tummy out on purpose. After an almighty effort, I connected and gave the girth another tug. Kitty took a dim view of this. Quick as a flash, she swung her head and bit me on the backside.

"*Argh!* Maaa, did you see that?"

"You must learn to keep an eye on what she's doing."

"That hurt!"

"Never mind. I'll tighten the strap, and you can help me fit her bridle."

I now had a sore backside, burning hands and a bash on my nose, but there was no point complaining. It was all part of life with our elderly pony.

As we slid the bridle in place, Ma reminded me of each fastener and strap's names and how they should be fixed. With my attention fixed on the confusion of buckles, I didn't spot the new tell-tale warning signs.

"Oww, my *foot!*"

"Oh dear, she is being irritable today," said Ma, pushing a triumphant Kitty so I could release my toe. "No harm done. Let's go for our ride."

Battered and bruised, I was plonked on Kitty's back, which was so broad it felt like sitting on a table. I hung onto her thick mane and waited while Ma disappeared into the stable. Out she clattered on Sioux, her horse, whose temperament and stature was completely different.

Our Irish cob was beloved by the family. Sioux had hooves the size of dinner plates and was generally enormous. Her skewbald deep chestnut splodges painted on a white coat were the reason for her name. I'm pretty sure I could have walked under her tummy. Not that she would have minded, Sioux was as placid as they come and possessed a maternal air. Ma dismounted, attached the lead rein to Kitty's bridle and hauled her into action.

The sun warmed our faces as we rode across lush meadows, the prize for our early efforts. Happy as a lark, I hummed and chirruped as Ma pointed out different plants while correcting my riding posture. Desperate as I was to go solo, the answer was 'No, you're not ready'. Disappointing, but probably sensible since I was still tiny. My time would come soon enough.

I'd love to tell you that our other animals had sweeter natures, but that wouldn't be true. Our gang of bantams was a handful. During mealtimes, they turned into a squawking mass of terrifying hooligans. And it was Di and me who had the job of feeding them.

The moment we appeared, beady bantam eyes locked onto the grain in our hands. We were stalked as avian tactics were calculated, but not for long. Within seconds the feathery missiles attacked, sending us reeling in agony, our shins covered in rake marks. They weren't our favourite family members.

We also had a flock of raucous geese with armour-plated beaks. They were excellent guardians but as badly behaved as the chooks. I remember laughing my socks off at Di being chased around the yard by a gaggle. And then they turned on me. Those beaks deliver a nasty pinch.

Despite the cheekiness of these characters, I was fascinated by them all. But there was an exception. House spiders. While I was never bitten, head-butted or clawed by one, something about all those eyes and those long hairy legs unnerved me. And our house was infested with them.

We lived in a large ramshackle house, which we shared with *Nain*, our Welsh grandmother. I remember little about her, except that she was a solemn, somewhat grim person. She seemed to sit an awful lot and read scary books, which I decided was very worrying and a bit witchy.

I'm sure *Nain* was a pleasant, refined lady, but even her appearance made me nervous. She permanently wore miserable, black garb, and tethered her iron-grey hair in a sad-looking bun. Her only accoutrement was the omnipresent lacy hankie she clutched. Also black. She smelled of lily of the valley most of the time, and mothballs on Sundays. I never worked out why.

While *Nain* used to have deep discussions in Welsh with Pa, she wasn't one for a cosy chat, at least not with me. So when I was addressed, it was usually a telling off for being too loud or naughty. My attempts at feeling persecuted fell on deaf ears.

"Di, *Nain's* been beastly to me again."

"That's because you are."

"What?"

"Beastly!"

"Am not!"

And so it went on.

Our Welsh grandfather, *Taid*, died when I was a baby. I'll always regret never knowing him. His career was dedicated to the slate quarrying industry. He was well respected in the community, and served as the Magistrates' Courts Chairman for our area. Yet, despite his public-spirited reputation, *Taid's* passions lay elsewhere. He loved the sea.

We had framed photos of *Taid* skippering his sleek Six Metre class yacht in races on stormy seas. The adventure thrilled me; I was convinced he must have been a swashbuckling hero. For *Taid*, the Welsh waters were in his blood. It passed to our father, and quickly became part of our heritage, too.

While he was born into a very 'Welsh' family for whom English was probably the second language, Pa did not have a Welsh accent. It was probably because he was sent to an English boarding school, followed by service in the Royal Navy during the Second World War.

While his accent did not give him away, Pa's looks did. He was a typically stocky, blue-eyed Celt with a shock of black hair. And faithful to his antecedents, he was relatively close to the ground. But what he lacked in stature, Pa made up for in personality.

Pa was the life and soul of social gatherings. He roared with laughter every day, sang like a bird, and had a bone-crushing bear hug. Pa was the best bear-hugger. He also had a temper to be reckoned with. Nobody was cheeky to our father, with the possible exception of his dog, Gus.

Our Great Dane, Gus, was nearly as tall as Pa. He could fill a room, and was the innocent perpetrator of mishaps as Di and I regularly toppled over him when he sprawled on the floor. A devoted disciple, Gus followed Pa everywhere, including to work. Off duty at home, he guarded us with a dribbly geniality. The best kind of childminder.

Being naughty was never ever a good idea with Pa around. Ma dealt with general mischief, but if we committed a grave sin, we would be summoned to his office at home. It was here where Pa's dragon-like wrath became truly formidable.

Access to the room was via two single doors with a little space in between. The first door was standard, but the second was covered in a felt soundproofing material. The fun *phloof* sound it made when pushed helped calm nerves as I plucked up the courage to enter.

Pa's inner sanctum was unnervingly impressive. Pictures of boats and slate quarries and dignitaries lined the walls. Crystal paperweights the size of cannonballs pinned down papers on the leather-bound desk, so vast it dwarfed Pa. Yet, somehow, he never seemed small.

His mariner's knife letter-opener lay casually on

the desk blotter, with his fat fountain pen alongside a roly-poly blotting arc. It looked like a seesaw. I waited, quaking in my shoes, while he finished reading a document. He placed it neatly in his teak in-tray and studied me with piercing blue eyes. Ominous.

Soft, menacing rumbles as the casters of his squashy Chesterton chair were pushed back. This was it. I braced myself.

"Explain yourself, Beth. What have you done this time?"

My descriptions burbled out in a rush of humiliated upset. But out they had to come. And there was no point lying. I tried that once. Never again. Pa was frighteningly perceptive, and I was a useless liar.

Pa sighed at my sorry account.

"I see. At least you were honest."

The inevitable barrage of shouts depended on the misdemeanour's gravity and would always be followed by a homily before the punishment was handed down. The ordeal, though truly dreadful, fortunately never lasted long. Chastisements varied. Being banned from riding for a week, extra chores for Ma and not being allowed to see my friends for a few days were favourites.

Life for Di and me in our labyrinthine home of intriguing rooms was fun. We had endless concealment choices for games of hide and seek, except for the disused servant's quarters. They were now used for storage, and even the access stairs looked too scary for investigations. In any case, Di assured me that armies of spiders lived up there. No-go. Obviously.

The ballroom housed the family's grand piano and an old gold-painted concert harp, which I latterly realised was appropriately Welsh. No longer used for its original purpose, this elaborate room had a whole new use for us children.

The parquet floor made an ideal roller skating rink. We dropped the stylus on a long-playing record and zoomed up and down and around in circles in time to scratchy music blaring from our ancient gramophone player. Herb Alpert and the Tijuana Brass was our favourite band. Nobody tooted better than Herb.

Stopping for a breather included a manic rendition of chopsticks on the piano, squabbles about who won the last race or twangs on a couple of harp strings before resuming our epic race series. With her sitting room next door, it was little wonder that *Nain* found us tiresome.

As a family of animal lovers, our indoor menagerie varied. It included a collection of terrapins with wanderlust. Much to Ma's exasperation, we'd often find them amiably pottering around the kitchen. We had several guinea pigs who, for some reason, hated each other. I found them curious, nicely fluffy, though disappointingly antisocial. Rodent-wise, Hammy the hamster was the best.

Many 'Hammys' touched our lives. Sometimes they were beige, other times they were cream, and once we had a chocolate coloured one. It didn't matter, they were always called Hammy. Despite mainly being asleep, when they woke up, our tubby cuties personified industry, busily whirring around on their beloved wheels.

Caged canaries trilled merrily in the conservatory. It was a sunny room filled with deliciously lemony scents, almost as tactile as Ma's furry-leaved pelargonium plants. Di and I loved sitting among the pots stacked in tiers against the warm windows, chattering to Ma while she tended her geraniums.

I was entranced by our birds, which were as yellow as can be. Yet despite loving their shrill song, I wanted to free them to join the garden birds that brightened our days. But Ma said 'no'. Cages kept them safe and protected from the elements. I was never convinced, although I understood the problems when it came to our cats.

Di had a slinky black and white cat called Lotti, and I had Thomas. I adored Thomas. He was a great big multi-coloured puss with a generous temperament and the patience of Job. Aside from being lip-smackingly mesmerised by the three yellow snacks flapping around in their cage, I couldn't fault him.

Thomas didn't mind if I stuffed him down the bed to keep my toes warm. Nor did he care if I hauled him onto my pillow for a snuggle. He was my comfort blanket when Di told me ghost stories at bedtime. And if I wanted a deep chat or an intrepid adventure in the garden, Thomas was always there. But there was one area where he let me down, and that was with spiders.

Thomas wasn't interested in spiders. He didn't want to eat them, swat them or lend a helpful paw when they sprinted in my direction. It was very frustrating. The worst kinds were the ones I met in the bath, which probably explained his reluctance to help.

Our bathroom was damp and freezing cold, which is not surprising since the only heating in the house came from coal fires. Stepping barefoot onto the icy lino floor should have been an incentive to jump into the hot bath. Not for me. I knew what lay in wait. That blissful moment of wallowing in a sea of bubbles with my favourite crocodile was usually ruined.

The iron bath was so huge I needed steps to

get in. It had a horrific hood at one end with an umbrella-sized shower head. Things lurked behind it. Regular as clockwork, out crept a spider. All eyes usually on stalks, though sometimes inset, legs poised – ready to dart. Big and hairy, they looked similar, which convinced me there was a cluster.

The top of my head was level with the bath's rim, so my foes had the high ground during encounters. With dreadful fascination, I gazed as my latest adversary skulked toward me. Options were limited. I could flick it into the water with my crocodile. I'd tried that. It landed on a froth of bubbles, which, to my horror, it used as a springboard to splat against the bath wall and shimmy up the side. This was when I realised spiders could scale sheer faces.

I remember being brave one non-bubble bath night. I courageously swatted my foe into the centre of the bath. It crumpled up into a crazy star, unfolded and whizzed across the water, up the enamel cliff face and escaped to sanctuary behind the showerhead. I concluded that spiders were indestructible, so I may as well learn to like them.

Our upbringing was pretty straightforward. We did as we were told, although we had our moments. One thing Ma couldn't abide was a fussy eater. I was that child who hated boiled eggs. Not that it got me anywhere.

I was that same child who sat sullenly staring at my rapidly drying yolk and soggy soldiers. Ma, ignoring my dilemma, did kitchen things, refusing to let me leave the table until I had eaten at least half of it. It was the same situation with minestrone.

"But Ma, why do I have to eat this stuff? It smells like sick, and it's got worms floating in it."

"Do not be rude. And remember, there are thousands of children around the world the same age as you, and even younger, who go without food. You must not be ungrateful."

"They're welcome to mine."

"Stop being impertinent. Minestrone soup is good for you."

I'd look to Terry and Timmy terrapins, back in their tank, for inspiration, and solidarity from the army of ants which permanently occupied the kitchen floor. There was none. Di suffered a similar fate with a hatred of eating bony fish. Even today, fish eyes leave her cold.

For Ma, time stood still during these low-grade traumas. With effortless focus, she allowed us to fester with minimal compromise. Inevitably, I would end up eating most of the egg, which went down like a bullet. The stone-cold soup was consumed too, sticky pasta included. For Di, it was the fish, bones 'n' all. Ma would have been an excellent trade union negotiator.

Going to bed was a similar story. There was no point moaning about our early bedtime during school terms. We had to go, and that was that. I didn't really mind; there was nothing quite like being snuggled up in bed with a hot water bottle, Thomas, and a good book.

As for schooling, it is often said that school days are the best days of a person's life.

Not necessarily.

The Wonder of Welsh Words

Merlen
This describes a small, mischievous species. Say it as it sounds with a rolled 'rrr', and you have the word for '**pony**'.

Chapter Two

'The Mabinogion and specifically the Four Branches, they have had quite an impact on Welsh literature and culture just as Shakespeare and Chaucer have on English literature.'

Professor Sioned Davies

Schooldays started well. Highcliff Primary opened every morning to welcome us: a gaggle of giggling boys and girls. The first ritual was always the same; a whole-school assembly presided over by our headmistress, Miss Bowser. She stood at the podium as we poured into the hall.

A study of youthful chaos, all it took was one stern look from 'the head' to send us into a frenzy of yanking up baggy socks and neatening pullovers. Pinching, nudging, tugging, we arranged ourselves more or less into class order and sat cross-legged on the floor. Expectant.

Smiles shone from proud little faces as selected children were praised for special achievements, a prayer was recited, and then we belted out a hymn. Music and song, it's part of being Welsh. But that wasn't all. A register was called, and each of us had to raise a hand when our name came up.

As a flibbertigibbet, try as I might to stay focused long enough to stick up my hand at the right time, it was a struggle. It usually ended up a bit like this.

"Jones, John"
"Yes, Miss."
"Jones, Bethan."
"Yes, Miss."
"Evans, Mark,"
"Yes, Miss."

"Jones, Beryl."

"Yes, Miss. Oops, sorry, no, Miss, that's not me."

"I am here, Miss."

"Thank you, Beryl."

"Jones, Beth."

"Yes, that's me, Miss!"

"I know."

"Selwyn-Jones, John."

"Yes, Miss."

And so it went on.

Primary school was where I first realised that most of us shared the same last name. Williams, Roberts, Evans and Jones were the favourites. Confusions were easily resolved by adding the person's occupation to their name. There was a Mr Roberts-the-milk, Mr Roberts-the-bread and Mr Roberts-the-blacksmith. Simple most of the time, though not always.

The limited number of surnames was tricky where school belongings were concerned. The lost property room was constantly stuffed with kit. Similar-looking bags, devotedly labelled by mums with the surname in capitals, followed by discreet initials, were often mistakenly picked up. It was the same with the uniform. I was forever going home in a hastily grabbed blazer three sizes too large.

I quickly settled into a happy routine and made lots of buddies, forming a special friendship with Siân (pronounced Sharn), a girl in my class. We had similar interests, including a love of animals. While our family kept ponies and horses, hers cosseted an assortment of donkeys. We both had hamsters, of course.

Siân's enchanting pets fascinated me with their ridiculously long ears and unusual markings.

"Any idea why they have that cross on their backs, Siân?"

"Not really. I asked Mum, and she said that donkeys are related to zebras, so maybe the cross comes from them?"

"They don't look very zebra-ish to me."

"Nor me. She also said something about helping to camouflage them."

"Oh. They look quite easy to spot."

"I thought so too."

"Still, I'm sure your mum is right."

We had many philosophical debates about our animals.

Occasionally, we were allowed to sit on one of the donkeys, but we usually helped Siân's mum with grooming and mucking out. It was a treat. In sharp contrast to Kitty, they were docile animals with velvet muzzles and kind, soulful eyes. They were grateful for any attention we gave them and loved being brushed. But positively the best thing about Siân's donks was the sounds they made.

Joyous hee-haws rang out across the meadows when we appeared with carrots and sugar lumps. They happily hee-hawed when we filled their water troughs, and they hee-hawed with interest when we cleaned their stalls. And sometimes, there would be a pause mid hee-haw when a donk was drawing breath. That's when you knew an extra loud one was about to come out. I'm sure they drove the neighbours crackers, but we adored them.

Primary school life was fun, learning was fun. Our classrooms were cosy, with windows overlooking gardens, and walls covered in world maps, baffling science tables and uniquely artistic masterpieces created by keen pupils. Teachers were smiley and filled with interesting information about most things apart from maths. For me, maths was boring.

We sat in rows at gnarled wooden desks, our legs dangling from fixed seats. The desks showed their age with grooves at the front and holes for inkpots. Dickensian. The day they gave me my first fountain pen was a thrill. It was supposed to aid in neat handwriting. That didn't happen. Instead, for years, I was covered in indigo-blue splodges.

The squiggles and scrawls on the desks' wooden lids riveted me. Strictly illegal, and woe betide anyone being caught defacing the surfaces, I was convinced the secret messages inscribed by children from yesteryear were important. Inevitably, I was dying to add my mark but never dared.

Our class sizes were small, so gigglers and note-passers were easily named and shamed. It was tough being a chatterbox. Tellings-off ranged from scoldings to being slapped on the knuckles with a ruler. Standing shame-faced in front of the class or being stuck in the corner also featured. Cardinal sins required a summons to the headmistress. Luckily I escaped those.

The school teaching techniques were based on chalk and talk. Reading, writing and arithmetic (the Three 'R's) were the fundamental disciplines, and much of our learning was by rote. None of this was difficult for me to grasp until it came to the times tables.

Academically, I was far more interested in the arts. I enjoyed the rhythm of reciting the times tables, though much to my parents' disappointment, never considered the mathematical side especially relevant. I didn't get a proper handle on problems either, being keener on the story behind them.

Geometry, I liked, but for all the wrong reasons. I was enchanted by the potential for creating intriguing shapes with the protractor and pencil. Sadly, my foray into fractions was dismal. But some subjects did grab my attention.

I loved nature studies. What could be more interesting than learning from books stuffed with page after page of illustrations, and fun facts about flora and fauna? And if we were lucky, we might go on a plant spotting expedition or bug hunt in the school grounds. And then there was Welsh. I suppose no school curriculum in Wales was complete without learning our native language. I'm not sure how much grammar I absorbed, but I remember enjoying the lessons.

Our teacher played a game whereby she held up a picture, and we shouted its name in Welsh. Ask me the name of apple or orange, or perhaps donkey or car in Welsh, and I can still tell you, but please don't ask me to include them in a sentence. Regretfully, my introduction to the language was short-lived.

Morning break time followed another ritual. Each of us was given a small glass bottle of milk and a biscuit. It was a government-funded practice that continued for years until Margaret Thatcher, a government minister, banned it in 1971.

Mrs Thatcher then served as Education

Secretary in Edward Heath's Conservative government. Her decision to stop milk for junior school pupils caused a national outcry. I'm not sure she ever got over her label, 'Thatcher, Thatcher, the milk snatcher!'.

Our dinky glass milk bottles had shiny silver foil lids. Any time from 9.00 am, we could hear the unmistakable sounds of Mr Roberts-the-milk's cheerful whistling as he chinked along the path with his delivery. He stole a secret wink at chortling pupils as he passed the classroom window, and deposited his crates of bottles outside. By break time, all sorts of things had happened to the contents.

In spring, the tops came ready-pierced by over-eager birds. The milk was often lukewarm in the summer, and during the winter months, the liquid was partially frozen and had to be parked against a radiator to help it thaw. The resulting mush of separated liquid wasn't appealing. No matter, a straw was stuck in, and it had to be drunk.

I remember little about mealtimes at school, but what happened after was always a mixture of huge pleasure and then tedium. With our teacher clucking behind, we filed out of the dining room in a mob of bubbling enthusiasm and yawns.

While our teacher settled into a chair, we grabbed blankets and sat cross-legged on the floor, gazing expectantly at her, waiting for our treat. Siân and I, always together, scooted to the front.

"What story would you like to hear today, children?"

"One from the Mabinogion, please, Mrs Griffiths!" we cried.

"Alright. Let's begin by learning about the book. Does anyone know where the stories came from?"

Huw's hand shot up.

"My da says they're all made up."

"He's right. Long, long ago, before the book was produced, people called Welsh bards journeyed across Britain and beyond."

"What are bards, please, Mrs Griffiths?" piped up Janice.

"They were important storytellers, poets, who often worked for kings. Their history goes way back to the sixth century. Remember, this was a time when there was no television or radio, so people were entertained through music and storytelling. They gathered around, just like we are now. Now then, you all know Mount Cadair Idris in Snowdonia?"

We nodded.

"They say it is the site of a giant's grave, which gave Cadair Idris magical powers. And, if you sleep one night on its summit, you'll wake either a bard or a madman!"

Huw was inspired.

"I definitely want to sleep on Cadair Idris and be a bard!"

"One day, perhaps, Huw."

Keen to continue, Siân asked the obvious question.

"What happened to the bards' stories, Mrs Griffiths?"

"They were usually memorised and often exaggerated as the tales unfolded. During the fourteenth century lots of these wonderful stories found their ways into two important documents called the White Book of Rhydderch and the Red Book of Hergest."

As Mrs Griffiths paused, we absorbed her explanation, wide-eyed. It was hard to imagine more thrilling books.

"It wasn't until much later, in the mid-nineteenth century, that Lady Charlotte Guest published your favourite book, Mabinogion. It is based on the famous White Book of Rhydderch and the Red Book of Hergest. That's why it contains all those myths about magical beasts and ogres, and the adventures of King Arthur and his knights. So there we are, children. Which of the stories would you like to hear?"

"Can we have the one about Rhonabwy's Dream, *pleeease?*"

We listened, rapt, exhilarated by each passage our teacher read. We had heard it before, but that didn't matter. The characters danced with our imaginations, engaging us as never before.

We groaned when the book was closed. It was time for our snooze. We dutifully laid out our blankets, heads filled with fantastic images, and snuggled down for half an hour's 'growing time' before the afternoon lessons.

Both Di and I attended the same school. She, being the eldest, was given a new uniform and new equipment. Hand-me-downs for me were fine, but the item I coveted was her black leather satchel. It had a flap fastened by straps and smart brass buckles. It could be slung, sat on, and used as a weapon. The bag was invincible, and I desperately wanted one.

When I finally reached the age to be given homework, I was unusually excited. It had nothing to do with the work and everything to do with having my very own leather satchel. Sure enough, one appeared on my birthday.

My satchel was brown, shiny and had a long shoulder strap. Loving it to pieces, I proudly stuffed Thomas inside and strutted around the house with his long-suffering head sticking out. If cats could sigh, Thomas would have.

In my excitement, I failed to consider the consequences of my magnificent gift. It signified homework, which reduced playtime, and generated new, unforgettable experiences.

The Wonder of Welsh Words

Chwedl
The 'ch' is soft and aspirated as in the Scottish 'loch' not 'church'. Add the following letters and you have the word, **'legend'**.

Chapter Three

'A Man without prudence is a ship without an anchor.'

Welsh Proverb

As soon as I got home from school, I wanted to play and chat about my day with Thomas. No such luck. I barely had enough time to give him a quick cuddle before homework began.

After a snack, Di and I were summoned to the table and had to stay put until our tasks were complete. Ma hovered with a duster, on hand to help if necessary, although we were expected to complete the work on our own.

At first, my assignments were easy. The only complications arose from illegible scribblings of the times table with a perpetually blunt pencil, and my story writing suffered from bouts of emotional leakage via a drippy fountain pen.

Di, huffing and puffing beside me, was onto more complicated stuff. Periodically, she sighed, gathered her papers and left the room. It wasn't until I got proper maths homework that I understood why the drawing-room door rattled from the shouting inside.

Pa loved maths and couldn't understand why we didn't. Di suffered a fire and brimstone reaction to her lack of interest in the subject. After a 'Pa session', she usually returned to the kitchen looking shell-shocked. My turn was to come, and I decided to be brave.

"Beth, why can't you understand this? It's simple!"

"I don't think so. I don't want to do it."

"Brace up, girl. That's an unforgivable attitude. I don't want to go to work, but I still have to."

"But what's the point of fractions?"

"We use fractions every day. Here's an example. After homework, you and Di normally share one of *Nain's* Welsh cakes, don't you?"

"Yes. They're yummy."

"They are. But the longer we sit here, the higher the likelihood is that Di will finish earlier and eat half of yours."

"That's not fair!"

"True. It also means that she might eat how much of the whole?"

"Three quarters?"

"Yes, exactly. See? It's easy. Now, sit down, and we'll go through this exercise together."

"Do we have to?"

"Sit!"

"Sorry, Pa."

"And stop looking out of the window. Kitty will still be there tomorrow morning!"

Using examples I was interested in, I grasped the basics but soon decided the more complex stuff was pointless. This was such a bad idea. Pa regularly exploded. I eventually escaped holding an exercise book bleached with rubbings-out and a puce father standing in the doorway. No wonder Di and I never took to the subject.

Our parents were stern about most routines, including going to church. No arguments. The family attended our local Methodist church service every Sunday morning. At the time, I did not know much about the denomination.

Methodism emphasises charity and support for the needy through good works. There is also a rich musical tradition, and Charles Wesley, one of the former leaders in the movement, was influential in writing much of the hymnody of Methodism.

Di and I had to wear our 'Sunday best', including matching woollen coats. They were scratchy, uncomfortable and heavy, even heavier in the rain. We probably looked like skinny versions of Tweedledum and Tweedledee, but our parents approved.

Our black patent T-bar shoes squeaked, and much to Ma's disappointment, my grey gloves were usually peppered with indigo ink splats. That ink got everywhere. Our parents were always immaculately dressed. *Nain* wore her special 'Sunday blacks', the ones which smelled of mothballs. Mothballs smell funny when they're wet.

Sadly, I didn't find the proceedings inspiring.

The church was always freezing, the pews were hard, and services interminable. An upside to the many, many prayers and psalms were the hymns. These were a good excuse for a boisterous warm-up. Thank goodness for Charles Wesley.

Our clergyman looked nearly as old as the church. An ecclesiastical chameleon, he was as grey as the walls with a shock of white hair and a grim cassock draped over coat hanger shoulders. He droned through the service until it was time for the sermon.

It took a while for him to reach the pulpit. He puffed up the steps, apparently spent when he got into position. But this was a façade. Filling his lungs with the glory of worship and true grit of a Welshman, Minister Jenkins imparted his words of wisdom in tones that ebbed and flowed like the waves of our coastal waters. Muddy.

Di and I were strategically jammed between Ma and Pa to prevent mischief. *Nain* sat devoutly on the end, fermenting. Lamentably uninspired, we knew a whispered chat was out of the question. Instead, we endured the tragic address by snatching sidelong looks at our parents, pointing at ladies with silly hats, inflicting secret sisterly pinches and silent giggles.

The end of the sermon was only

distinguishable from the beginning and middle by the tenor of our minister's voice and a touch of drama. With his voice, now ragged with exhaustion, he peered heavenwards with rheumy eyes and slammed the bible shut. He paused, momentarily enveloped by a cloud of dust. And then, with a wavering finger, he pointed at the row of numbers on a pillar. It was time for the final hymn.

Thrilled, we excitedly grabbed our hymn books and jumped up as the organist ground into action for the last hurrah. Soon the church was alive with the sounds of stirring music. Impromptu harmonies laced the main melody. It's a Welsh thing; we can't help ourselves. Voices like birds, and occasionally not, the celebration of song was what mattered most.

We poured out of the church into refreshing perma-drizzle, said appropriately sombre things to Minister Jenkins, and dashed home for our day's highlight. Ma's Sunday roasts were legendary.

It didn't matter what Ma cooked; every roast tasted delicious. She loaded our plates with Yorkshire puddings, which I quickly learned to drown in gravy and salt, just like Pa. If we were very lucky, we were treated to Ma's sensational chocolate pudding creation, which dripped gooey sauce. Calorifically off the scale, and completely delightful.

Playtime after lunch varied. We grew up at a time when reading, music, and board games like Monopoly formed our indoor entertainment. I don't remember watching much TV. As a born tomboy, I mainly wanted to play outside.

Our slate-roofed home stood on a hill overlooking paddocks and a body of water called the Menai Strait. This narrow tidal area separates the isle of Anglesey from the Welsh mainland and carries almost as many stories about its mischievous temperament as the dragons I felt sure existed. A notoriously treacherous stretch of the Strait is known as the Swellies. Its fearsome reputation dates back centuries. It wouldn't be long before I had first-hand experience of its precarious nature.

In years gone by, ferries traversed the fast-running waters. With vessels at the mercy of malicious tides and altering conditions, crossings could be dangerous. In the nineteenth century, to aid safer travel, two bridges were built to span the waters between the mainland and Anglesey.

Di and I were intrigued by the stories we'd heard about the Strait in school and asked Pa to tell us more.

"You both know about tides and how they flow?"

"Yes, Pa," we chorused, rolling our eyes. I didn't, but it was a shame to ruin a good story.

"There are differential tides at the two ends of the Strait, which cause powerful currents to flow in both directions through the Strait at different times."

Di wagged her head knowledgeably.

"What happens?"

"You've been through once, Di, but you may not have realised what you were looking at. If expert advice is not taken, these conditions can create unstable conditions. Can you remember seeing patches of circling water between the two bridges?"

"Yes."

"Those were whirlpools. We were sailing through the Swellies, one of the most dangerous sections. Rocks near the surface cause what's known as overfalls and whirlpools like the ones you saw. As you'll guess, they can be dangerous and occasionally cause boats to founder on the rocks. This was where a training ship called HMS Conway was lost in 1953."

Now we were getting to the juicy bit.

"What happened to the ship, Pa?"

"On that terrible day, the ship's officers ignored

the advice of local mariners. In a disastrous turn of events, the ship ran aground on flat rocks called the Platters."

"No!"

"I'm afraid so. And the situation worsened. As the tide fell away, the ship's back broke, leaving HMS Conway wrecked on the edge of the Strait. Traces of her remains are still visible today."

"Wowee. Can we see them?"

"One day, Beth, but now you both need to get on with your homework."

"But Pa, what about our end of the Swellies?" cried Di, desperate to avoid her sums.

Di had scored an ace. We knew he wouldn't be able to resist another seafaring yarn.

"Ah, well, just one more story, then. Navigating the Strait from the southwest Caernarfon end carries different risks. Frequently shifting sandbanks cause changeable depth variations. This spot is called the Caernarfon bar."

"So, what happens to them?"

"Good question, Beth. The sands change their height and position with the tides. There are many reports of boats capsizing or running aground on the Caernarfon bar. Nobody wants to be caught out there."

"Ooh, no," we gasped.

"One of the greatest tragedies took place in

1785. A boat carrying 55 people became stranded on the Caernarfon bar. Attempts to refloat the boat failed, and it was swamped."

"What happened?" exclaimed Di.

"The alarm was raised, and rescuers set off from Caernarfon. But, conditions were terrible. The combination of high winds, nightfall and the fear of running aground themselves meant the rescuers could not approach the sandbar."

"That's awful!"

"It was. The tide rose during that night and swept away those still stranded. Only one soul survived. Imagine that? And now, you two, no more stories. Off to finish your homework!"

"Smashing stories, thank you, Pa. I bet Beth has nightmares about shipwrecks now."

"Will not!"

I did.

As allured as we were by the infamous watery world bordering us, Di and I had lots to captivate our interest in the garden. Still very young and naive, we had absolutely no idea how lucky we were to live in such a beautifully appointed property.

A raised veranda wrapped around part of the house. For me, it was an intriguing feature, but not because of its architecture. Beneath the floor lay a mole kingdom. There were hordes of them, and they infuriated several household members.

Lotti, Thomas, and our gardener, Bailey, spent hours stalking them with limited success. I was pretty glad about that and went on stakeouts, hoping to see a pair of shovel paws pop out of a newly excavated earthy hill.

On the occasions that Bailey managed to trap one, he did something odd. The hapless body was pinned to the fence to deter incoming foreign moles. They stayed there for months and ended up looking like desiccated furry oven gloves. It all seemed awfully heathen to me.

Our rockery was an adventure playground, with little gravel paths winding around enormous boulders and teeny weeny plants. Beyond was a copse, with trees begging to be climbed and a soft base that magically turned bright yellow at the end of winter and dark cobalt in spring. I've loved daffodils and bluebells ever since. In the wood and meadows, we played cowboys and indians with friends and embarked on mushroom foraging missions. Ma's favourites were the type that grew to the size of footballs. We dutifully gathered several, which she cooked for tea.

Another section of the garden was filled with graceful roses. There was a unique appeal about this place. Our job was to harvest fallen petals for Ma to make into jam. More usually, Di and I wandered, wide-eyed, around the sensory wonderland, entranced by the kaleidoscope of colours and scents.

Blooms were velvety to touch. Different perfumes made us wrinkle our noses, we challenged ourselves, giving each aroma a silly name. Roses flowed from old urns, they curled high above us, winding over ancient wrought iron arches, and they festooned beds. Knee-high, shoulder high, even higher than that. There were big floppy petals, sophisticated neat ones and little tinkers.

Beyond the roses was Ma's sunken garden. It was her grand title for a boggy spot, which she dug out to house a vast old bath. This was another wonderland for nature observations. Frogs, toads, and newty type creatures lived here.

They hopped, croaked and slithered in and out of the pond, fascinating me and regularly terrifying Ma. I'm not quite sure why she ever started the project. And then we had a massive pyramid of sand. It was Di who told me all about its secrets.

"Can you see all those little leaves sprouting out of the sand?"

"Yes, what are they?"

"Pull one. I dare you."

"No, Di, I'll get into trouble!"

"No, honestly, you won't. Look, watch me."

Di grabbed the feathery stems at their base and out popped a fat carrot. This was a surprise.

"Cor, it's a whopper. I didn't know carrots lived here!"

"Yup, and see all those dark lumps next to them?"

"Yes, what are they?"

"That's all cats' poo."

"*Euuw!*"

"Yes! Ma doesn't know, so promise not to tell her. It'll be why our carrots are so ginormous."

We explored the outbuildings, inside and on top. Ma stored apples in an old bothy, which was a handy hangout when emergency refreshments were needed. The dairy was fun too. Di saved me on countless occasions when I plummeted off its sloping roof. It was a great sledging run.

And while our instincts were always to play, Ma had other ideas. She was a stickler for tasks and determined we should pull our weight from a young age. A chore I particularly hated involved a plant I quickly learnt to loathe. I had a valiant go at resisting.

"But Ma, I'm not strong enough."

"You must try, Beth. The more you try, the stronger you will become. Now, go and join your sister in the field, and come back at lunchtime."

Vanquished, I traipsed out to find Di and help her pull up a dreaded weed called Ragwort.

This tall plant has flat-topped yellow daisy-like flowers. It might look nice, but it isn't. Ragwort contains chemicals toxic to livestock and is blamed for the deaths of horses and other animals. With the risk of Sioux or Kitty being poisoned, the plants had to be removed.

Our weed-hauling career continued for years. At the end of each stint, we dragged ourselves out of the fields, looking like a couple of waifs with stinky green hands and wrenched arms that felt twice their original length. Less terrible was helping in the vegetable garden.

Under the watchful eye of Bailey, Di and I each had a patch to tend. Tomatoes and lettuces were my favourites. They were easy to grow, and there was something particularly satisfying about watching those tiny stems morph into blobby red fruits. The baby leaflets that gradually developed into large, floppy edible leaves were positively marvellous.

Bailey, failed mole hunter, was in charge of pest control. He kept slugs under control with his secret brew involving beer, and ensured the market garden gates were closed to prevent a chicken and goose invasion. But these measures did not affect his archenemy – the Cabbage White.

The larvae of Cabbage White butterflies were the bane of his life. He tried attracting insect-eating birds by planting masses of flowery herbs to no avail. Caterpillars steadfastly munched their ways through his crops. Poor Bailey was a slave to his brassicas.

As a last resort, in conference with Ma, Di and I were supplied with a glass jar each and given a penny for every Cabbage White we harvested. We did little to reduce the problem, but we earned extra pocket money.

Ma was a born gardener and stocked all the borders with glorious plants. We enjoyed the fruits of her labours indoors too. Our house was perpetually decked with vases filled with seasonal sights and scents. Floral displays were diverse, and often included roses, sweet peas with their delicate perfume, and the aromatic overtones offered by innumerable herbs. Di inherited her creative talent. Sadly, I did not.

Once the jobs were done, we could play. Our carpet-flat lawn saw many fiendish croquet encounters. One might imagine that this game, which involves hitting a wooden ball with a mallet through hoops, is tame. Not with our family. It was a battle where devilish tactics were employed.

We also played tennis, with mixed results. Everyone wanted to partner Pa. Conveniently forgetting he had a couple of tiny-tot daughters, he took no prisoners and played like a pro. To save Di and me from concussion, Ma eventually put a stop to his missile service, and he was reduced to pootling the ball over the net, underarm style.

Our family's competitive flair showed itself on the water too. Following the tradition of *Taid's* seamanship, my parents sailed a yacht called a Fife One Design. A sleek 24-foot racing machine specifically built for the local waters.

Every weekend during the season, our parents would go racing. Ma was a naturally talented helm, so she steered while Pa crewed. Once the race began, Pa barked instructions. He yelled when Ma was a split second out and ranted when the wind wasn't up to puff. After every race, they returned with blow-by-blow accounts of near misses, tussles for the best passage, wins and losses.

Their stories delighted Di and me. We were desperate to reach the age where we could join them. Sadly, their experiences were short-lived. Despite their winning partnership, Ma eventually got fed up with Pa losing his temper every ten seconds.

A sensitive soul with a strong character, Ma refused to race with him. It was a shame for Pa because he had to concede that Ma was the better helm, and they were a brilliant team who won many races. After that, our family outings on the water became gentle days out or fishing expeditions.

As an outdoorish kind of family, Ma was an obsessive picnicker. She prepared heaps of goodies for treks into the fields, onto the shore, over to Anglesey or just at home on the front lawn. This was a favourite spot for lots of reasons.

We sprawled on rugs with Gus, now a grizzled old boy, and the cats, munching on various yummy snacks while we watched the world go by. Yachts tacked past, zig-zagging to catch the breeze and larger vessels chugged in straight lines to open water. Closer to shore, we spied boats swinging lazily around on their moorings as the tide turned. All by themselves.

When I was a little older, we took picnics on rides. Ma bought a thoroughbred bay horse called Neenah. The Irish mare was gorgeous to look at, but she was very nervy and spooked at everything, including her own shadow. It fell to Di and me to carry the goodies.

Di rode Sioux and, to my delight, looked like a peapod perched on top. I had Kitty to myself. It came with mixed blessings. It's strange how physical pain becomes embedded in one's memory. I have a clear recollection of one such pre-picnic session that involved our old pony.

The Wonder of Welsh Words

Pili-Pala
Pronounced 'pil-ee pal-ah', this word meaning **'butterfly'** possesses a gentle delicacy.

Chapter Four

'Tell a gelding, ask a mare and discuss with a stallion. Pray if it is a pony.'

Unknown

Kitty had developed mild laminitis in her later years. This miserable disorder affects tissues bonding the hoof wall to the coffin bone it encases. In severe cases, it can be excruciatingly painful.

The problem for our ageing pony was overeating. She was a tubster. Kitty was especially prone to flare-ups during the spring when she spent all day scoffing fresh grass shoots. We had to manage her diet, which meant being stabled for part of each day.

This simple care routine, along with keeping her hooves clean, kept the condition at bay and the last bout had cleared up nicely. I could now ride her again. As I was about to find out, being stabled did wonders for Kitty's tummy but nothing for her temper.

Ma opened the kitchen door and smiled at the banks of cheerful daffodils. She had a plan.

"Come along, girls, it's a glorious afternoon; we'll go for a ride to the woods."

While Ma created one of her famous picnics we went off to prepare the horses. To save time, Di said she'd help me tack-up my old pony. Dying to get started, I sprinted ahead to Kitty's stall, completely ignoring my annoying sister's frantic yells.

"Beth, wait! Don't open her door until I get..."

Too late.

In my enthusiasm, I had forgotten that after being stuck in her stall, despite her dotage, Kitty might be feeling pretty frisky. The second I slid the bolt back, she began a relentless advance.

"Back, Kitty. Back. Stay *there!*" I squeaked, trying to block her way.

Kitty carried on regardless. This was a first in my relationship with our Shetland pony. I had been bitten, butted and kicked, but never slow-motion trampled before, and it hurt.

Di dashed up to find me embedded in the soil. Grabbing my arm, she hauled me up.

"Are you okay?"

"Nooo," I howled. "I've been squashed!"

Ma trotted up on Neenah.

"Di, hold these reins, please. Pull up your sweater, Beth, and show me where it hurts."

Snivelling miserably, I showed Ma the offending areas.

"Ah yes, I see. And Di, please stop *giggling*. This will have been sore."

Di lurked in the background, sniggering at the perfectly formed hoof shape appearing on my ribs. There was another on my right shoulder. I had been imprinted with Kitty's signature.

"Sorry, Ma, but they do look funny!"

"Perhaps they do, but you mustn't laugh at your sister's misfortunes."

Ma gently prodded, testing for full movement, and dusted me down.

"A little bruised, but you're otherwise fine. Good. No harm done. Now, let's catch Kitty, and next time, wait for Di or me to help you."

Still mopey, I trailed after Ma, rubbing sore spots, which to Di's glee, blossomed into yet more hoofmarks.

We saddled my old pony and set off. Passing through several fields, Sioux and Kitty plodded along amiably, ignoring Neenah's neurosis as she flinched at flies and imaginary ghosts. It's just as well Ma was such an accomplished horsewoman.

We reached the shore track leading to the woods. The beach, stony and inaccessible for horses, was bursting with minuscule life. Even from our position, we could see the crabs scurrying busily. It was an ideal spot to pause for a quick examination.

We tethered the horses and started collecting pretty fan-shaped and conical shells before checking out the rock pools for inhabitants. Engrossed, we picked through slimy seaweed, scraping at stinky mud to access new and exciting discoveries.

Brown shrimps blundered before escaping to the sandy depths. A sea anemone stuck to a rock, its brightly coloured, frilly topknot swishing in the water. As I deliberated how limpets managed to cement themselves to surfaces I spied one of my favourite creatures.

"Ma, I've found a starfish!"

"That's a great find. Well done."

"Guess what, Beth? I learned in school that they eat mussels."

"Ooh, how do they do that?"

"It's really weird. They use some of their arms and stick their tummy into the shell. They do something yucky which mushes up the mussel into soup."

"That's horrid!"

"Yeah, it's really, *really* gross. The teacher said something about juices and goo. It probably gets everywhere. I'll tell you more at bedtime. I bet starfish grow massive. Might even eat children."

"Di, stop it. You know how sensitive Beth is. You'll give her nightmares. Now look, girls, here's an interesting jellyfish."

"Dare you to touch it, Beth."

"Di!"

"Sorry, Ma."

The interest I had in jellyfish mercifully

replaced my fast-developing trauma about sci-fi starfish.

In this area, we had lots of jellyfish. I was fascinated by their gloopiness. Blooms of these amorphous creatures fed in the waters and some were caught by tides and washed onto the beaches. Pesky things they were too. We were regularly stung by tentacles or tendrils that had become attached to boat mooring ropes.

The compass jellyfish was a common variety. Its yellowish-white body is marked with brown splodges around the fringe and V shapes radiating from a central point. It genuinely does look like a compass. Ma drew our attention to a different species. I knelt to take a closer look.

"I like these. They're all blobby and shaped like the top of *Nain's* Sunday best hat. What are those pinky rings on its back?"

"I'm not sure, but they are distinctive. Do you both remember that whopper we found close to the boat mooring?"

"Ooh, yeah, it was gigantic."

"Humongous, bigger than Beth!"

"It was, and it was called a barrel jellyfish. Now come on, let's get on with our ride. We have a picnic to eat."

We clambered onto our mounts, stuffing shell

trophies into our saddlebags, and headed to the woods. The clearing we found overlooked the mysterious Strait. A backdrop of towering pines protected us from the breeze, but even they couldn't dampen another sound that animated so many of our days.

Lambs in a meadow farther down the track bleated insistently. They were hungry, lost or fed up and wanted their mums. Out came our rugs and Ma's promised feast. It was another blissful afternoon filled with chatter and squabbles.

Whilst a pastoral setting graced much of our home, the property had a completely different facet. Its heritage was aligned with many generations of North Walians joined in an occupation synonymous with toil, danger and great pride. Slate quarrying.

In the south, coal, known as black gold, was the lifeblood for many families. Here, it was sleek, grey slate. Our home's drive led to a small docking complex initially bound to the industry. During the height of the quarry's success, narrow-gauge railway wagons brought slate here to waiting cargo ships.

Eventually, the quarrying industry declined, and the docks slowly transformed into a pleasure craft marina. As children, we had no idea about the significance of this change and its crippling impact on hundreds of local families. For Di and I, there were a million reasons to find this nautical maze a thrilling place.

At one end was the dry dock with its cavernous workshop. It was a world of interesting sights and odours. The pungent mixtures of sawdust, glue and linseed oil pervading the interior were weirdly addictive. Emlyn was the master shipwright and we adored him.

Di and I often visited Emlyn with Pa. The covered work area was an ever-changing hotchpotch of intriguing rigging. Boat ribs looking like dinosaur bones, a mighty mast laid on workbenches, slats that would eventually knit together like a jigsaw to form a wooden deck. Occasionally, the hull of a boat would be in the dry lock, ready for repair or fitting out. It was all mind-boggling.

It wouldn't matter whether Emlyn was in the middle of a job by himself, or working with one of his men. The moment he saw us, his periwinkle blue eyes crinkled in delight. He'd down tools and saunter over with a broad grin that somehow caused no problem for the cigarette lodged in the gap between his two front teeth.

He always spoke in Welsh with Pa, which we didn't understand, but that was fine. There were many things about Emlyn to captivate our attention. His blue dungarees were perpetually covered in sawdust. His pockets bulged with extendible measuring sticks and sticky pots that dribbled gunk.

Better still, Emlyn sometimes stubbed out a half-smoked cigarette in his palm and stuck it behind his right ear. I always wondered if that yellow patch on his hand hurt, though never dared ask. His left ear gripped an oblong pencil. Impressive.

After talking to Pa, Emlyn tested Di and me on a few words in Welsh and then chatted to us in fluent English, always cheerful, always cheeky. And without fail, we pleaded to see his latest project.

With an indulgent wink, Emlyn beckoned us into his enormous workshop. He was never too busy to show us his masterpieces. Minute pencil marks, perfect repairs, an exquisite finish on a completed assignment. Even at my young age, it was easy to see how meticulous he was about his craft.

The other person I idolised here was the watchman, Idwal. He was a square-shaped man with snowy white hair. He wore black trousers, a black jumper and a black coat. His seaman's Breton cap was black, as were his big boots.

Infinitely old, Idwal patrolled the docks at a steady pace. Placid, peaceful, utterly dependable.

Every time I saw Idwal, I'd race up, chirruping greetings. He would stop, ease himself onto one of the iron mooring bollards and pull out a packet of Woodbines for a smoke. Deep chats weren't possible as he wasn't a fluent English speaker, but his expression and lifetime of warm smiles spoke volumes.

Occasionally, I went on patrol with Idwal. It was an important thing. We might pause to watch the iron bridge as it screeched and rumbled to perpendicular, enabling pleasure boats to manoeuvre from one lock basin to another.

The personalities of dock users varied in their behaviour. Some yachts glided smoothly through, skippered by nonchalant helmsmen having side chats with crew members. Others veered precariously from side to side at the hands of novices snapping instructions, getting splashed and using fenders as guides. There didn't seem to be an in-between level of competence.

We observed sailors alighting from their moored boats. Scaling the impossibly slippery iron rung ladders inset into the dock walls wasn't easy. Harder still without the proper footwear. We witnessed several skids and the occasional shed moccasin, lost to the greasy depths. Idwal watched them slowly disappear, and sighed.

In companionable silence, Idwal and I crossed the docks via old lock gates. Each had a skinny walkway, just wide enough for one person. By hanging onto the chain link guardrails and treading the gnarled timber planks, we traversed, pausing in the middle. Watching the mucky water churning below was fun and scary all at the same time.

Opening the ancient lock gates was equally mesmerising. Oily chains clunked and rolled on their stays, gradually wrenching the gates apart. Water gushed through the widening gap, revealing new slimy stuff attached to the lower sections; it was a marine biologist's gold mine.

The far side of the docks was backed by a steep hill and an interminable flight of even steeper slate steps. These led to the village, where Di and I were regularly planted on charity fundraising days.

Our parents were staunch supporters of charities, especially the RNLI (Royal National Lifeboat Institution) and RSPCA (Royal Society for the Prevention of Cruelty to Animals). As children, our job was to look angelic and rattle collection boxes on the street. It worked a treat.

The village was full of quirky shops. I never saw a note pass hands, but it was in the bank where we were given special book-shaped money boxes bound by a fat padlock. We treasured those, delighting in the satisfying jangle when pocket money coins were saved.

The butcher's shop black and white tiled floor was covered in sawdust, and had nightmarish animal carcasses hanging off hooks. It was a gruesome place. Weirdly, it was always filled with little old ladies. Ma said they bought chops, which meant nothing to me. Then there was the grocery store. Strange things happened there.

This was the place where Ma endlessly browsed. It was worth enduring, though, because Di and I were given a weekly treat. Oddly, Ma put everything 'on the slate' instead of paying. I assumed it was because she thought it unseemly to handle money. It was years before I learnt that it was a credit system.

The seaward side of the dock opened to a tidal harbour. A dinghy trailer often occupied the long slipway, ready to launch its occupants into a seafaring adventure. Our little motorboat was kept here.

We had friends who lived on Anglesey, directly opposite the harbour. Instead of taking the hour's drive by road, it was easier to hop in the boat and pootle across the water. There was a slipway to their home, so we didn't even get our feet wet. But for us children, some of the best fun we had in the boat were early evening fishing trips.

When the tide was adjudged suitable, Ma packed goodies, and we loaded the boat with gear. Nothing fancy. Di and I had a hand line each with feathers. Our goal would be to fish for mackerel or pollock, both prevalent in our waters during the summer months.

With Pa in charge, we chugged off on expeditions through millpond-flat water, searching for a suitable spot. There was something inexplicably inspiring about the greenish water passing below us, deceptively benign, guarding a thousand secrets. My imagination ran riot with visions of the mysterious creatures assuredly dwelling in its murky depths.

Our passage took us close to the Anglesey shoreline, near the magnificent stately home, Plas Newydd. Tree boughs with graceful branches tickled the water's surface; it looked like a riverbank rather than the seashore. Just how I imagined Wind in the Willows must be.

With rarely a soul in sight, it felt like we had the whole Strait to ourselves. Transported to a timeless existence, we listened to the haunting calls of curlews as we watched oystercatchers and redshanks wading on spindly legs in search of supper. And then Pa would tell us to prepare our kit. This was never a quiet process, although it was supposed to be.

Our simple fishing hand lines had several feathers spaced at intervals. The brightly coloured feathers and tiny shiny metal fish shapes rotated on a spindle in the water. Each had a hook attached and thereby lay the challenge. My mishaps were frequent.

"Paaaa, my hooks are all tangled up."

"I taught you to stow your equipment carefully, Beth."

"I tried, but they've got stuck in the cushion."

"Right, *right!* Di, take the wheel."

"Yes, Pa."

"Move over, Beth. I'll sort it out."

It was never that easy.

"H...how on *earth* did you manage to get all five hooks snagged in your cushion? Stand up and don't fall overboard. I can't remove them all with you sitting there."

Inevitably, Pa was seething by the time he had me unhooked. I was miserable, Di was smug as hers were nicely tethered. Ma handed out sandwiches.

There is something strangely calming yet exciting about fishing. Even watching the feathers flicker out of sight was oddly hypnotic. The boat moved peacefully through the water, not too fast, just enough for our feathers to spin and wiggle as a tiny fish might. With this came anticipation.

Whispers and quiet chat filled our boat as we trawled through the silent waters. We knew that too much noise might alert the fish. Snacks helped stop giggles and growling tummies, as did whispered advice from our parents on how to use our equipment to their best effect.

Our lines were secured to cleats on the stern. Sometimes we tweaked them to simulate movement and attract the fish, or tugged them lightly if the boat was stilled. A finger resting on the cord sensitised us to that imperceptible test nibble.

"I've got one. I've got a *bite!*"

"Well done, Di, now be careful, don't yank on the line; otherwise, you'll lose your catch."

"Okay, can I pull it in now, though? Ooh, it's tugging like mad!"

"Yes, try by yourself."

It was the same situation for me, although if the catch was a big one, I needed help.

A flash of green, iridescent blue and silver as the fish reached the surface. These were mackerel, voracious feeders in these waters. The catch was made. Pa removed the fish and cleaned the tackle before re-baiting if needed. We only took enough to eat, and the meals prepared by Ma afterwards were sensational.

Fun fishing trips, riding in the fields, playing in the gardens, and dock adventures eventually ended with a decision made by our parents. We had no idea what lay in store, and the news was shocking.

The Wonder of Welsh Words

Pysgota
Pronounced 'puhs-gota', this is the word for **'fishing'**.

Chapter Five

From the poem *Snowdonia*
...As I breathe the mountain air,
And gaze with deepest awe upon
This land beyond compare.

Andrew Blakemore

"**G**irls, we are moving to a new home."
Di started pouting.

"Why, Ma?"

"We have the use of it because of Pa's work, just like this house. There's nothing to worry about. We think you'll both be very happy."

"So every time someone gets a new job, they get a new house?"

"No, not at all. There are special reasons why it's part of Pa's work."

"What reasons?"

"You're far too young to understand."

"Aw, but we love it here."

"Yes, I know, but you will adjust. The subject is now closed."

"Will it have as many spiders?"

"That I do not know, Beth. Let's hope not."

The reason why Pa was given a house remained a mystery, which was annoying. Still, Ma had *that* look, and the conversation was over. Soon, excitement overcame anxieties. We started stuffing toys and books in boxes as we prepared for the move to our new home, Ty Fawr. Everything was going smoothly until we suffered two desperately sad losses.

Within weeks of one another, Gus, Pa's beloved Great Dane and our matriarchal Shetland, Kitty, died. Both succumbed to old age with the grace of souls who had fully enjoyed life. They relished their last days and passed away peacefully in their sleep. Despite this, it was the first time Di and I had experienced loss. We found it confusing, difficult to absorb, and, inevitably, it caused tears and misery. Pa was quiet for days. We knew it hit him hard.

Gus's absence in the house was palpable. It felt empty. Gone were the clatters of his clawed paws as he galumphed up and down the passages. Never far from Pa, our noble old boy had treated us like his treasured wards; a faithful companion and guardian of the family.

Although Kitty's techniques were less gentle, she taught Di and me so much. We had known these animals our whole lives. They were part of us, family. We missed them terribly yet accepted Ma's assurances that their time with us had ended. She quickly filled our heads with distractions about the new house, which eventually helped assuage our grief.

I instantly fell in love with our new home, which was like a Russian Matryoshka doll. Gardens and paddocks surrounded Ty Fawr, flanked by woodland and meadows, all protected within a walled farm estate. This, in turn, was part of an extensive tranche of land in Wales, all originally owned by the same family. I was convinced our house was its jewel.

Ty Fawr's comforting square shape was appealing. Large windows, arranged in perfect symmetry on each floor, invited natural light into rooms. The central conservatory porch stocked with fragrant plants was warm, exuding bonhomie to all comers.

Virginia creeper decorated the front walls; shades of green to deep red, strikingly beautiful all year round. I wondered whether it was climbable. I never tried. But perhaps finer still was the graceful magnolia tree. It was one of Ma's favourite plants.

The tall, goblet-flowered, white beauty grew against the front wall, daring to upstage the creeper behind. It flowered from the spring through to summer, lacing window frames with delicate petals. And when its season was done, the show still wasn't over. Blooms fluttered to the ground, forming exquisite bridal carpets.

My bedroom was directly above the porch. I clambered out of my window onto the flat roof on sunny days, and it was here where I had a short-lived foray into chemistry experiments. Heatwaves are rare in Wales, but the lead-covered porch roof was boiling when they occurred. In a moment of supreme inspiration, I decided to try frying an egg on the liner. Fortunately, it didn't cook. Otherwise, I might have met a sticky end from lead poisoning.

I spent hours snuggled on my window seat with a book and Thomas, getting side-tracked by the views. Who wouldn't? Beyond the gravel drive, there was a circular paddock. It was empty when we moved in. I dreamt of the day when it would corral my own horse, waiting to take us off on adventures. But there was more to this stunning view.

Regal mountains lined my horizon, often snow-capped, and always immense. They were mesmerising. The peaks formed part of Eryri (Snowdonia) National Park, a vast tract of rugged terrain extending 823 square miles (2131.56 square kilometres), the largest national park in Wales.

This was a place we learned so much about at school. Lakes, cwms and mountains were the settings for ancient villages, towns and Welsh magic. I hugged myself gleefully. Tales from Snowdonia have thrilled young and old for centuries.

Enjoying the dramatic view reminded me of a favourite love-hate myth involving a hound. The tale caused me horrible angst the first time I heard it at school, reducing me to tears. Legends like this were not for the faint-hearted.

It was Mrs Griffiths who first told us about Gelert.

"Now, girls and boys, are you all sitting comfortably?"

"Yes, Mrs Griffiths," we cried, desperate to get on with the post-lunch story.

"Well now, Prince Llywelyn Fawr for once had been hunting without his faithful hound Gelert. He returned home to a terrible, gruesome scene."

"Ooh, what happened?"

"Just a moment, Geraint, and I'll tell you. Blood was everywhere, and his son's crib was empty. He looked across the room and saw Gelert with his mouth covered in gore. Horrified, he believed Gelert had killed the child."

"That's *awful!*"

"It was, Janice. In his rage, Llywelyn killed Gelert, stabbing him with his sword."

"No!"

"Yes! Moments later, Llywelyn heard a baby crying. He ran towards the sound and found his son, concealed, safe and sound. And right there next to the little one lay a huge dead wolf. Shocked, at that moment, he realised it was his Gelert who had bravely defended the baby and killed the wolf."

"Awww, what a terrible thing to happen to Gelert!"

"It was, Beth. Prince Llywelyn broke his heart at killing his beloved hound. A gravestone was dedicated in memory of Gelert. It is in Beddgelert. We'll go on a school trip there one day. So there we are, children. Now settle down for your nap, please."

Finding a soothing Welsh myth to lull us into slumbers was often challenging.

We all found tales about King Arthur gripping, especially since many of his exploits allegedly occurred nearby. There are those who claim that the shadowy Llyn Ogwen (Lake Ogwen) contained Excalibur. Pa told us the story one gloomy day as we drove through the area.

The clouds were slate grey, matching the scenery. Mount Tryfan, towering above us, brooded on one side of the road, but darker still were the waters of Lake Ogwen. It's a strange, bewitching place. As we followed our ribbon road between the forbidding features, Pa pointed at the water.

"This, girls, is a very famous lake."

"Why? It looks cold and miserable."

"Cold, yes, Di, but on a sunny day, it's stunning. Now, you've both learnt all about the King Arthur tales from the Mabinogion, I imagine?"

"Yes, Pa."

"Some think that after the battle of Camlann,

where King Arthur died, Sir Bedwyr, his one-handed warrior, took his sword."

"Was that Excalibur?"

"Yes. He took Excalibur to the Lady of the Lake here in Llyn Ogwen."

I looked at the inky, fathomless depths with a new interest.

"That's exciting. Is it ever so deep?"

"Actually, it isn't. I know it looks that way, but it's one of the shallowest lakes in North Wales. It is only ten feet [three metres] at its deepest point."

"Ooh, and it's huge."

"You're right, Beth. This stretch of water covers 78 acres [31.5 hectares], which is big. They say that when he died, Sir Bedwyr was buried on Mount Tryfan."

I looked up at the austere mountains. It felt like we were at the bottom of a cauldron. Were there different tales about witches stirring a magical brew in the lake? Possibly.

The sun broke through clouds; rays flashed off wavelets, dazzling sparks of light. It reminded me of another question.

"Pa, what about dragons? Didn't red dragons live here too?"

"You and your dragons, Beth. They're so *boring!*"

"They are not, Di!"

"Pipe down, you two. One of the best stories about dragons comes from Dinas Emrys, a rocky hillock close to Beddgelert."

"Please tell us!"

"It's the legend of King Vortigern and the red dragon. The king wanted to build a castle on top of Dinas Emrys, but his castle walls collapsed every night. Angry, he asked the sorcerer, Merlin f..."

"*The* Merlin? Merlin, the wizard?"

"Yes, the very same, Di. The king asked for Merlin's advice. He told the king that his walls would continue to fall. And can you guess why?"

We knitted our brows, but no, we couldn't make any sensible suggestions.

"It was because two dragons were fighting deep underground, beneath the hill, and their battles caused the earth to shudder."

"*Cor!* So what happened?"

"King Vortigern and his men dug into the mountain and released the two dragons. With fire and fury, and brimstone and smoke, the red and white dragons continued to fight until, eventually, the white dragon fled."

"Hooray!"

"The red dragon returned to his lair in peace. Vortigern's castle was built and named Dinas

Emrys in honour of Merlin, and we have celebrated our Welsh red dragon since."

Ridiculously inspired, I pleaded for another tale.

"Alright then. Since we're driving through the area, just over there," he said, pointing towards Mount Tryfan, "close to the mountain is a second, smaller lake called Llyn Idwal."

"Like Idwal who works at the dock?"

"Yes. Exactly the same name. It lies in an area of glacial debris. At the top is a big dark fissure, a crack, in the rocks called *Twll Du*. Any idea what it means in English?"

We shook our heads.

"It means Black Hole, though it is commonly known as Devil's Kitchen."

Di squeaked.

"Brilliant! Why?"

"Steam is often seen rising from the crack, which looks like a chimney. When that happens, they say the Devil is cooking."

We craned our necks, searching in vain for vapour plumes.

"Ooh, that's great. It doesn't look like he's cooking now, though."

"Ah, true. And it's from the top of lake Idwal where druids hurled curses and lightning at Roman invaders."

Pa told top stories.

I would come to know some parts of Snowdonia well, but those stories and the breathtaking views were enough at this stage of my life. There was so much to explore in Ty Fawr. Nooks, crannies, indoors and out, we couldn't wait to investigate.

The Wonder of Welsh Words

Draig
One of my favourite mythical creatures. Pronounced as, 'd-rrra-ig', this is the word for **'dragon'**.

Chapter Six

**Bodnant Garden:
'I have no doubt at all that this is the richest garden I have ever seen.'**

Harold Nicolson

Ty Fawr's kitchen French windows invited us to enjoy the walled garden. Potting sheds had hidey-holes in corners and gnarled apple trees with giant limbs beckoned 'climb me!'. We raced up and down the lush lawn and played tag around podgy fruit bushes. It was our very own secret universe, filled with wonder.

Slate steps led to a maze of borders, vegetable plots and mighty Victorian glasshouses. Inside, they felt tropical. We played around the raised beds, cranked decrepit rusty pulleys to see what might happen, and rummaged in the old boiler room looking for important things. Hide and seek could take hours.

Ma was in her element and loved the greenhouses. Mostly. Despite having a tired air, their conditions were ideal for propagating a multitude of exotic vegetables and fruits. They also housed grapevines, which had been there for years. But there was a problem.

Spiders.

By now, I had harnessed my fear of the beady-eyed stalkers. Ma had not. We always knew if she was in one of the greenhouses by the squawks. For such a ladylike person, she could holler like a banshee.

We were helping Ma with the vines one day

when Di poked me in the ribs, silently gesturing at an unfurling blob. We watched, transfixed, as an interested arachnid slowly abseiled from a vine's limb. A hairy whopper. It momentarily hung, suspended above Ma's head. Then it landed, fairy-footed, on her shoulder. Now we were in a fix.

If either of us warned Ma, she would scream. We were awfully close for that kind of volume. Equally, we couldn't sneak off as we were on pot-filling duty. Hoping it might sidle down her back to the floor, we exchanged secret sniggers and decided not to say anything.

The spider, a sociable sort, had a different plan. Gathering all of its legs, it scuttled down her arm and paused on her gardening glove. This was when we learned that spiders can jump.

"Argh! *Arrgggghhhh!*"

As Ma screamed, the offending spider, presumably shell-shocked by the sheer noise, leapt off her hand and sprinted into the foliage. It was ages before she calmed down.

There were fewer traumas associated with the other outbuildings. We had stables, which were perfect for Sioux and Neenah. There were also kennels, which housed a couple of anxiety-prone collies. I loved these dogs. They belonged to the estate shepherd, who was also our neighbour.

Meg and Fly came from a long line of shepherding dogs and were dedicated to their task. They were friendly, although working dogs through and through. Most of Meg's movements were done at the crouch, and Fly compulsively rounded us up. It was Fly's bouts of neurosis that got him into trouble.

Fly could not stop chasing cars. It was the tyres. He had a thing about them. The problem was so acute that he'd latch on and refuse to let go. He had been slow-motion run over at least once and turned a cartwheel in time to the rotating wheel. Poor Fly was condemned to quarters at the end of each working day to save him from himself.

Having a family living next door was a brand new experience for us. The eldest of their three children, Gavin, was the same age as me. Cerys was a year younger, and Gwen was about three years old. It's just as well their mum was a nurse because Gwen had curious habits.

Aside from hating any form of footwear, Gwen was a specialist in sticking interesting objects up her nose. Usually food, she progressed to tiny pebbles, impressing us with the number she could shove up each nostril. It took Mrs Bolton ages to get them out.

Living with a shepherd next door was fun. As

spring approached, Mr Bolton's flock was penned close by. Waking to the plaintive bleats of forlorn newborn lambs, unrelenting *baaaaas* of mums rushing to help, and playful *meeeehs* when hi-jinks began were enchanting.

It was during lambing time when we occasionally took care of wards. Mr Bolton sometimes returned with lone youngsters to foster. After a crash course in lamb nannying, we helped out. I was astonished by the resilience of orphaned youngsters and loved working with them. Bottle feeding was the best. Plucky woolly mites with wiggly bottoms, they butted insistently, trying to hang onto the rubber teat.

Ma tutted indulgently at our latest charges skipping around the kitchen.

"They're getting under my feet, Beth. Take them back out to their pen, please."

"But they're cold, Ma. It's freezing outside."

"Oh dear, well, alright. But do keep them away from the Aga. I'm trying to cook."

The estate was also home to a successful pheasant shoot. The gamekeeper lovingly reared these animals, so lovingly that flying was a challenge. I suspect that just as many were accidentally run over as were shot by visiting 'guns'. Sunday meals often featured feathery roadkill.

I'm not sure whether the inspiration came from having two farm dogs in our midst or longing from our parents. But to our rapturous joy, two new pups joined our family. Paddington was a floppy English Setter, the apple of Ma's eye, and Monty was a steel blue Great Dane.

Our house echoed with *yips*, *yelps* and disgruntled *meows*, and a new set of chores for Di and I. Puddle clearance duties. Monty started life huge and quickly grew huger. He lolloped around on puppy Scooby-Doo paws, so big we thought the rest of his body would never catch up. Paddington had a different frame altogether.

Paddington was sleek and elegant. His long, silky coat was feathery and flowed when he ran. He started almost white, and to my delight, black blotches appeared as he developed – unbelievably cute.

Both dogs were gentle, although Monty's natural inclination to jump up with an exuberant '*I love you!*' usually ended in either Di or me being flattened. Paddington was far more graceful and quickly developed a habit we never broke. Paddy loved to roam. Now and again, he slunk off on a private jaunt. Fortunately, the estate was linked by a lattice of little-used private lanes bisecting fields and farm buildings, so he didn't come to any harm.

However, belonging to a bird-hunting breed meant he was often in trouble.

Mr Edwards, the gamekeeper, was a regular visitor on Paddy's away-days. With a long face and moans about his pheasants being traumatised, he'd haul a smiling Paddington, attached to a length of binder twine, out of his Land Rover. Despite Ma's efforts, she could not persuade Mr Edwards that Paddy didn't possess an ounce of bird-hunting instincts. He usually left in a huff, which sent Ma into a failed etiquette fluster. Paddy, on the other hand, was supremely relaxed, ready to plan his next stroll.

Ma tried hard to train Paddington. Off she'd march in her Barbour jacket and wax country hat, deadly serious, with her enthusiastic companion by her side. She'd stand in the middle of a field, tooting on the dog whistle, attempting to teach Paddy the nuances of recall. Sometimes Paddy responded. Often not. If an intoxicating whiff floated past his nose, the lesson was doomed. A canine airhead, he'd forget all about Ma and set off.

I joined Ma on several of these sessions. Watching her pupil disappear into the distance caused her great exasperation. With nothing for it, we'd set off in pursuit and eventually return with a contented Paddington, dead keen to give it another go.

One of my favourite people in the world was a regular visitor during this period, and he caused Ma even greater frustration. It was Uncle Barry. Both Di and I worshiped him. He regularly turned up in his clapped out Hillman Imp and filled our world with colour.

Uncle B had cerebral palsy, which affected his mobility and speech. Not that either of these piffling inconveniences held him back. Uncle B was an undying optimist who grabbed life by the scruff of the neck, worked hard and took every opportunity to travel. One of his chief pleasures was teasing his big sister, our mother.

One could usually hear Uncle B before seeing him. That unmistakable 'Haw haw haw' guffaw, followed by *'really*, Barry!' as the siblings fell out over yet another triviality. He was one of the happiest people I have ever known.

Uncle B was a gifted botanist who lectured at Cardiff University. Walks with him were marvellous. We delighted in discoveries, accidentally learning as he pointed out new wildflowers or herbs with healthful properties. Our outings felt like plant safaris and we never came back empty-handed. At the end of each expedition, we proudly presented our samples to Ma. Our spoils were examined and then stuck in the ground, cooked, or distilled. Ma made delicious elderberry cordial.

Uncle B also encouraged us to visit local stately home gardens. Plas Newydd on Anglesey, Erddig near Wrexham and Bodnant, which was a particular favourite. Haughtily refusing to go anywhere near his ramshackle Hillman Imp, Ma piled us into our Ford Escort and off we'd go.

A visit to Bodnant Gardens was awe-inspiring. I was bursting with questions the first time we visited this secret treasure.

"Why are the gardens so special, Uncle Barry?"

"Ah well, they're very old, even older than your Ma, haw haw haw."

"Barry, *really!*"

"A man called Henry Pochin established the gardens in the 1870s. He and his family filled them with wonderful plants collected by famous explorers. Have you heard of Ernest Wilson, George Forrest and Harold Comber?"

"Um, no."

"They were Victorians who travelled the world, collecting unusual plants. And lots of them ended up here."

"Wow!"

"One of my favourite exhibits is the grand laburnum arch built in 1880. The design is based on pergola walkways of the sixteenth and seventeenth centuries. They say it's the longest and oldest of its type in Britain."

"That's brilliant."

"I know. Imagine an arch nearly two hundred feet long [60.96 metres] covered in golden flowers. If we're lucky, we'll see it flowering today. But beware!"

"Ooh, what?"

"If you don't want to get bees in your bonnet, you'll have to duck. They have lots and lots here!"

Bodnant was breath-taking. Ma swooned at the magnolias – sensational beauties introduced from China in the late 1800s. Uncle B gave us a running commentary as we ambled among different sections. Another of his favourites was the riot of unique rhododendron hybrids bred in the garden from the 1920s. Their pastel shades were exquisite.

We were ravished by masses of exotic and alpine plants. Mixtures of shy and extrovert varieties, some peeped between rockery stones, others were dazzlingly gregarious, waving cheerily from urns and borders. And then we saw a collection of UK Champion Trees. I had no idea what that meant. Uncle B was the obvious person to ask.

"Good question. The Champion Trees are important examples of their species because of their enormous size, great age, rarity or historical significance. See that whopper over there?"

"Coo, yes. What is it?"

"If I'm not mistaken, that is a *Pinus Ayacahuite*, a Mexican White Pine. These can grow immensely tall, up to 147 feet [30-45 metres] and above. This one's a beauty, isn't it?"

"It is!"

"Mind you. You wouldn't want to be standing too close when one of its cones falls. They'd leave a nasty bop on your head, haw haw haw."

"Ouch, yes! How many champions do they have here?"

"Let's see," he said, thumbing through a pamphlet. "Ah yes, according to the Tree Register, the garden is home to around forty British Champion Trees, the best examples of their kind, and 130 Welsh Champion Trees."

"Wow, that's loads!"

"Haw haw haw, it is! Now, let's have a look at those interesting ponds. If we're lucky, we might see a frog snoozing on a lily pad."

It was always sad when Uncle B's visits ended. He and Ma bickered their way through his stay, Pa enjoyed his company in the evenings after work, and Di and I marvelled at his depthless plant knowledge and constant giggles. Happily, it was never too long before he returned.

As we settled into life at Ty Fawr, there was a new development in our future that would make life even more entertaining.

The Wonder of Welsh Words

Gardd
Since I spend much of my time here, I should know what this means. It's **'garden'**, pronounced 'garrth'.

Chapter Seven

'Wales has more than its fair share of ghostly goings-on.'

Amy Pay

Fat Dogs and Welsh Estates

Life in the Welsh countryside was safe. It was safer still on the farm estate. Employees and their families occupied the handful of houses nestled in enclaves. Neither cars nor homes were ever locked. Front doors were usually ajar, welcoming impromptu visitors.

We could roam where we pleased so long as we were back for mealtimes or bedtime. We made dens in the gardens and surrounding woods. Makeshift tree houses sprouted from the boughs of mighty oaks, and intrepid explorations took place across meadows. Then, one Christmas, our horizons widened a little more.

Exciting!

I woke up to find a lightish weight at the end of my bed. I gave it a toe-poke. It rustled. Obviously not Thomas, he was snuggled up on the pillow. The dogs weren't allowed upstairs, so it couldn't be them either. Still half asleep, I pondered for a millisecond. Of course. Christmas Day!

I can't remember when I first knew that Father Christmas didn't deliver the presents. It didn't matter. Every gift elated me, however simple. It started with the stocking left on our bed overnight by a stealthy parent. The routine was always the same. I pulled out treat after treat, marvelling at the number of goodies that could be squashed into one knee-length sock. The regulars included a tiny Christmas cracker, sugar mouse, walnut, a penny, satsuma, chocolate coins, and a teeny weeny book. Then there were the extras.

A favourite comic. Mine was *Dennis the Menace and Gnasher*, and Di's was *Bunty*, which was ridiculously girly. There might be a gift attached. Whizzers were fab. They looked like a tiny steering wheel and flew across the room like a boomerang. *Nain* was especially disapproving of those. The *Dandy* Thunder Bang came a close second, mainly because it made a spectacular noise. Brilliant for booby traps, never brilliant for parents.

A special pen, crayons, a slim Basildon Bond writing pad, everything wrapped. Alternating between satsuma segments and chocolate coins, I tore off the paper and examined each one. My remaining treasures were then re-stuffed, and I charged upstairs to Di's room for a sock-contents comparing session.

Once we'd scrutinised each other's gifts, we raced downstairs, hurdling sleepy dogs and hungry cats as we galloped into the drawing-room to examine the Christmas tree. Was my wished-for present there? I checked every gift. Disappointingly, there was nothing that bore the slightest resemblance.

Christmas morning progressed as usual. Our whined pleas fell on deaf ears. We were banned from opening presents until after lunch. The torment of waiting was filled with dog walks and morning chores. Mine involved jobs with the horses. Di helped Ma indoors and then came out to find me.

"Wanna have a snowball fight, Di?"

"No, it's not fair. You've got Monty on your side."

"He doesn't count. Go on, please…"

"Ow! That hurt. Right, you're in for it now!"

Hands frozen from heroic snowball battles, squabbles, sniffly noses and the tempting wafts of Christmas turkey eventually brought us scampering back inside. We crowded around the warm Aga with the dogs, daring one another to touch the boiling hot oven doors.

"*Ahem*, girls! For goodness' sake, get out of the way, please. And take those dogs with you!"

Ma made strange tutting sounds.

Finally, we sat down to eat, with Pa's new spindly-legged gramophone player blaring carols from the hall. Christmas crackers were ceremoniously pulled, and plates heaped with turkey, Yorkshire puds and seas of rich gravy. Battalions of vegetables were eased around the edge and we dug in.

Christmas pudding was next. In Pa's sole contribution to the feast, he drowned the dessert in brandy and set it alight. Blue flames soared in the air, singeing his eyebrows and horrifying *Nain*, who was convinced her paper crown was about to be incinerated. It was a top party trick.

Doorstep portions were delivered to our plates with dollops of sickly brandy butter and ladles of white sauce. There was the usual promise of a lucky silver sixpence hiding somewhere in the fruity depths, so we had an enthusiastic dig around. We never found one. I'm sure the whole thing was a hoax.

Desperate to open our presents, we rushed into the drawing-room and flopped by the tree. The anticipation was agony. Ma was a world expert at stringing things out. Eventually, one present at a time, we carefully peeled off sticky tape so Ma could re-use the paper. A highlight would be the giant hardback book both Di and I received from our Great Aunt Rhiannon each year. They were usually fairy tales and absolute treasures.

Gazing with wonder, we reverently removed the dust jackets and turned glossy pages, marvelling at the illustrations and accompanying stories. Publications of this quality would later become known as coffee table books. They were too big for most bookcases and too beautiful to hide.

Working through our gifts was a thrill, even though none of them answered my secret dream. Eventually, all that was left were two small envelopes. Ma gestured for us to open them. Assuming they were book tokens, we glibly unpeeled the flaps and stared, intrigued by the contents. Treasure hunt!

"Attention, girls. Read the question carefully."

"Okay!" we squeaked, not getting past the first line.

"Follow each clue, and the last one will take you to your main presents."

Main presents? This was unbelievably fabulous!

Off we sprinted, a mixture of quarrels and excited squeals. The clues sent us to every floor in the house.

Turning into rainbows, we ran through the coloured lights cast from the landings' stained glass windows. Then we tore down to the cellar and into the grimy coalhole, a creepy place at the best of times.

More clues had us hunting around the scullery, dining room, and then the long hall where we found one stuck to the telephone. We charged into the kitchen, falling over one another in our eagerness to reach the egg basket. There lay a blue notelet.

The clue went something like this:

Into the garden, you will go, to a hothouse where grapes do grow. Your presents are in a musty place, next to that machine with a rusty face... And be careful of the spiders!

"Greenhouse!" we yelled in unison.

Off we dashed, with two over-excited dogs pelting alongside. A sheet covered two objects in the old boiler room doorway. We hauled it off, and there they were. Two bicycles. Both had seen better days, but that didn't matter. They were rideable, and they were ours. Our Christmas wishes had been answered.

With bikes, there was no stopping us. Our drive led to a deer park, a prairie-like expanse of open land with a lane running through the middle. Deer had long since been replaced by crops, which rendered the cattle grids at either end of the half-mile stretch obsolete. That didn't stop them from being a death trap for cyclists.

The metal cylinders rattled and rolled menacingly under our bicycle wheels. Plucking up the courage to ride over them usually started with dares.

"See how slowly you can ride over the grid, Di."

"No, that's silly."

"Go on, scaredy cat. I bet you can't stay on if you go dead slow."

"Of course I can, but I'm not going to."

"I dare you!"

There was a deep pit below. Unless we gathered lots of speed, there was a risk of sliding in and somersaulting over the handlebars. We both suffered bloody knees and bent bike wheels from those rollers.

Enclosed fields bordered the park. An especially high iron post and rail fence ran the whole length on one side. Many years before, exotic animals including bison and bears were kept here. Now it housed a new species. For a good reason, entering this wooded pasture was strictly forbidden.

A herd of rare cattle roamed the meadowland along with their guardian, Baron, a colossal carthorse. We admired the compact, perfectly formed bovines from afar. They were commonly white, with black noses and black tips around their ears. Sometimes a black calf would be born. They were timid, beautiful animals.

As for Baron, he was absolutely vast. His forefathers would have worked the land, but his job was to look after his herd. He always seemed pretty wild to me. If we came close, he thundered up, neighing like a charger, massive hooves hammering across the ground. On occasions like that, we were glad there was a barrier between us.

The deer park became a bike race track and link to the estate farm buildings and home of another family with children of similar ages. The Griffiths lived in a rambling old manor house. It was stuffed with dogs, cats, and hamsters. Also gerbils, which were endearing but a bit dull. Outside, flocks of assorted fowl milled around, and ponies occupied fields close by.

With shared interests, we quickly became best friends, and the manor, which started life in the Middle Ages, became our second home. The family was always pretty cheerful about the situation, well, mostly, but I wasn't convinced. I had reservations. It was the ghosts. There were several.

I can't remember why. It was probably something to do with muddy boots, but we were never allowed to use the front door. Instead, we rode our bikes into the cobbled courtyard and entered through a cellar door.

Despite it being a catacomb of dark rooms filled with an infinite number of ancient tools and furnishings, it was probably the least haunted part of the house. After jettisoning our boots amongst the herd of similar footwear, we clambered up steep, age-bevelled stone steps to the pantry.

A commanding feature of the manor was its wood-panelled dining room and cavernous fireplace. It had a baronial feel and we children weren't allowed to enter. Many of the other rooms retained their original dark, uneven oak floors. The ceilings were low and saggy, which was awkward because Mr Griffiths was tall. Constantly bashing his head against the massive beams can't have been pleasant. The leaded windows had heavy iron catches, and lattice panes which made the world look quirky when looked through.

In contrast, the kitchen, with its brightly painted walls and lino floor, was modern and cheerful, and filled with the homely wafts of Mrs Griffiths' wonderful cooking. Upstairs was another labyrinth. I may not have a psychic bone in my body, but even I felt a peculiar atmosphere when I was up there alone.

Floorboards sometimes creaked without being trodden on, which was odd. Some rooms felt dank and prickly, while others were warm and cloying. Lights didn't always behave properly and sporadically flickered. Doors occasionally slammed all by themselves. The upstairs bathroom was for emergencies only.

We usually played in the kitchen or Clare and

Jane's rooms, but not Mark's. In his bedroom, now and then, the books in his bookcase were mysteriously reshuffled during the night. Never tipped out, just badly rearranged. Even the animals didn't linger in there.

The setting outside was just as intriguing, or creepy, depending on how one felt. The manor's chapel stood opposite the main entrance. I only have fleeting memories of it as a dark, sombre place with a level of gravitas even children instinctively respected.

Halfway down the drive, a yew tree hedge screened a sunken garden from view. Di had an opinion about these.

"See these yews, Beth?"

"Yes, they're just trees."

"Ah, but they're not *ordinary* trees."

"What d'you mean?"

"They've been planted on top of dead people."

"No!"

"Yeah, I read about it. In the olden days, every time they killed someone, you know, horridly, they stuck them in the ground and planted a yew tree on top."

I've never felt the same way about yews since then.

Steep granite steps led to a lawn with a pond, which had a fountain in the middle. Apart from the yews, this was a great place. We splashed around in the watery base, chasing damselflies and counting frogs leaping over lilies. As they bounded, their croaks echoed around the high walls protecting the garden. It was said that the apparition of a lady in Elizabethan dress appeared here. I was happier spotting tadpoles.

A flight of terraced gardens on the far side of the gravel drive had a different spectre. It was the only one I wouldn't have minded seeing. Among the Tudor formal flower borders, a ghostly greyhound padded. The story goes that he was lost during a hunt and had returned to look for his master.

I suppose it isn't every family that gets to chat about their favourite ghoul, but that's what happened. Sounding like a bunch of mini ghostbusters, debates took place about the merits of each one. Mark was underwhelmed with the greyhound, declaring his poltergeist and floating books to be far more interesting.

Exploring the endless manor buildings was always an adventure. Probably my favourite part was its disused stable block. Our first innocent exploration was a thrilling revelation. We had no idea that it housed a fantastic secret.

A splendid doorway off the courtyard led to a series of magnificent stables. Tremulous, we crept over the herringbone brick floor and shoved open the first heavy stable door. Wood panels seated vertically in the base formed half the interior. Above were railings with metal balls on top. A horse could peep through these. Even the back wall, with its green and white tiles, looked smart.

There were iron mangers and hayracks and tethering rings fixed to the back walls. Someone had evidently designed the stables to house much-valued animals. Mark returned to the passage and started poking around pieces of furniture.

"Wow! *Quick*, everyone, come here."

We rushed out to join him. And stopped dead. We stared at the substantial glass case propped against the wall, astonished. Clare started brushing away years of dust, and gasped.

"It is. It really *is* a horse's head!"

Half appalled, half fascinated, we joined in. The more we cleared, the more the form took shape. Inside, it was still pristine. Nothing could possibly detract from the noble air of what was once a magnificent animal. I was overwhelmed.

"Gosh, he looks so…alive."

"True. Not scary at all," said Di, wiping the wood frame with her hanky.

"What's his name?"

Mark rubbed the brass nameplate at the base, and gulped.

"You're *never* going to guess what. His name was Brigadoon, and he won the Grand National! I can't read the date properly, but it looks like eighteen something or other."

We gazed at Brigadoon for ages. Amazed, not frightened. It felt strangely humbling to be in the presence of this tribute to such an outstanding steeplechaser. It wasn't until much later that I learnt more about the history of the grand stable block and the cherished racehorses nurtured there. Brigadoon was its prize.

Still pre teenagers, we delighted in rummaging around for old saddlery, records, more evidence of racing and interesting horsey stuff. And dream about what it was like to ride from those stables into the grand courtyard on a world-famous racehorse. Our mounts weren't quite the same.

The Griffiths children were as horsey as us and the girls had ponies. This caused renewed pleas to our parents. We now lived in a place surrounded by fields. We could safely ride all over the place by ourselves. It was perfect. Couldn't we have ponies? Please?

No.

Our parents were resolute. Until we could ride competently and demonstrate proper care, there would be no ponies. We would continue to share Sioux under supervision. We were doing pretty well on the animal husbandry side of things, but they had a point about our abilities in the saddle. This led to weekly riding lessons at stables on Anglesey. We loved riding school.

Here, we learned how to school a pony, jump, and the rudiments of dressage. I say rudiments because it was never a discipline that interested me. I regularly got into trouble for forgetting the routine halfway through. Speed, and leaping over obstacles were far more exhilarating.

We rarely got to choose which mount to ride, but I had my favourites. We went on treks, riding through the lush countryside and learning about road safety. In the more advanced classes, we enjoyed gallops over fields with natural obstacles.

Our improving equestrian skills fuelled renewed appeals to have ponies. For a while, the answer was still 'no'. Our parents had a secret horsey plan up their sleeves, but they didn't let on. Instead, smaller animals gradually arrived.

A new hamster (Hammy two) was given as a birthday present. His cage was alongside Hammy's. Peering at one another with those tiny, sticky-out eyes, they had interminable sessions on their wheels, busily trying to out-trundle one another. Cute as they were, we were more enamoured by the chickens that came next.

Ma developed a passion for silkies, a breed

rarely seen in our area. They had fluffy pompoms on their heads, super-soft plumage and feathery feet. These features, together with their endearing natures, immediately stole our hearts. Coffee, Chocolate and Vanilla, so-named because of their colours, were like downy teddy bears.

Any worries we may have had about the dogs seeing them as tasty titbits were soon dispelled. Paddington didn't seem to register that they were birds and ignored them. The only danger they were exposed to from Monty was being accidentally trampled.

Silkies have no natural waterproofing, so their coop was in the walled garden to protect them from the Welsh elements. Mind you, they spent little time in it. Being a family who preferred animals to be free when possible, they mostly foraged around the borders and plots – and kitchen. Our lettuce crops were never the same after their arrival.

Another birthday brought Buck for me and Liza for Di. The Dutch rabbits had a white blaze on their noses and a white collar. Buck was a rich grey colour, and Liza was mainly black and looked like a bunny version of Di's cat, Lotti.

Brushing them, cuddling them, we played endlessly with our bunnies. They were sweet-tempered and long-suffering. And they became a solace when I suffered my first devastating animal loss.

The Wonder of Welsh Words

Cwningen
We loved ours. Try saying 'cooneegen', and you have the word, '**rabbit**'.

Chapter Eight

**Beaumaris:
'The greatest castle never built.'**

Anon

My purry boy, Thomas, died.

This was the cat who never hissed, spat, or scratched. He was the puss who endured the indignity of being carted around like a rag doll. Thomas, with his deep, soothing purr, was my comforter when I was sad and hot water bottle when cold. It was my Thomas who taught me how to be gentle with all animals.

I sobbed my heart out when he was gone.

I moped around the house, inconsolable for days. And it was my big sis who cheered me up. Scary stories were set aside. Instead, Di gently teased me, came out on dog walks and played with me and my toys. Eventually, I perked up, but it took a long time. I shall never ever forget Thomas, my generous, big-hearted boy.

Having an older sibling means that they often get to do stuff first. This included leaving primary school ahead of me. Although we saw little of one another except at playtimes, I have one enduring memory. It was an incident at Beaumaris Castle during Di's last year.

For me, the excursion was fab for several reasons. First, the castle was built, at least partially, by the infamous King Edward I, which gave me the excuse to quote his chortle-worthy nickname, 'Longshanks'. He was over six feet (1.8 metres) tall, which in the thirteenth century was pretty lanky.

As usual, the school visit was an excuse to ply us with information. Mrs Roberts, history buff, couldn't resist educating us about his activities.

"Longshanks, children, was the king who returned English royal authority after the reign of Henry III. He made Parliament a permanent institution."

Mary, keen as mustard on detail, piped up.

"What's one of those, Mrs Roberts?"

"Parliament? It is anything to do with public affairs. In his case, it was where nobles and clergymen agreed taxes and laws."

Mary, knitted brows, nodded sagely, still foxed like the rest of us. We waited for Mrs Roberts, hoping for an improvement in her story.

"But there were downsides to this medieval royal. King Edward was a cantankerous man. Does anyone know what cantankerous means?"

Eric, class swot, flung his hand in the air.

"Grumpy, Mrs Roberts?"

"Well done, Eric, that's right. Now, everyone, close your eyes and think of the grrrumpiest person you know."

Eyes squeezed shut in concentration. It was easy, Pa, on a maths homework day.

"Right, children, it looks like you have a suitable picture in your minds. King Edward was even grumpier than that! His men respected him, though he was often criticised for other actions, like his brutal conduct towards the Scots."

"Nooo!" we cried in mutual solidarity with our Celtic counterparts.

"Yes, I'm afraid so. His actions earned him another name; 'Hammer of the Scots'. His behaviour wasn't much better with the Welsh."

Thrilled and appalled, we urged Mrs Roberts to continue.

"The king launched many terrible campaigns against the Welsh defences. It began the symbolic act of crowning the heir to England's throne as the Prince of Wales. I'll tell you about that another time."

Mrs Roberts had ignited our interest. She increased it further by explaining that his warring behaviour left a legacy that we loved. King Edward had castle mania. During his reign, he was involved with the building of seventeen castles in Wales. Ironically, although created to protect himself against Welsh invaders, they became cherished country symbols.

I have always been fascinated by castles, and I was born in the correct country to fuel my fancy. Wales is a veritable hotbed of fortresses, featuring more castles per square mile than any other country in Europe.

As we clambered onto the school bus, my mind

was crammed with images of castle life. Dashing heroes thundering about on chargers, ladies looking like Maid Marion hiding in their chambers, and archers bravely defended their lords during skirmishes. Dungeons, murder holes and feasting halls, these were genuinely thrilling places, and Beaumaris Castle was one of the best.

The day of our excursion dawned brightly. As the school coach coughed into life, someone whispered the first line of *Ten Green Bottles*. That was it. The coach erupted into song. We were on about verse nine when we crossed the Menai Suspension Bridge.

You had to hand it to our teachers. Whenever we approached this overpass, someone felt compelled to remind us about Thomas Telford and his iconic design.

"Who can remember when the bridge was finished?"

"Eighteen something?"

"Good, Marcus. It was completed in 1826 and crossed the Strait at its narrowest point. And it was very famous at the time because it was the biggest suspension bridge in the world."

"Gosh!"

"Look up now, children. There are sixteen of these great big chains. They hold up five hundred and seventy-nine feet [176 metres] of deck."

"Could big ships sail underneath, Mrs Roberts?"

"They could, Rebecca. There are a hundred feet [thirty metres] of clear space below us right now. It allowed tall sailing ships to pass underneath."

Lots of wow factors there. Still, *Ten Green Bottles* has greater merit for pupils.

We headed east for Beaumaris, snatching sea views to our right from the coast road. Mrs Williams, an indefatigable fact-supplying guru, took over the educational baton by going Viking.

"Here's another interesting fact, children. The town began life as a Viking settlement. It wasn't until the thirteenth century that it was re-named *Beau Marais* by the Normans. Does anyone know what that means in French?"

We knew the first word, but the second had us floored.

"Well, never mind," she continued. "It means 'Fair Marsh'. It sits beside the water at the head of the Menai Strait and was the perfect spot to build a castle."

We thundered down the coach steps and formed disorderly lines, equipped with a smidgen of knowledge, packed lunches, pads, pencils, and someone else's blazer. Holding hands with our best friend and desperate to get cracking, our tour began.

Did we know the castle design was made up of perfectly matching turrets? No, but that was interesting and kind of clever. And did we know that it was never finished because King Edward had to go and sort out the revolting Scots? Poor Scots! No, we didn't know that either, but it did sound sort of funny.

Wide-eyed with wonder and feeling the size of ants, we scurried around the immense, near-perfectly symmetrical fortress, eyes filled with awe at tubby turrets reaching for the sky. Miss Evans, teacher in charge of crocodile lines, sensed a captive audience.

"Attention, please, children, can anyone guess the number of arrow loops in the outer walls?"

By anyone's standards, this was a top question. Hands shot up.

"Ten, Miss?" peeped a natural pessimist.

"No, many more than that, Huw."

"Could it be a hundred, Miss?"

"Lots more than that, Janice."

"Can I have a wee, please, Miss?"

"Yes, in a second, Belinda. Any other arrow loop guesses?"

"I know, I know," squeaked Thomas, school bragger. "Two hundred!"

"No, even more, Thomas. There are three hundred loops here. Let's see if we can count them all."

With cries of 'Oooh!' we dashed around, arrow loop counting. It took ages.

We munched lunch on a grassy knoll where we listened to more stories about the castle, King Edward I's last fortress. For him, it was a dream that never did quite come true, and yet even half-built, we could all appreciate what a formidable place it was.

With our trip almost over, the moat and dock area was the last place for a detailed investigation. As we meandered alongside the murky water, Siân made an important frog discovery and beckoned for me to have a look. Instead of following the path, I nipped across a grassy patch. I was mid-stride when Di started yelling.

"Beth, Beth! *Stop!*"

Splosh!

I was in the moat.

Di regularly rescued me when we were little and she was the one who hauled me out. Furious at having a soggy little sister, she started lecturing me.

"Why did you try to run across the moat?"

"I thought it was grass."

"It's weed growing in the water. Can't you see the difference in the colour?"

"It looks the same as the grass."

"Well, it isn't. *Everyone* in the universe can see that. Honestly, you are so embarrassing!"

It was an unceremonious way to end a splendid afternoon, one that rapidly led to questions about my ability to distinguish colours. I was convinced I could see them perfectly well. Di disagreed. Ma said the optician would decide.

The optician handed me a book with circles on each page filled with random coloured dots. I later found out that it was the Ishihara colour perception test. My job was to point out the shape or number pattern among the dots. I huffed and puffed my way through several, only managing to distinguish a few.

The optician gave me a knowing look and showed me a couple more. This was when I thought I'd cracked it. I could see those. Nodding sagely, the optician withdrew his book and confirmed that I was red-green colour blind, just like Pa.

Di was triumphant because she now had a defective sister. I remained in denial. As it happens, it has presented no problem in the usual course of life, but I would never make an airline pilot and was told to be especially careful around moats.

Besides life lessons, riding lessons and unfruitful maths lessons with Pa, being a musical family, our parents decided we needed to take piano lessons. I didn't mind the idea of it, although I found practising scales boring. My biggest problem lay with the teacher.

For one hour each week after school, Ma took me to Mrs Barton's house. Her role was to get me through as many grades as possible, ideally up to grade three, before going to the big school. Fat chance of that.

My inability to progress had little to do with musical talent and everything to do with bodily movements. Mrs Barton had galloping dyspepsia. Being brought up as a polite child, I didn't dare mention anything. Instead, I suffered in silence when her tummy rumbled and gurgled like a volcano ready to blow. I sat, solid as a rock when she turned burps into ill-disguised coughs and didn't bat an eyelid when the exertion set off bouts of flatulence.

My agony worsened when Mrs Barton cradled her hands over mine to help me form a chord. We were now uncomfortably close. My nose was stuck under her left armpit, which was as ripe as her botty coughs. Every lesson was dire.

I eventually plucked up the courage to tell Pa. He roared with laughter, gave me one of his bone-crushing bear hugs, and told me it was good character-building stuff. Ma was far primmer. She said I must feel sympathy for other people's problems and persevere. I never took to the piano after that.

With Di in her final year at primary school, it was time to choose the secondary school that would take us through the rest of our education up to university level. Our parents were determined to scrimp and save to provide the best education they could for us. At least that was their aim.

The Wonder of Welsh Words

Castell
Pronouncing this word for '**castle**' is trickier than it appears. It's an 'll' word, the cause of many facial contortions for non-Welsh-speakers. Try smiling, combining 'h' and 'l' and blowing at the same time. Once you've mastered that, combine 'cast-ehl' and you've cracked it!

Chapter Nine

'Cats are the best people.'

Jeni Rizio

Having undergone her unusual Victorian governess-tutored education, Ma wanted us to continue conventional education. Pa had attended boarding school when he was very young. He advocated instilling independence and discipline into a child at an early age. There was more than a smidgeon of the Duke of Edinburgh in our father.

They agreed that Di and I should also go to a boarding school for girls. It boiled down to two affordable options in Wales. Di could choose which she liked best, and after much humming and hawing, she made her final decision. Entry exams were passed, documents completed, and the preparations began.

The list of essentials went on for pages. Bales of nametapes were purchased from a Dickensian-sounding company. Every single garment had to have a nametape sewn on by hand. Socks, undies, blouses, towels, flannels, skirts, cardigans. It was interminable.

The uniform requirements were immense and ridiculously expensive, so Ma resorted to using the school's second-hand clothes shop to get Di kitted out. I watched, half incredulous, half amused by the provisioning.

"Go on, Di, put that big long cloak on again."

"Why?"

"You look like a vampire bat, especially when you pull the hood up!"

"I hate you!"

Did Di honestly need three pairs of navy blue over-undies for sport? What was wrong with the mountains of white under-undies she was required to have? And three pairs of grey over-undies, especially for hockey? And what was so special about hockey that scratchy grey culottes had to be worn? Part of me was secretly dying to find out.

Special stationery had to be bought. And then maths kit, different pencils, erasers and a fountain pen with Quink ink. Another new item of equipment to be sourced was a very impressive trunk. I badly coveted one of those.

Di's trunk had round edges with wooden supporting slats. It had to be big enough to contain all her clothes for one term. It was. I could easily lie in it. She also needed a tuck box. This was filled with food treats, supplied at the beginning of term by Ma, and after that periodically sourced with pocket money from the school tuck shop.

On the day Di left home aged eleven-and-a-bit, Ma took a photo of her standing beside the magnolia tree. Wearing regulation T-bar shoes, white ankle socks, a grey skirt and blazer with extra-long sleeves, she looked neat as a pin.

I went along with Ma to drop Di off. We were still a distance away from the entrance when Di started digging me in the ribs.

"Look, look over there."

"What? Where? Are we here?"

"Not yet, but there it is!"

"Wowee!"

At the top of a hill stood a castle. At least that's what it looked like to me.

"That's it?"

"Yes!"

"Has it got proper battlements and things?"

"I don't know, but I'll find out. Yeah, probably."

As we drew into the courtyard, I immediately felt jealous. I was desperate to stay and play in this fantastic place. But now was not my time. We left Di busily making friends with lots of other newbies. She waved happily as we drove off, looking forward to the next stage in her education.

It was strange without my big sis at home. Even though Monty and Paddy were the focus of my attention, I missed her badly. I was even glad to have the chores and homework as a distraction. I also had more time to play with Gavin from next door. He had recently been given a posh Raleigh

Chopper bike and wanted to take it out for a spin. This presented me with a new and brilliant idea.

"Let's bike across the deer park. We can take Monty with us."

"Okay, but he won't eat my wheels like Fly does, will he?"

"Noooo, he's a Great Dane. If we can get him over the cattle grids, he'll be fine."

We started well. Monty padded amiably alongside, with Gavin proudly wobbling on his Chopper, clutching his tall spindly handlebars with ribbons flailing off either end. He'd clipped a playing card to the front fork with a clothes peg to make the ensemble extra impressive. The clickety sound the card made as the wheel rotated was excellent. I quite fancied one of those. Still, I didn't think his bike was as fast as mine. There was only one way to find out.

"Fancy a race from the middle tree to the end, Gavin?"

"'course, but what about Monty?"

"He'll be fine. It's not very far, and he can run with us."

Off we zoomed, Gavin clicketing, me whirring, and Monty lolloping. There wasn't a breath between us. It was all going so well until, out of nowhere, a pheasant popped up from the crop.

Mesmerised by Gavin's clickerties, it strolled into the middle of the lane and stopped directly in front of us.

Monty, child guardian, lunged at the bird to clear the way. I yanked my brakes, but not much happened; Gavin, still mastering his, started weaving. Neither of us stopped in time. We ended up in a jumbled heap of scratched bikes and slobbery dog. Variously wounded, we gave up and decided that making dens was safer.

When I wasn't having misadventures with Gavin or our other friends, I messed around with our animals. Excitingly, one of the silkies occasionally produced an egg. They didn't lay very often, so each was treated with reverence.

Our bunnies had grown, as had Buck's ardour. Now keen to spend all his time attached to Liza, another cage was bought. But it was a different animal altogether that stole my heart. Ma called me into the kitchen after school.

"Beth, I want you to close your eyes and hold out both hands."

"Why?"

"I have a small surprise for you. Quickly, now."

Instantly bursting with excitement, I jammed shut my eyes, and thrust my hands forward.

Funny noises came from somewhere near Ma.

Squeaky, insistent. An animal. Ever so gently, Ma placed a small, wriggly, furry creature into my cupped palms. I opened my eyes, and staring up at me, was a tiny ginger kitten.

"Oh, Ma, I, I...thank you ever so much!"

"You needed a new companion, and this little boy needs one too. He was abandoned, so will need lots of love and care."

"Don't worry. I'll love him forever!"

He squirmed, wanting to play and explore, so I gently put him on the floor. As I watched, enchanted, Lotti appeared. Horrified at the young imposter, she inflated to twice her size and gave him a haughty hiss. The kitten, oblivious to the warning, pattered up to *meow* hello. I grabbed him just in time to avoid a swipe.

"Uh oh, you. Lotti's the queen around here. You'll have to mind your manners with her. I need to give you a name. Um, what'll it be? Oh, I know. Perfect, I've been learning about a Greek hero. You're so brave I'll call you Hercules."

Mew!

Hercules quickly became my new soul mate. I adored him. He was a bright spark with a feisty character and courage beyond his capabilities. Hercules got stuck up trees, wedged in tiny spaces and lost in fields. He stalked everything, caught nothing and when he'd worn himself out, he'd lie on my lap in purry contentment.

During this period, education took a different turn in the family. Pa, still race sailing every weekend, was approached by a couple of friends who had bought ocean-going yachts. Strange though it sounded to me, they were nervous about sailing them on the open sea and asked for his help.

Having sailed all his life, the technical rudiments were simple for Pa, but he was less confident about navigation. One of his friends was keen to sail over to France, the other around Ireland. The opportunities were too enticing for him to turn down. Pa studied for the Yachtmaster Offshore qualification.

I was clueless about his studies and asked Pa to explain.

"I'll be learning some new subjects and revising others I already have experience of."

"But why bother with them if you already know all about the subject?"

"Revisiting existing learning is always useful. It

refreshes our knowledge. Several topics combine to qualify me as a Yachtmaster if I pass the exams. It's a well-respected qualification worldwide for several nautical disciplines."

"That sounds exciting."

"I'm not sure about that, but passing the qualification will mean I can competently skipper a sailing vessel up to 78 feet [twenty-four metres] long at sea over 150 miles [241 kilometres] from a safe haven."

Most of the syllabus proved to be familiar territory for Pa, but some elements interested and frustrated him. Navigation and chart plotting were testers. Out came charts the size of tablecloths, a needle-sharp pencil, a set of parallel rules, and a divider.

The dining room table became a skipper's cabin as Pa plotted his way through theoretical passages. Woe betide anyone interrupting him in mid-plot. It all looked a bit too mathsy, so I gave him a wide berth.

Familiarity with international maritime signal flags used to communicate with ships was essential, as was the NATO phonetic alphabet. This was used for onboard radio communication. It was something, for some peculiar reason, Pa decided we all needed to learn. During the lead up to his exams, he developed a habit of barking out letters.

"V?"

"Vine, Pa?"

"No, Victor."

"G?"

"Erm, Golf!"

"Yes, good."

And so it went on. It was the same with knots. This niche knowledge was simple for Pa as he had been tying different knots forever, but apparently, we needed to learn too.

"Tie me a sheet bend knot with this rope, please."

Joining the two lengths of rope he handed me, I could manage. It was with some of the more complicated ones where I got stuck. The bowline, used for mooring a boat to bollards or rings, was impossible for my little fingers.

"No, that won't do. If you tie it like that, the boat will slip its mooring. Try it again and while you're doing it, tell me what J stands for."

"Juliet?"

"Yes, good. Now, let's have a look at that knot."

"Can we use your spike to undo it, Pa?"

"Yes, yes, alright."

Pa was never without his seaman's knife. It was

a folding mechanism with spike attachment used for jobs like unlaying rope for splicing, untying knots and a variety of other mariner related jobs. I desperately wanted one.

Disappointingly, it was considered that I was more likely to skewer myself by accident than use it for its original purpose. Instead, I was later given a six-inch sheath knife for my thirteenth birthday, which I proudly attached to my jeans belt. Go figure!

Pa juggled his studies with a demanding job that caused him occasional overseas travel. Still, as predicted, he passed his exams. He could now skipper his pals' yachts, which would open incredible new horizons for me later on.

It wasn't only Pa who was involved in projects. With no formal education but bags of natural business acumen, Ma decided to augment her weekly housekeeping money. She used our privileged surroundings and set up a small business buying, training and selling ponies and horses. It was slow going at first because funds were limited. Profits gained from the sale, livery or training of animals helped fund future purchases and equipment.

For me, the very idea of having more livestock was fantastic. More exciting still was the announcement our parents made soon after.

The Wonder of Welsh Words

Cath
One of my favourite animals. Using a soft 'th' as in 'bath', pronounce the word as it looks and you have, '**cat**'.

Chapter Ten

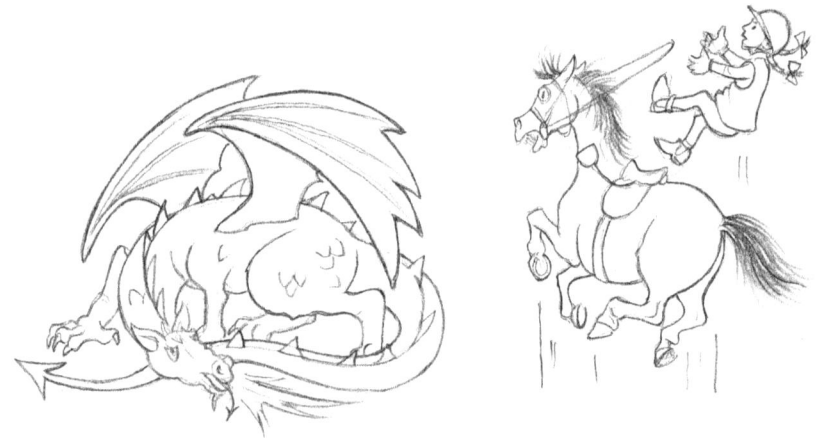

'In riding a horse, we borrow freedom.'

Helen Thomson

Di and I would finally be given ponies. It was a new chapter in our equestrian lives, and we couldn't wait.

As half-term came, Di had barely settled before I started grilling her. Was it fun? Had she made loads of new friends? Were the teachers as nice as the ones at our primary school? Her responses were non-committal.

The big school wasn't quite what Di expected. It was ever so rulesy, and the food was yucky, not at all like Ma's. The lessons were...ugh, although drama classes were great. And she had some lovely new friends. One was from France, and her new best friend, Mandy, came from Liverpool. School was okay.

We sat among the dogs while I filled Di in on our home news. Kitten Hercules, of course, came first. In between bouts of using her as a climbing frame, he flopped, purring, on one or other of us, vying for lap time with slinky Lotti. Superbly snooty, our feline diva continued to be sceptical of the young ginger upstart.

Our combined adventure was imminent. They often sold horses and ponies at our riding stables on Anglesey, and that's where we were going. Tomorrow we would choose our steeds. Sleep that night was almost impossible.

We set off bright and early in jodhpurs and

ankle riding boots, clutching hard hats. Giggling, pinching one another, Di gabbling with a Liverpudlian twang. We hurried into the menage to find four ponies waiting. While we cooed at them, Ma and Mr McElroy talked suitability and money. Di was first.

She had taken an instant shine to a liver bay, and I wasn't surprised. Ponni was alert, friendly and possessed bags of pizazz. She clambered aboard and took Ponni through his paces. The sun bounced off his shiny brown coat as he strutted around the arena. He'd be a handful, but Di was smitten. The deal was done.

My choices were between a diminutive Welsh cob bay gelding and a much higher piebald mare. First, I tried out little Llewellyn. Despite his amply rounded tummy, he was perky and dead keen to get going. I immediately felt at home as we trotted and cantered around the arena.

"Can I take him over some jumps, please, Mr McElroy?"

"Yes, try the cavaletti first."

I pointed Llewellyn at the low wooden obstacle, no more than calf height. He flew over. We tried some bigger jumps. He was quick; he was accurate, and I was in heaven. Flushed with delight, I trotted back. Before I could say anything, Ma intervened.

"Try Molly now. She may be a better size for you."

"But Ma, I don't need to. I love Llewellyn."

"I can see that, but he is small. Come on. Molly is a fine-looking mare."

Molly didn't have the same wow factor for me. Well, none at all. We plodded amicably through her paces. Yes, she could jump, but grazing was more interesting. Hauling her head up with the reins was quite hard. We returned after an uninspired display.

"I know what you're going to say, Beth, but Molly is the better pony for you. She looks reliable. She is younger and a much better height. I know she's strong to manage at the moment, but you'll grow into her."

I looked wistfully at Llewellyn. It's true, he was pint-sized, but I could have had so much fun with him. I sighed, knowing there was no point arguing. Molly and Ponni were bought and joined our family the following day.

Di and I spent hours playing on our ponies before she returned to school. Molly, being black and white, was quickly re-named Apache. It was an ideal name since I was still in mid-cowboy and indians phase. I lived in the cowboy boots and fringed waistcoat Pa had brought back for us from a business trip to America.

Ponni mostly galloped around the big field totally out of control, with Di hanging on for grim death. In contrast, I pootled around bareback on Apache stalking imaginary bison. Eventually, we converged in the middle – Di, breathless.

"How's Jug-Head going?"

"Who?"

"Apache. Her head does look quite juggy."

"Awww, don't be mean. At least she doesn't bolt like Ponni!"

"Does not! He's just, well, okay, he does a bit. He's great, though!"

Di returned to school full of beans. She had her new pony, and was looking forward to telling her chums about the half-term adventures. And to ensure that Ponni didn't run totally wild, Ma promised to exercise him while she was away.

True to her business ambitions, Ma soon bought a new horse. Along came a magnificent Arab gelding. Tall for the breed, he held his classically dished head high, flicked his tail and danced around the paddock. Khan was spirited, but Ma managed him beautifully.

Having Apache created opportunities my bike could not fulfil. Now that I was allowed out on my own, I rode her across country, including visits to the pheasant rearing pens. Being an amiable soul, so long as grass was available, I could tether her to a bush or tree while I conducted my investigations.

The pheasant rearing site was intriguing. Numerous aviaries stood around a lightly wooded area next to an old ornamental lake. Some pens contained parent birds and depending on the time of year, others were filled with squawking adolescent poults preparing to meet their destiny.

Under Mr Edwards' no-nonsense tutelage, I learned the rudiments of gamekeeping. General characteristics of the birds came first. My suggestion that the youngsters were nutty was apparently entirely wrong. They were calm when handled correctly. He told me about their diet, how to make pens predator-proof, and offered sage words about hygiene. His husbandry worked.

Mr Edwards whistled up his released poults, which came sprinting out of crops and meadows at mealtimes. His adult birds strolling around the estate were veritable fatties. Rearing birds was a captivating process.

Mr Edwards also kept a small army of broody hens. He said they were an essential part of the rearing programme because hen pheasants were useless mothers. I wasn't sure whether he was joking or had a chicken obsession because he did have some strange habits. Many years later, I would realise the wisdom of his words.

Thousands of pheasants were reared under our gamekeeper's expert supervision. He nurtured each one as though it was his child, which was possibly his only flaw. They were awfully tame. Mr Edwards prowled his domain like a tiger with gun in hand, guarding his brood against predators. Rather like Bailey, our old gardener, he attached his small predator kills to barbed wire fences as a warning to similar species. I considered the miserable lines of dead moles one day.

"Mr Edwards, isn't pinning moles to the fence a bit pointless?"

"Why would you say that?"

"Well, moles are short-sighted. I don't think they'd be able to work out what all those bodies are. And anyway, they mostly live underground."

"It's the general shape and smell, you see. When they pop up, they can tell, those moles can. It stops them making a mess in my pens, for a while anyway. Done it for years, I have."

The local arable farmer did the same with offender crows caught pecking seeds. Fortunately, neither he nor Mr Edwards applied the same treatment to slain foxes.

When a batch of pheasants was old enough to be released, Mr Edwards' expression of pride was priceless. He and his dogs made sure they were herded to the correct zones at the right times for shoots. He was resigned to their fate and knew it was a job well done. The estate gamekeeper was a countryman through and through.

Di and I regularly went on long rides during the holidays, often with Clare, the eldest of the Griffiths' girls. We explored distant meadows and pockets of woods within the walled estate. Mr Griffiths, as estate manager, knew every nook and cranny, including the old buildings.

We were at a loose end one day, so Mr Griffiths sent us off on an adventure to find the old mausoleum. The estate's principal family members had been laid to rest here. He said we mustn't go in, but we were free to explore outside. This was far too exciting a prospect to turn down. We set off, a merry band of ghost hunters, racing across fields and trekking through woods. Finally, we found the approximate site and started casting around.

At first, we thought we were in the wrong place. Di yelled. She'd discovered a partially concealed track. We tethered the ponies and started groping our ways down the brambly, tree-lined path, grumbling, tumbling and unpicking prickly thorns from our clothes.

Facing us were trees. Dark, foreboding varieties.

"Ooh, look, Beth. Loads of yews. Remember what I said about why they were planted?"

"Don't, Di!"

Fighting through to a clearing, we spotted railings ahead. Wrought iron stakes with arrowhead finials corralled a sombre Gothic-style building. We had found it, the mortuary chapel with an octagonal bell tower.

Whispers hissed among us. Who dared to scale the fence for a closer look?

"Go on, Beth, you're the littlest. You climb over."

"No fear, Di. You go!"

"Not likely! Clare, how about it?"

"What me? No way. There are real live dead bodies in there!"

Nobody was keen. Someone suggested drawing straws. Nope, it was far too creepy. Gripped with the eeriness of the dank setting, we crept around the outside, straining our eyes, trying to see through the windows. Was someone or something staring out? The possibility seemed plausible.

In truth, there wasn't much to see, but the imagined spectral eyes were quite enough. We scurried back to the ponies and charged back home. After that visit, Mark's bookcase spook seemed positively chummy.

Trekking with Ma was fun, especially because

eats were involved. One of our favourite rides was to the old boathouse. Off we went, a colourful ensemble. Our painted steeds, Sioux and Apache, sauntered in harmony while Di and Ponni thundered around in circles nearby.

The ride took us to the mainland edge of the Menai Strait and a miniature tumbledown dock. This square-ish structure was built during the nineteenth century. It was initially used as a depot to transport coal and other supplies to and from the estate. It now served as a wondrous private adventure playground for children.

We could teeter along part of the existing quay playing pirates, and negotiate slippery steps to the water. A rubble of stones on the north side provided an artificial breakwater, stemming those mischievous tides. We tried to picture the boats coming in to dock. They couldn't have been huge. Still, it would be a tricky manoeuvre.

The boathouse looked newer than the dock. I don't remember anyone living in it, although we decided that sitting on its veranda looking out to sea must have been pleasant. But the most fun we had here was messing around in rock pools.

After our snacks, the hunt was on. We spent ages fishing around the stony shoreline for shells. Squeals rang around the dock walls when one of us narrowly avoided grabbing a stranded jellyfish or lifted a particularly gloopy lump of seaweed to reveal sidestepping crabs.

There were loads of different seaweed varieties in these waters. Some had long, flat strands. This was called serrated wrack. Others had pods, which were poppable if squished extra hard. Ma knew about them all.

"Beth, do stop bursting the seaweed pods, please. Your hands are getting filthy."

"Sorry, Ma. What's it called?"

"That variety is bladderwrack."

"Top name!"

"*Ahem*, I thought you might approve, Di," said Ma. "Now, girls, do you know the name of this type?"

We shook our heads.

"This is called sea lettuce. And, in fact, we can eat it. I must prepare some for us soon."

We ate most things by then, but I'm not sure anything would have persuaded us to eat that yucky-looking stuff.

The one I liked best was called gutweed, also known as sea kelp. It looks like manky hair and was wonderfully slimy stuff to slide through your fingers, or your sister's hair. That always caused a satisfyingly extreme reaction.

After boathouse trips, the ride home was smelly. Our knees and backsides were soggy, and drying seaweed slime was strewn everywhere. As with all seaside excursions, we were stocked up with interesting shells. And although these were great outings, the farm was even better.

One of my favourite places to hang around was the estate farmyard, with its rustic mixture of ancient moss-covered stone buildings and hints of modernity.

The agricultural smells, sounds and activities were intoxicating. I loved the sweet-scented hay, the faintly nutty aroma of grain, and that oily whiff of newly shorn sheep. Even the acidic pongs coming from piles of steaming silage were weirdly nice.

The sheep dip and marking processes fascinated me. I watched for hours as Meg and Fly went through their paces, effortlessly herding their woolly charges in and out of fields and into their deep insecticide bath.

The deep throaty roar of the bull calling his girls electrified me. The gentle lowing of cattle comforted me. And the plaintive bleats of newborn lambs searching for their mums always melted my heart. There was something reassuring about the machinery, too.

Depending on the season, tractors hauled trailers back and forth, sometimes loaded with wobbly straw or hay bale skyscrapers. Clunky farrows, seeders, tillers, and ploughs with their broad blades still soily with use. They were transported to their places of work. But there was one activity that took place every single day, and that was milking.

The farm had a herd of black and white Holstein Friesian dairy cattle. Without fail, the cows filed out of their field twice a day, crowding the lanes as they ambled towards the milking parlour. It was a practised routine, skilfully managed by cowmen and their zig-zagging collies. Cars, trucks, ponies and bikes, we all had to stop while the procession took its course.

The dairy was easy to identify. Outside, there was a ledge in the half wall. Big metal, multi-gallon milk churns were stored here, ready for despatch. These were the traditional trappings of the milking process, but things were changing.

The milking parlour was a clean, airy building furnished with what looked like sci-fi equipment. Each cow seemed to know which stall was hers. Once the girls had settled down to their meal, the kit was fitted. It was a peaceful operation.

Under the supervision of Janet, the milkmaid, I only saw the inner sanctum a few times. Watching those machines performing their rhythmic roles, making funny suction-pumping sounds, was mesmerising. And just to make my visits even more special, at the end of each round, a mug of creamy uber-fresh milk was placed into my hands. Delicious! Experiences like these convinced me that I wanted to work with animals forever and ever. Perhaps I wouldn't be a cowboy after all. A career in farming felt just right.

It was around this time, when we had an animal-related experience of a completely different kind. And it thrilled Di and me to the core.

The Wonder of Welsh Words

Gwymon
Slimy and endlessly interesting, the word for **'seaweed'** is pronounced, 'gwi-mon'.

Chapter Eleven

'Slate quarries – the most Welsh of Welsh industries.'

Dr David Gwyn

"Girls, the Household Cavalry is coming to stay. They will set up camp in the big field."

"Fantastic! Can we go and see them? Are we allowed to ride their horses? Stroke them? Can we talk to the soldiers?"

"Settle down, Beth. They're called cavalrymen, and this is exactly why I have told you in advance. No, their camp will be strictly out of bounds. You may not go unless you have permission."

"Awww, Maaaa," we howled.

"There's no point complaining. They will be swamped preparing for Prince Charles's Investiture at the castle. We will have one or two of the officers for drinks, so you might be able to speak to them if you're very well behaved."

As the date drew near, the meadow became a hive of activity. As men milled around, a collection of tan-coloured tents popped up like mushrooms. We were engrossed but didn't dare venture too close. Instead, we took to riding in a field extra-close to the fence, craning our necks for sneak peeks. Lurking.

Ma and Pa hosted a cocktail party that included guest representatives from the cavalry. Di and I performed our usual canape-offering service. In my case, these were apt to be fraught affairs. The opportunities for accidentally tipping a tray of nibbles over someone's dress or trousers were limitless. Happily, neither event occurred.

Sadly, we didn't have any deep chats with our new heroes, but being genuine horse lovers, a couple were invited back to view our animals. Whilst my coloured pony held little interest for them, Sioux did.

The Household Cavalry was searching for a new drum horse and took a shine to our big skewbald mare. These horses carry gold-coated kettle drummers plus a solid silver kettle drum and banner over each wither, so they must be strong. They also have to be docile enough to be controlled by reins attached from their bit to the drummer's stirrups.

They thought Sioux fitted the bill in almost every respect except one. Shire or Clydesdale cross horses are typically used for this role, and our Sioux wasn't quite tall enough. None of us was upset when they decided not to make an offer after all.

The day of the Investiture came. Ma and Pa were guests at the ceremony and went along in their finery. But we didn't miss out. Despite being aged and frail now, *Nain* came with us to the roadside, where we joined thousands of others to watch the Royal party make their way to Caernarfon Castle.

As it transpired, our *Nain* passed away at the end of that summer. I look back on that day and wonder what she thought of the pomp and ceremony. Prince Charles, the future King of England, was now officially appointed the Prince of Wales. It was a celebration of everything Welsh, yet so very English. Did she approve? We will never know.

Fidgeting animatedly, Di and I watched, enthralled, as we spotted our new heroes clattering past. Their uniforms with horsehair plumed silver helmets shone, as did their cuirasse chest armour and buckles. Leather saddlery glowed with a dark lustre, the coats of their black mounts gleamed with health and vigour.

And while these dazzling sights thrilled so many, the scenes were a foil for others. Not many, but enough. As youngsters, Di and I had no idea about the turbulence surrounding the event.

The 1969 Investiture drew fierce criticism from some Welsh nationalists, who recognised it as symbolic of English occupation in Wales over the centuries. There were demonstrations, civil unrest, bombs planted. We were naively unaware of the angst.

A Netflix episode of *The Crown* described the philosophical conundrums. While much was over-dramatised, there were truths. The royal historian,

Robert Jobson, revisited those days in a biography, citing a radio interview about the event with Prince Charles, who said:

'It would be unnatural, I think, if one didn't feel any apprehension about it. One always wonders what's going to happen... As long as I don't get covered in too much egg and tomato I'll be alright. But I don't blame people demonstrating like that. They've never seen me before. They don't know what I'm like. I've hardly been to Wales, and you can't really expect people to be overzealous about the fact of having a so-called English prince to come amongst them.'

In contrast to the protestors, on 1 July 1969, we experienced a mutual sharing of unrestrained pride and joy with multitudes of cheering families. The entire route to Caernarfon Castle was lined with troops and spectators. Cheers, flag-waving, and cried wishes of good luck and thanks. Embracing British pomp with happy hearts.

During the centuries-old Investiture, as custom required, the Secretary of State for Wales read the Letters Patent in Welsh, while the Queen bestowed upon Charles five pieces of insignia: a sword, coronet, ring, the gold rod, and the kingly mantle. The moment had come.

Charles took the oath:

"I, Charles, Prince of Wales, do become your

liege man of life and limb and of earthly worship and faith and truth I will bear unto thee to live and die against all manner of folks."

It marked the start of a new historic chapter for our country and coincided with a momentous event.

Shortly after the Investiture, a major slate quarry in our area was closed. Ironically, the magnificent slate dais upon which Prince Charles was invested was crafted by the very quarrymen who lost their jobs. Like many generations of male workers in North Wales, Pa worked in the slate quarry as had *Taid*. Entire communities grew up around the site, which started operations in the 1770s.

Youngsters aged fourteen and less began an apprenticeship, learning how to split slabs of slate into roofing tiles. It is said that sixteen could be produced from a two-inch block. Imagine that? And they turned out hundreds every day.

As industry boomed, a workforce of three thousand flat-capped quarrymen clattered up winding slag waste paths to the quarry huts. They wore clogs to protect their feet from shards, debris from the production process. This practice continued well into the 1950s and was commented on by a former quarryman, Alun Wyn Evans.

"My father and brother were at the quarry and

my uncles too, and most of them lived in the same street. You could hear their clogs as they walked along the street in the morning. That's what most men wore because they were warmer and more comfortable."

Wales is quoted as having 'roofed the industrial revolution'. In its heyday, the quarry was the second largest globally, producing 90,000 tonnes of slate every year. Eventually, the demand for slate lessened, and consequently, worldwide orders. Investment dwindled, and inevitably the quarry had to be downsized. The workforce was reduced. During this challenging period, Pa took Di and me to the site.

My youthful impressions were of a vast, barren landscape, too enormous to absorb. A grey world smudged with silvery yellow lichen. Hills of smithereens, viciously sharp slabs dwarfing humble stone and slate huts. I wondered who lived in those. There was a tiny single gauge railway supporting rusty bucket cars filled with slate, a massive industrial wheel, and so much more.

Pa led us to the workings. One side of the mountain had been stripped. Stark, stepped sections. Chiselled areas called galleries where the slate was quarried. The other was as nature intended. Unblemished, green, lush. Way below, I could see men working. They looked like ants. I tried but couldn't count them.

"How many people work here, Pa?"

"We used to have thousands of men, but there are about three hundred and fifty now."

Pa pointed towards a group.

"See those quarrymen? They'll be blasting soon."

Di tugged Pa's sleeve.

"What does that mean?"

"It's a controlled explosion which blasts slate slabs from the mountain. They'll be taken from the rock shelf and brought to the sheds to be cut and split."

"That sounds dangerous."

"It is. These days, we have several safety precautions in place. It wasn't always the case, though."

"What happened?"

"Years ago, one of the most dangerous jobs was getting the blasted slabs down from the shelf galleries. Without the help of machines, quarrymen had to swing with a rope wrapped around one leg as they dislodged the slate. There were many injuries, and some men were killed by rockfalls."

"That's awful."

"It was tragic. And it was one of the reasons

why a hospital was built here by the owners in 1860. It isn't used as a hospital now, although they still give first aid to quarrymen with superficial injuries."

"What, like fingers being chopped off?"

"No, Beth, that isn't what superficial means. More like cuts and grazes. Come with me, girls. I'll show you some of the other buildings."

I took one last look at the galleries. Tunnels disappeared into the blackened bowels of the mountains, sites of triumph over a job well done; anguish, injury and toil, too. I shuddered.

Pa took us to a shed with rows of tables where slates were sawn. The ground was dusty and covered with teeny weeny bits of slate. There were piles and piles and yet more piles of slate – far too many to count. All neatly stacked, each was unique, each perfectly fashioned. Motes hung in the air. No wonder so many quarrymen suffered illness from dust clogging their lungs.

The hospital was alarming and exciting all at the same time. There were lots of iron beds, leg and arm braces hanging on hooks, and a room with implements where surgeries took place. One room had a cabinet with little drawers labelled with the names of herbs. I recognised some from nature walks with Ma. They must have been medicines. I spotted a strange-looking bed.

"Pa, why is that bed on those weird-looking wheels?"

"It's a stretcher. They attached it to a special tram on the two-gauge railway. Getting to the injured quarryman was often difficult because of the places they worked. Using the tramway transported them to the hospital more rapidly."

"Did they have doctors here?"

"Yes. One of the most famous was Dr Mills Roberts, the quarry surgeon."

"Did he put people back together again when they were hurt?"

"Yes, Beth. There's a famous story from years ago where a man suffered a terrible accident and had to have parts of both arms removed."

"That's terrible!"

"I know. Dr Mills Roberts and a colleague made a contraption which allowed the brave man to hold a spoon and knife to eat with, and he could take his hat off when going to chapel."

"Who cared about his hat?"

"He did. Being respectful and taking off his cap in the chapel was very important to him. The quarryman was very grateful for the help he was given."

"The poor, poor man."

We continued in subdued silence, shocked by

visions of the horrific injuries many quarrymen had sustained.

"What is that queer thing, Pa?" asked Di.

"It's an X-ray machine. In 1900, the quarry was one of the first British hospitals to receive one. They could take special pictures of an injury with this machine to find out whether a bone was broken or out of place."

"Gosh."

"And what was in this shed, Pa?" I said, keen to know what was behind the closed door.

"Well, this is the mortuary."

"What's one of those?"

"It was where the quarrymen who lost their lives were laid before being taken away."

"Oh, Pa, quarrying sounds frightening."

"Sometimes it was, and perilous. But safety standards improved enormously over the years, as you'll see now. Come on, let's go and watch the blasting. There's no one down there now. It's safe."

We returned to the quarry edge and looked down to where the final preparations had been made. A siren sounded.

Boom!

We stared, awestruck, as a muffled explosion way below sent gouts of dust-filled smoke into the air. Shrapnel fragments clattered against the gallery ledge. Another chunk of slate had been dislodged, another bony piece of the mountain's soul.

"Pa, do the quarrymen get scared? I bet they don't like working here at all."

"Quarrymen are hardworking, brave men who support and help one another. I have enormous respect for them. I'm sure they get nervous sometimes. That's natural. The conditions can be appalling."

"I think they're heroes."

"Try to understand that this quarry is in their blood, ours too. Their brothers, fathers, uncles and grandfathers probably worked here, and families grew up in the area. There's a bond, a close-knit community spirit."

Our visit with Pa had a lasting impression on Di and me. We were surprised and confused when we were told that the quarry had closed. Overseas orders had dried up, they said. The receivers were called in. We didn't understand the significance of either.

Communications between management and quarrymen were poor. Inevitably, the closure led to a deeply troubled period for many in the slate quarrying community. While Pa, whose specific role Di and I never fully understood, battled with work, we continued much as before. Ma focused on managing our home, doing everything possible to make life run smoothly. But there was optimism, too. For me, there was a new chapter on my horizon. And I was excited.

The Wonder of Welsh Words

Llech

Pronouncing this is trickier than it appears. Now that you can pronounce the 'll', pop an 'eh' sound in the middle followed by the soft 'ch', and you have the word: **'slate'**.

Chapter Twelve

'Three things give us hardy strength: sleeping on hairy mattresses, breathing cold air, and eating dry food.'

Welsh Proverb

It was my final year of primary school education. School was a home from home, and I loved it. I had made lots of friends. I learned from teachers who nurtured us with energy, humour, and gentle persuasion.

The summer term ended with the school sports day. We all looked forward to this annual event, even the non-sporty types. Everyone took part as a competitor or helper. Parents were invited, which heightened the excitement, and it all began in an orderly fashion.

Miss Jones, our sports teacher, lined us up in classes to select teams. Anxious eyes darted around. Nobody wanted to be on the same team as Caryl. She couldn't run for toffee. (Poor Caryl.) Thomas couldn't throw, so he was to be avoided, and Beryl needed a wee every three minutes so she'd be largely absent.

After several subdued moans and sniggers, we were organised. We donned our coloured team bibs and filed over to the sports field. Helpers had laid out essential equipment, including trestle tables, one of which was heavy with refreshments. It was a hot day, so we'd need those.

The judges' table was festooned with rosettes and trophies. Mr Brown, maths, was in charge of recording results. He was ideal for the job. Weirdly, he always brought his desk, which looked odd sitting beside the running track. Miles, spontaneous pants-wetter, didn't possess a single sporting instinct but was a whizz at counting. He was Mr Brown's aide.

As parents took up their seats on the trackside, we searched for familiar faces. We were strictly forbidden from displaying unruly behaviour. Instead, we stole bashful grins and shy waves. Beryl sighed.

"Look, my grandpa's here!"

"That's nice."

"I know, but I hope he doesn't start burping. He's horribly loud when he gets going."

Glancing uneasily at her grandpa, Beryl trotted off to join her team.

Mr Davis, geography, fired his starting gun to call us to order. A courteous hush fell as our headmistress declared the event open. Highcliff junior Olympics had begun.

The egg-and-spoon race was our first event. Competitors scooped up oversized hard-boiled eggs with a dessert spoon and began teetering down the track towards the finish line. Parents, usually such pleasant people, instantly combusted into a roaring mob.

"Come on, Johnny, *run!*"

"Pick it *up* again, Janet!"

"Clever boy. Well *done*, Dewi!"

And so it went on.

Next was the dreaded hula hoop contest. I was picked for our team, and I have no idea why. I'm just not bendy enough in the right places. We lined up and began twirling. Despite several energetic swivels, my hoop was going south. And I wasn't the only one having difficulties. Alice, mostly standing like a statue, was watching her apparatus slide. And, as all hula hoopers will know, there's only one outcome once that starts to happen.

"Wiggle, darling, *wiggle!*" shrieked her distraught mother.

Her encouragement was for nought; Alice's dismal expression said it all. The hoop had settled around her ankle socks.

Meanwhile, Sue, shaped like a test tube, was gyrating like a pro. Evidently destined to be a belly dancer, her hula hoop whirled like a spinning top. She was the runaway winner for the blue team. I managed a solid second last for my red compatriots.

The starting gun went off for no apparent reason. Mr Davis, puzzled, examined his imitation firearm for signs of defect. There were none. This happened without warning throughout the afternoon. Mr Davis was trigger-happy.

Other events followed. They banned me from the standing discus event on health and safety grounds. It was a sensible decision. Regardless of trying my best, it was anyone's guess where it would end up. Luckily for our team, we had Geraint. A stocky lad. The crowd gasped in awe as he expertly flung his missile. It landed a country mile from anyone else's, gaining boisterous cheers from the red team and thunderous bellows from his proud da. Our boy had come good. Geraint gained us lots of points.

The next three races held hazards of their own. You'd think the sack race was a relatively benign sport. Far from it. Bloody noses were not uncommon in the event as competitors, hands occupied with holding up their hessian death traps, keeled over.

For those like Sally, a studious girl who lacked any form of natural coordination, this was a test fraught with snags. Devoid of natural hopping instincts, she concluded that the only way to progress was to run up the inside of her sack. It took ages for her to reach the finish line.

The wheelbarrow race was risky for the 'barrows', not that the parents cared.

"Patrick, keep your arms *straight*. You're collapsing!"

"Come on, Dilys, pick yourself *up*. You're fine!"

"Push, Teddy, *push!*"

We never did find out who Teddy was.

The three-legged race held similar challenges, as it would. One leg of a competitor being strapped to another of their partner is never easy. The tricky technique involved synchronised movements and caused a multitude of on-track bickers, tumbles and unravelled cords.

Howls of derision mixed with praise rang out from the horde as contenders valiantly staggered down the track. The green team, hot favourites, knew what they were doing. Streaming ahead with their strange bunny-hop method, they won by several lengths, leaving a tangled heap of opponents behind. For the track events, it was a different story.

Running competitions operated relatively smoothly. They were my minor forte. I galloped along the track with confidence, finally contributing to my team. The last team event was the 4x100 yard relay race. Mr Brown read out the scores, and it was a nail-biter. Our team was running second to the blues. This was the decider for the Sports Day team trophy.

There were two boys and two girls in each team. Ours was a mixed bag of abilities. Michelle was to go first, and she was basically a gazelle. Our two middle runners definitely weren't, but they were keen as mustard. I was fourth, running anchor.

You could cut the atmosphere with a knife as we lined up. Mr Davis pulled his trigger, and we were off. Michelle streaked away, hotly followed by Dewi for the blues. He had longer legs. We expected him to pass her, but she miraculously held him off. Jane and Gareth in the other teams bumbled gamely behind but lost distance fast.

Running was the easy bit. The real clincher for these races was passing the baton. Was there any finesse involved? None. Thrown, dropped, fumbled and occasionally exchanged, it was the luck of the draw whether a 'receive' was made. The dire interceptions were playing out three times. There were several outcomes, none of which were lost on the frenzied mass. With the Sports Day team trophy at stake, decorum was doomed.

Pupils screamed, parents bawled, everyone willing their own to execute that slick swap.

"Let it *go*, Dafydd!"

"No, no, *noooo*, you've dropped it again. Stop and pick it *up*, Chrissy!"

"Stay in your lane, Dewi!"

"Stop crying, Janice, just pass it, for *goodness' sake!*"

Our third runner puffed around the track towards me. Gasping for breath, she reached the exchange zone and chucked the baton in my general direction. To everyone's surprise, including my own, I caught it and was off.

Thanks to our gallant Michelle, it was an easy run. I crossed the line in first place to hysterical screams, some of triumph, others of woe. Our red team had won the coveted Sports Day trophy.

Adults and children milled around the refreshments tables. Parents sipped dreadful coffee while their chattering offspring noisily sucked orange juice through straws. Everyone munched slabs of Bara Brith. The traditional Welsh fruit cake, or 'dead flies', as it was affectionately termed, is flavoured with tea, dried fruits and spices. It stuck to our tummies like glue.

Prize-giving would follow, but there was one more event to come. The parents' hundred-yard dash, and it was a toe-curler for many of us to watch. For some parents, the competition was a personality-transforming activity. Fathers, in particular.

Pa was away on business; I was pretty glad about that. Siân wasn't so lucky. We watched pensively as suit jackets were cast off and ties jettisoned. Short, shorter, round and slim, shoulder to shoulder, and a bit squashed. Twenty dads lined up – mouths set in grim determination.

The starter gun fired, and they were off. The ground rocked as they stampeded down the skinny track like a herd of bullocks, using elbows as weapons, grunting, fighting for position. Siân's dad was jostled in the middle. There were anxious moments as Dewi's dad tripped, bringing Diane's dad down with him. It wasn't comfortable viewing.

As soon as it had started, it was over. With a triumphant roar, David's dad broke through the winning tape. We'd witnessed broken limbs at these events before. Today was just a fractured temper or two, a relief, on the whole.

Our prize-giving finale came as a tame contrast. Parents, bursting with pride, watched their little ones receive trophies. Nearly everyone was awarded something. Even Miles, for being a top counting aide. It was another momentous end to our year and a fitting way to end my primary school career.

The summer holidays flew by, following their usual pattern with trips to the beach, long dog walks and adventures on ponies with our friends. Halcyon days. Simple country living. But whether or not we liked it, the everyday jobs had to come first. Di and I shared out the duties. She was stuck with the indoor housework, which was fine by me. Being outdoors was far more interesting. I usually mucked out stables, and then we tidied up the other big and small animals together.

Hammy hamsters regularly went temporarily AWOL when our attentions were momentarily diverted. We managed to keep the canaries safe but during one of these sessions, Liza and Buck tried to establish a new home.

Being cage-haters, Di and I often played with our bunnies on the front lawn. We followed the usual pattern, with the pair succumbing to strokes and grooming sessions before hopping nose-to-tail in circles. Buck was an ardent suitor.

Monty and Paddington found the bunnies boring and snoozed beside us. Not Hercules. An interested cat, he decided to join in and leapt between us. Both bunnies took fright and jumped into the rockery. It wasn't a small rockery. Di and I scrambled over boulders and around dwarf conifers after our rabbits, terrified they were gone for good.

"Di, you're such an idiot. Why did you let Liza go?"

"I couldn't help it. Hercules pounced on her!"

"He did not! He was only coming to play."

"Anyway, look, Buck's gone now too."

Our squabbles alerted Ma, who rushed out with

a bunch of carrots.

"Do be careful of the alpines, Beth. You're ruining my sedums."

"Sorry, Ma."

"Oh dear. Come off *now*, girls. I have only just planted that patch of campanula."

Ma continued to scold us about her precious alpines. She shooed Hercules away and sent me off to gather a bunch of dandelions. They proved the perfect snare. Buck gave up mountain climbing in favour of a nibble on his favourite snack. Liza quickly followed, and we scooped up our precious bunnies. Full of juicy stems, they were perfectly content to be stuffed back inside their cages.

Bad weather days still meant the outdoor stuff had to be done. Rain, being a regular visitor to Wales, meant we were habitually soaked. But that was fine. We cosied up in front of coal fires with our cats, dogs, and favourite reads. Di quickly became hooked on Jean Plaidy's books and consumed dozens. I'm sure it's why she was so good at history in school. After Enid Blyton, I progressed to Anna Sewell's *Black Beauty*, *The Silver Brumby* by Elyne Mitchell, and Monica Dickens's *Follyfoot Farm* series. Anything to do with animals.

Our playroom was on the top floor, which we loved, apart from the flies. We shared it with billions. I wouldn't have minded, but they always seemed such pointless creatures. They zoomed around the bay windows for half the year, squadrons of dive bombers bashing into us and our toys. And then they started to die. Crazy buzzers, mostly upside down, sometimes sideways, coming to a sticky end in one or other of our games. We never got rid of them.

The cork-floored room was strewn with board games, a rocking horse, books and two big old Victorian dolls houses, which had been passed down through the family. *Taid's* old lead clockwork train set plus miles of railway lines were periodically fixed together, as was my particular favourite. I spent hours and hours setting up and rearranging my farm.

The end of the summer holidays came, and with it, the next stage of my schooling. It had been at the back of my mind the whole time. Naturally, I assumed the big school would be the same as Highcliff. Why not? As Ma sewed interminable nametapes onto every single item of clothing, we packed the endless smalls and not so smalls into my posh new trunk. Then she filled my tuck box with homemade goodies. I was ever so excited.

Ma took the obligatory beginning of school year photos. Me, aged ten, socks wrinkled around my ankles as always, Di looking neat and tidy. Both wearing blazers with extra-long sleeves, which she promised we'd grow into. We packed the car with two enormous trunks, plus other school paraphernalia. Di and I took our places in the back seat, half eager, half uneasy. And we were off.

During our journey, we caught fleeting views of the Menai Strait, Puffin Island, which really does have puffins living on it, and Conwy Castle. The comforting peaks of Snowdonia slowly disappeared from view as we headed towards England. Mountains were replaced by fields, little towns and the endlessly long drive to my new school.

The penny dropped.

This time, despite having been before, it felt different, desperately different. The faux gothic castle walls, the archways and crenellations suddenly looked more foreboding than thrilling. It looked enormous and scary. I felt horribly small.

Di was unloaded first. As we left her, she wagged a knowing finger at me.

"Remember, Bethy. You're not allowed to speak to me here."

And with that, she hugged Ma and skipped off to find her pals.

We drove to a different part of the school, where I was deposited at Amelia House, Junior Block. Lots of other children and parents were milling around. We lugged my kit up the steep stone staircase, hanging onto the metal rail as we headed to the dormitories where my housemistress, Miss Barren, was waiting.

Cheerful hails of 'Hello, how was your summer?', 'Ooh, you've grown!', 'Did you have a magic birthday?', 'Where did you get so suntanned?' echoed around the corridors as the second-year girls were reunited with their friends. Miss Barren ushered Ma and me into a large dormitory, shushing excitable girls as she went.

We dragged the trunk to my iron-framed bed with a horsehair mattress. It looked like the old cot we had seen in the quarry hospital. There were eight identical beds in the room. Ma sighed and helped me open the trunk.

Out came Elly, my favourite elephant toy. Ma placed him gently on the pillow alongside my folded nightie. Miss Barren took charge of my tuck box and tapped her watch. Ma turned to me.

"It's time to say goodbye now, Beth."

I meekly followed Ma back down to the car, where she gave me a peck on the cheek.

"This is for the best," she said. "Lingering does nobody any good. Now go and get yourself organised."

All of a sudden, I was close to tears. I waved goodbye with a lump in my throat and stood, utterly lost. Wondering what to do next.

There was a tap on my shoulder.

"Hi Beth, I've been looking for you everywhere. It feels awful, doesn't it?"

Siân had arrived. We hugged and dashed upstairs to find that, mercifully, we were in the same dormitory.

As girls filtered in, we quickly made friends and settled into our new routine. We learnt that the school was highly structured. After two formative years in Junior Block, girls would be allocated a middle school house, which became that person's home away from home. Each house had dormitories and was run by a housemistress, and each teacher was affiliated with a house.

Pupils were awarded house points for honourable conduct, academic achievement, sports and other competitions. And there were lots. Debating competitions, music competitions, ballroom dancing competitions, the school sports day, they were all run on an inter-house competition basis.

Each year ended with the house earning the highest number of points winning the coveted House Trophy. Think Harry Potter's Hogwarts, and you have it. Come to think of it, there were close similarities with our school buildings too, except our staircases didn't move.

The first days flew by. There were new people to meet, new names, places and procedures to remember, and new rules – so many rules. Many of which I couldn't see the point of at all. One of these concerned associating with girls in the senior school. As juniors, we were forbidden from speaking to the seniors. Including siblings. Exceptionally, fifteen minutes after supper was set aside each day for 'Sisters' Talk'. Chatting to Di in a stark room seemed incongruous and artificial. It was, but I had no option.

Miss Barren informed us newbies that we might feel homesick, which was natural. And I did. I was dreadfully homesick. It didn't take me long to decide that a boarding school for young ladies wasn't for me, but I was stuck with it. We all were.

The Christmas term started in early September and finished in late December. We had a half-term break in the middle. Either side was an exeat, where girls were allowed home for the weekend. I remember anxiously counting the days, hours, minutes in the run-up to the first exeat. Each girl packed her overnight case. We lined up in the freezing cold courtyard, waiting for our parents to arrive. What would home be like? Would things be different?

The Wonder of Welsh Words

Ysgol
I spent years in them so I should know this one off by heart. This is the word for **'school'**, pronounced, 'us-gol'.

Chapter Thirteen

'Teg yw edrych tuag adref.' ('It is good to look homewards.')

Welsh Saying

Di had gone to stay with her pal in Liverpool, so I was on my own. I dashed through the front door into a wall of fur. Monty, and he was ecstatic. With Ma tutting in the background, I giggled, fighting off his sloppy licks, looking around for his cohort. If there's anything that can put the world to rights, it's a happy dog.

"Where's Paddy, Ma?"

"He's in disgrace, I'm afraid. He strayed to the pheasant pens again. I'm sure he isn't doing any harm down there, but Mr Edwards is rather cross. I've had to keep him in the walled garden during the day while I air the house in case he decides to go on another excursion."

Unless there was a blizzard or driving rain, Ma always had several doors and windows wide open. Of course, there was no need. We lived in an enormous, draughty old house in Wales – not the tropics. Di and I spent most of our childhood wearing at least two pullovers. Nevertheless, she was convinced it was good for our health.

I released Paddington from his latest purgatory. Floppy and soppy as usual, he lolloped around me before padding off with his lanky mate, searching for an open door. I grabbed my bag and rushed upstairs to the bedroom, where I found my ginger ninja. I looked around for Lotti, but she was nowhere to be seen. Thinking nothing of it, I smiled at my boy.

Hercules was curled up in the middle of my bed, fast asleep. He opened a sleepy eye and yawned, slowly unfurling his firebrand legs into a luxuriant stretch. For a feline welcome, that's pretty much as good as it gets.

It seemed an age since I'd last seen my feisty little puss. I hunkered down with Hercules, who started his slow, throaty purr. It was therapeutic, comforting. It was all part of being home.

"Beth, come on, lunch is nearly ready."

"Alright, won't be a mo."

I galloped up to Di's room in case Lotti was asleep on her bed. No, not there either. I nipped into the playroom to have a quick chat with both Hammys. That didn't last long. All I could see was beige bottoms. They were fast asleep in their nests.

I heard the front door bang downstairs. That could only mean one thing.

"Pa!"

Pa gave me one of his bear hugs before asking the inevitable.

"So, how is the maths going?"

"Um, not awfully well, really."

"Brace up, Beth. You must tackle the subject properly. It isn't difficult."

"I suppose not. Anyway, Ma, where's Lotti? I can't find her. I bet she's sad without Di being here."

"Oh, dear, didn't Di tell you?"

"Tell me what? What's happened?"

"I'm afraid Lotti went missing two weeks ago."

"Aww, that's rotten. I hope she's alright. Can we look for her before I go riding?"

"Yes, after lunch. I have been calling for her every day at suppertime, but no luck so far."

"Poor Lotti, it must be awful being lost. I hope she isn't frightened."

"Yes, I know. Now, let's not get silly and miserable. Tell us about school."

Ma had set the ground rules, so there was no point dwelling on the subject. Nevertheless, I decided to go out with the dogs on a search as soon as possible.

As we tucked into an epic lunch, I gabbled about school. I found myself chuckling about incidents, telling silly stories, stuff about new friends, loving that Siân was with me. Wanting to make it all alright. And I suppose it was. I was just a home girl.

I took Monty and Paddington across the fields, calling and calling, hunting thickets, woods and finally, the outhouses. There was no sign of Di's graceful black and white beauty. Crestfallen, I went to see the other animals. The chickens were perky, apparently still gracing us with the occasional egg. I headed to the bunny hutches and found Ma dispensing rations.

"We have two lop-eared rescue rabbits now. They were used in a testing laboratory."

"The poor things."

"I know. It was being closed, so I offered to take two."

"I am glad. Were there any others?"

"Yes, but they've all gone to good homes."

Intrigued by our newcomers, I peered into the cages and out gazed two massive bunnies with the longest ears I had ever seen.

"Gosh, Ma, they're huge! Can I get one out?"

"No, not yet. They're still very nervous. Just be very careful about how you handle..."

"Owww! It bit me!"

"Oh dear, I was trying to tell you to be careful. Ah, yes, it has taken rather a chunk out of that finger. Never mind. Wrap it with my hanky and clasp it tightly to stem the bleeding."

The bunnies were never cuddly types, and they did have teeth like carving knives. I should know. I was sliced several times. Eventually, they realised that they wouldn't be harmed ever again. Lop and Hop relaxed into their new surroundings, enjoying limitless food and the novelty of fresh grass under their paws.

With a fat dressing on my finger, when I wasn't searching for Lotti, much of the exeat was spent riding. I mostly rode Apache with Ma bobbing around on Ponni, fussing about needing Di back to exercise her pony. Neenah had been sold, which I didn't think was a bad idea. She was gorgeous but always seemed a bit nuts to me. But we still had proud Khan.

With Sioux and Khan still to exercise, Ma called to her dapple grey Arab in the paddock. Khan raised his head, intelligent eyes, always keen. His ears, with those characteristic inward curving tips, flickered with interest. He snorted and trotted over to us.

"Ma, why does he always hold his tail so high?"

"Many Arabians have one or two fewer vertebrae in their spines than most other horses. Have you noticed how compact he is?"

"They're *all* more compact than Apache, but I suppose he is."

"It's because of this difference that Arabs like Khan carry their tails up. Holding it higher is easier and more comfortable for them."

"I think it looks smashing."

"Yes, I do too. Now come along, let's get you aboard Sioux. We need to get on with our hack."

The exeat passed in the blink of an eye. I hadn't seen Gavin or the girls next door or been across the park to say hello to Clare, Jane, and Mark. There hadn't been enough time, but that didn't matter. Home was all I wanted.

Pa took me back to school. The ball in my tummy started growing as we entered the courtyard. The grey slate roofs, slick with water, glinted darkly in the twilight. Raindrops stained the granite walls in austere veils. Foreboding, unfriendly. I looked up at my daddy, eyes welling with tears.

"I don't want to stay here anymore, Pa."

"Come on now, Bethy, buck up. It'll be half term before you know it."

"And we didn't even find Lotti."

"I know, but let's not give up hope. There's always hope."

Tears streamed as I clung to Pa, hugging, not wanting to let go. I waved as he zoomed off, feeling overwhelmingly daunted. Would I ever get used to being at boarding school? At that moment, I felt I couldn't.

Though I couldn't have known at the time, our beautiful Lotti never did return home. I'm glad that Pa had given me that precious gift of hope to ease the emotion.

I joined the bustle, seeking out my friends. We

slipped back into an often uneasy routine. Uneasy because most of us were flibbertigibbets who struggled with the plethora of regulations we had to remember. And woe betide anyone breaking them.

Having been brought up in an ordered environment, I was used to rules. The problem I instinctively had and still do was their purpose. For me, there has to be one. Protocols surrounding 'Lights out', when we were supposed to sleep, were problematic. There were frequent infringements. At 8.30 pm sharp, Miss Barren stomped down the corridor. A disembodied arm snaked around the door, reaching for the electricity switch.

"Lights out, now, girls. Goodnight."

"Goodnight, Miss Barren," we chorused at thin air.

Requiring a roomful of girls aged between ten and eleven to fall asleep instantly was a big ask. Giggles permeated the room. Tiny torches flickered as girls started reading under blankets. A secret chat was shared. None of this was lost on our housemistress.

Miss Barren had the hearing of a bat. She prowled up and down the corridors, lurking, rapping sharply on doors to quell noisy rabble-rousers. If symptoms persisted, disciplinary action was taken. The door flew open. Our housemistress filled the space like a galleon in full sail.

"Janis Ellis," she thundered, "I can hear you all the way down the corridor. In my study now, please. And the rest of you go to sleep!"

Shamefaced, Janis slunk after Miss Barren to be lectured on noiselessness.

Repeat offenders were given lines. Tuck, dispensed like war rations, might be denied, letters written to parents admitting shameful behaviour. These rules I accepted, but being forbidden to leave our dormitory after 'lights out' was an impossibility. The moment the light switch was clicked, I needed a wee. I tossed and turned and stuck my head under the pillow, willing the urge to pass. But it didn't. It got worse. There was nothing for it. I had to go.

The consequences formed a sorry pattern that plagued me throughout my two years in Junior Block. Grabbing my dressing gown, I sought Miss Barren, who was usually moored outside a dormitory bedroom.

"May I visit the washroom, please, Miss Barren?"

"No, you may not. You should have gone before lights out. Go back to bed this instant."

I returned to the dorm, trying to forget about it. Of course, I couldn't. Soon after, I plucked up the courage to try again. This time I bypassed our housemistress and crept down the corridor towards the toilets and new challenges.

The building was decrepit, as were the floorboards, which were riddled with woodworm. The threadbare runner carpet was constantly fringed with sawdust. Despite being stealthy, now and again, I trod on a wobbly plank. The *creak* was like activating a landmine.

Miss Barren, triumphant, rumbled around the corner, catching me in the act.

"You disobedient child. My study, now!"

These were regular occurrences. Sometimes the crackly tracing paper toilet sheets gave me away; others, it was the cronky woodwork. I was told off, often given lines. But I still had to go.

After insistently pleading my case, I would be frog marched to the nearest toilet. It's probably why I have never turned down the chance of having a 'precautionary visit' when the opportunity presents itself.

Sundays at school were bittersweet and involved a battery of particularly silly rules. The silliest involved dressing in our 'Sunday best', for church. It was a whole school event. Passing muster before we joined the others was fraught. Miss Barren lined us up.

"Beth, your shoes are dirty. Go and clean them quickly."

"Cerys, gloves. Where are they? And your cloak. Do not forget your cloak!"

"Diane, pull up your socks. You look like a rugby player."

"Jacky, dirty! Your skirt has a mark on it. Dab it off immediately."

I shall never know why these details were so religiously adhered to, and this is why.

Once ready, we assembled in the courtyard, class order, with prefects first. Regardless of the weather, we formed pairs, linked hands, and began our march to church. A dot on the horizon. It wasn't the distance so much as the terrain that caused problems. Our route took us down a steep flight of chiselled steps into the school park. It was a sizeable expanse of grassland, maintained by a flock of sheep, who deposited as much as they consumed.

Our long crocodile was herded by teachers, flanking us on either side. We plodded over stony ground, treading on sheep poo, lots of that, and negotiated clumps of wet grass. By the time we reached the gates, shoes were filthy, socks had wrinkled, and at least one girl had slipped and covered herself in muck. And we were often drenched.

We filed, hand-in-hand, down the church nave, taking up positions in our appointed pews. Prayer books came out of pockets and were replaced by grubby gloves. Pupils were hemmed in by prefects or teachers, and periodically glared at for excessive fidgeting or an outbreak of titters.

The natural aroma of mildew, so quintessentially ecclesiastical, could not compete with the pungency of fresh dung. And so we all sat, along with devout sufferers, quietly brewing in an environment that possessed toxic qualities. For at least an hour.

Sunday afternoons were free time. We were allowed to explore the 'in bounds' parts of the school, which in itself involved a sub-section of instructions. We were also required to write to our parents about the week's activities. My inky epistles were a mixture of chat about my best pals and sports. Without exception, they ended with questions about the animals and, during this period, special pleas for news about Lotti. Ma's replies were non-committal. I missed home all the more.

The end of term finally arrived, and with it, the school Tableau. This was organised by our drama teacher, Miss Foley. Tableau was a festive concert where the Christmas story was presented on stage with pupils in costumes, posing silently in a series of static scenes. The school choir sang carols with umpteen verses, which allowed time for scenery changes and actresses to alter positions.

Who would play Mary, Joseph, and the three kings? These were hotly contested roles, as was the Angel Gabriel. It was unclear why since everyone had to stand stock still on stage. Angel Gabriel did have posh wings, though.

Siân and I were among those chosen from Junior Block to take part. We were thrilled with the honour and waited excitedly to find out which roles we would play. Miss Foley blustered in with her clipboard and pen. And drew breath.

The Wonder of Welsh Words

Eglwys
The place of worship revered by so many. This word for '**church**' is pronounced, 'egg-lewis'.

Chapter Fourteen

'Tyfid maban, ni thyf ei gadachan.'
('The child will grow, his clothes will not.')

Welsh Saying

The major parts were handed out. Di bagged a king role and was overjoyed, especially since she'd be in charge of myrrh. Imagine her disenchantment when it turned out to be an empty gravy boat from Chef's kitchen.

Miss Foley reached the bottom of her list and gave Siân and me a kindly glance. Our hopes of being chosen as minor angels were dashed. We had run out of angel parts.

"Girls, you will both play sheep."

Sheep? We didn't know there were any in the nativity. Still, they were parts, and we accepted our responsibility with great pride.

Endless rehearsals followed. There were teething troubles with Gabriel, who kept getting her wings stuck in the scenery. Modifications were made, reducing their impressive wingspan. It was a bitter disappointment to Gabriel, but reducing the risk of avalanche from a dislodged backdrop was a relief for everyone else.

It was the last dress rehearsal. Problems persisted with the kings' beards, which had been stuck with the wrong glue and kept sliding off. Aside from that, it ran like clockwork. There wasn't much for Siân and me to worry about. Posing on hands and knees for three minutes in four different tableau scenes wasn't that complicated.

Parents flooded into the great hall on the opening night. Ours rarely attended school functions but made an exception for the Tableau. I peeped from the wings. There they were in the middle row, ready to start doting. It must be hard being proud of a sheep. At least Di had made it to relative stardom.

"Try not to *baa* in your scenes, Beth!" chortled my sister as she disappeared in search of the glue pot.

Packing for the Christmas holidays produced excited shrieks, laughter, teasing and shouts. Miss Barren's fog horn reprimands went largely unheeded as girls scraped trunks along corridors, down the steps and into the courtyard. It was home time.

Having been away for an eternity, I embraced my surroundings with new gratitude. The view of the majestic Snowdonia mountains from my bedroom with their icing sugar peaks. The winter-sleepy gardens with wild bunny tracks in the snow, frosty fields and diamond-tipped grass, I couldn't be happier.

It was during the holidays when Ma took Di shopping. Much to my sister's joy, her blazer sleeves no longer looked like drainpipe ends. Di's hands had appeared at the cuff. She had finally grown, and there were consequences. This teenage sprouting caused the hems of her jeans to wag cheekily around her ankles. Apparently, it was not a good look.

I had already been subjected to Di and her clothes shopping indecisions. Watching her humming and hawing over endless, almost identical garments was a fate worse than death. I declined to join them. Staying at home was a much better proposition.

I slipped on Apache's bridle and took her for a bareback ride. Having circumnavigated several pastures, I ended up in the field with Khan and General, a big old hunter staying with us for a few weeks. We trotted over for a friendly chat.

For some reason, Khan had taken a shine to General. Despite being the least threatening pony in the world, he decided Apache should not be allowed near his new friend. As I leant forward to stroke General's nose, Khan spun around and lashed out.

Thwack!

Mercifully, he missed Apache but kicked me squarely on the shin.

A split second of shock. No pain. And then it hit. Scared to look at my leg in case it had been severed at the knee, I screamed blue murder. Apache was totally undisturbed by the noise. Instead, she took my hullabaloo as a cue to graze.

I tried to pull up the reins but couldn't, and fell off.

Now I was in a pickle. I was in the middle of a freezing cold field, unable to walk, and no one was home. I crawled back to the house and did what I had never dared do before. I called Pa's office.

"H...hello, Miss Edwards. It's Beth. May I speak to my father, please?"

"Hello, Beth, nice to hear from you. I hope everything's alright. Let me see if your father is free."

"Beth? Beth, what's wrong?"

"I'm sorry to bother you, Daddy, but Khan has kicked me, and Apache is still in the field with her bri…"

"Never mind Apache, are you alright?"

"No, ever so, really."

"Stop sniffing and tell me what's wrong."

"Well, I've hurt my leg, and I can't get my boot off."

"Can you see any blood coming through?"

"Um, yes."

"Right. Stay there. Do not move. I'm coming over now."

Pa zoomed back home and studied my battered boot.

"Can you feel your foot and wiggle your toes?"

"Yes, just about."

"Can you raise your leg from your knee?"

"Yes, but it hurts," I whimpered.

"We'd better get you to hospital for a check-up."

Off we went to the Casualty department at our local hospital. Now named Accident and Emergency, this was where prompt aid was given without needing an appointment.

We joined fellow patients in the waiting room, decorated with a collection of miserable festive paper chains. A limp crepe paper lantern hung from the ceiling, partially obscuring a killjoy sign on the hospital noticeboard:

Please do not bleed on our decorations.

A merry reveller staggered in. He'd peaked too soon. Still bursting with bonhomie, he didn't seem to notice that the end of one of his fingers was missing. Brushing aside his wife's attempts to stem the crimson geyser, he burst into song. It's a Welsh thing.

Mercifully, a nurse appeared and took us into a curtained booth. She cut off my boot, which revealed a deep gash to the bone, but no fracture. I was patched up, and we returned home to a concerned-looking Ma, and Di who managed to look sympathetic for about ten seconds.

While Di unbridled Apache, Pa explained the situation and returned to work.

"Right, Beth, no riding for a while, I'm afraid."

"Oh, Maaaa."

"I think your bandage is far out," trilled Di, plonking Hercules on my lap. "Wanna see my new jeans? They're funky!"

"Di! Please stop using that *dreadful* slang."

I, and my enormous bandage spent the next few days mostly luxuriating in the warm kitchen. And I wasn't alone. The Aga was perfect for heating frozen limbs after messing around outside. Dogs, cats, and humans, we all got under Ma's feet.

Christmas decorations twinkled merrily. Cheery crackling fires warmed rooms; all impossibly cosy. To serenade us, Bing Crosby boomed Christmas favourites from Pa's gramophone in the hall. Despite having a crocked leg, Christmas at home felt extra special that year.

The school Easter term was much shorter. No longer newbies, my pals and I finally remembered which areas we could roam around and those that were taboo. We contravened fewer rules, and lessons seemed less daunting. Still, I always looked forward to Sister's Talk. My big sis, much tougher than me, was a reassuring rock whenever I came unstuck.

By the time we reached the holidays, spring had sprung. Pristine snowdrops stepped aside for bumptious daffodils, whose bold yellow petals heralded the advent of sunny days. And crocuses, masses of them, formed multi-coloured carpets everywhere we went.

Never short of a creative idea, Ma cajoled Di and me into picking endless bunches of daffodils. We sold these to the local 'on the slate' grocery shop. I'm not sure what happened to the money we earned. Strange things happened with currency in that place.

Fields rang with the voices of newcomers. Countryside music. The *meeeehs* of lambs, the *moos* of calves, and the exuberant cries of cock pheasants all celebrating the season of rebirth. And while there was much going on outside, Ma was busy too. More business dinner parties were being held.

The house, which was customarily filled with flowers anyway, started looking like a botanical hothouse. Ma replenished vases with fresh, sunny daffodils, irises and lilies mixed with greenery. She finished them with a flourish, a flimsy branch or shoreline treasure we found during walks. Ma was incredibly artistic.

As strangers, usually associated with Pa's work, arrived for cocktails or dinner, Di and I fulfilled our usual duties before leaving the adults to their evening. We served canapes, chatting politely with guests. Having no idea who these people were, we quickly learned the art of small talk. Ma was a supremo at being able to chat about nothing in particular. In our cases, having a plateful of nibbles to stick under someone's nose if the conversation dried up was a particularly handy ruse.

Many of the visitors were colourful characters and always pleasant. Some I vaguely remember, one I will never forget. This man, a staying guest, had twinkly eyes and laughter lines. He took the time to talk to Di and me about our animals. I immediately liked him.

The following day, I was up early, just in time to gaze at the sun as it soaked Snowdon's peak with dazzling rays. A perfect pony trek day. Misdemeanours forgiven, I smiled at Khan in the paddock and hauled on some clothes to go and say hello.

Dragon's breath surrounded the Arab's head as he snorted, surveying the new day with approval. I called. He tossed his head and floated over, his silvery mane and tail flowing. I watched him dance across the ground, captivated by his silvery grace.

"Good morning, Beth. He's a beauty, is he yours?"

It was the kind gentleman from the dinner party. He leant on the paddock rails next to me.

"Oh, hello, good morning. Um, no, Khan is Ma's horse. I'd love to ride him one day."

"Well, be patient, and perhaps you will."

The gentleman started chatting about his animals and the circus his family had been involved with for generations. I was enthralled. My eyes were the size of saucers as he described how he had grown up working with African animals, many of which he had performed with in shows.

As I gained confidence, I asked more questions about the lions, tigers, and the elephants in their care. His respect for them was evident. He told me about the vision he had for families to enjoy the wonders of African animals in a more natural, liberated setting. Different to a circus. It was his special project, and it was why he was visiting our part of Wales.

Mesmerised, I was bulging with questions. I was halfway through my list when Ma appeared.

"Ah, Jimmy, there you are. Breakfast is ready when you are. And Beth, do stop chattering. Mr Chipperfield[1] is extremely busy."

My early morning companion winked at me.

"It sounds as though this is my cue to go. Now, don't forget, stick to your studies, finish school and always care for your animals properly. And watch Khan, he's a spirited horse, but I have a feeling you'll enjoy riding him if you have the opportunity."

Sadly, I never got the chance to ride Khan, but

there would be a momentous event in my future to complete my equestrian bliss. It was something I had no idea would happen.

The Wonder of Welsh Words

Mynydd
I've climbed many. Pronounced, 'mun-eth', this is the word for, **'mountain'**.

---

1. Chipperfield's Circus became one of the largest in Europe with a Big Top that could hold 6,000 people. The circus later diversified into safari parks.

Chapter Fifteen

'Llanddwyn beach. Longer Than Childhood Summers.'

William Gerwyn

My two-year stint in Junior Block was finally drawing to a close. Settling into the boarding school way of life took a long time. I, and my friends, had moped and coped our way through and learned a few tricks along the way.

Junior Block plots involving impromptu apple pie beds were favourites. The chosen victim was usually close to a birthday. Suspicious for days, these girls would gingerly feel their way into bed, eventually assuming the risk was over. An oversight.

That unmistakable *rrrripping* sound caused peals of laughter to ring around the dorm as the victim stuck her foot through the top sheet. It had been folded back on itself and torn on impact. A great wheeze for the plotters, but not for the girl.

Predictably, Miss Barren, stalking nearby, charged in, demanding to know what was going on. Her reply was a roomful of noiseless girls, heads on pillows, pretending to be asleep. Temporarily foiled, our housemistress barked out a vicious line-writing threat and retreated in a huff.

Perhaps our greatest junior triumphs were the midnight feasts – it wasn't just a St. Trinian's lark. Careful planning was required. Tuck was kept back and stored in pillowcases along with break-time stale biscuits. The chosen night was always a full moon.

At the appointed hour, each girl, ever so stealthy, crept out of bed and dragged her pillow stuffed with goodies over to the big bay window. Counterpane tents helped dampen the sound of sniggers. We were ready to begin.

Gathering our nighties, we huddled in a tight circle as someone produced a book of spooky stories. Typically, it would be Janice. An unusual girl, she had harboured a strong sense of the macabre from an early age. Under the pale light of an eerie moon and the feeble glow from a pencil torch stuck under her chin for ghoulish effect, she started.

'Oohs' and 'Eeuws' were hissed as she recited a grisly detail. Gripped by the story, hands absently dug into pillowcases, peeling half-unwrapped Refreshers off cotton material. Crumbly Rich Tea biscuits and melty Chocolate Buttons, the booty was equally shared. That was the rule.

Eventually bored with Janice's book, we took turns telling our creepiest story. Wide-eyed, we scoffed our feast, collectively terrifying ourselves, setting off nervous titters. Stage whispered reprimands to quell the noisiest made things worse, especially for Phillipa.

If Philly got the giggles, we were sunk. Philly snorked. She couldn't help the surprisingly realistic imitation of a warthog, nor could she help the volume. Poking her in the ribs didn't help; it made her louder. Inevitably, this set off everyone else with dire consequences.

Janice heard the first creak. A rickety floorboard straining under the weight of a hefty footfall. Jamming one hand over her mouth, she feverishly pointed towards the door with her other. It could only be Miss Barron. We froze. Philly honked.

Scraps flew as we scampered back to our beds, slamming heads on pillows, trying to suffocate gurgles. The door squeaked as a hand snaked to the light switch. We were doomed.

Miss Barren surveyed the aftermath of our feast.

"How *dare* you! Look at this mess. You know perfectly well that eating after lights out is strictly forbidden. Own up, girls. Who is the ringleader?"

Miss Barron was up against it. We were firm friends, and there wasn't a snitch among us. After a brief silence, Miss Barron grunted. There was a touch of menace about her demeanour.

"I see. If you're not prepared to own up, you must all be punished. Out of bed now, and follow me."

Hiding smirks, we meekly followed our housemistress down the corridor and sat cross-legged outside her sitting room. It was freezing;

the floor was hard, and we stayed there for over an hour. It wasn't an isolated incident. I think Miss Barron was relieved to see us progress to middle school.

The summer holidays were filled with endless delights. Di and I spent most of the time outdoors, and each holiday marked several horsey occasions. It might be a country show, equestrian event or gymkhana. We occasionally got involved in the latter with remarkably average results.

Our local branch of the Pony Club ran several rallies and gymkhanas. General tuition ranged from pony care to different riding techniques. The competition elements aimed to encourage worthy traits such as sportsmanship, strength of character and self-discipline. Pa approved.

Aside from being great fun, gymkhanas are designed for riders to concentrate on improving their speed, stopping ability, turns, mounting and dismounting quickly and picking up objects while mounted. At least that's the theory.

Think mayhem, and you're pretty close to the mark for ours. Screaming young riders, bolting ponies, lost saddlery and bewildered stewards, it was all part of the fun. Di and I loved them, even before we had our steeds.

We used a school mount when Pony Club competitions were held at our local riding school.

My choice was Noddy, a scraggy fourteen hand bay. Noddy had no finesse, but he was fast and dead keen. These were mostly assets for gymkhana events. The Bending race was one of my favourites, and Noddy was a star. But there was a drawback. Although he could weave his way around upright poles like a pipe cleaner, my pony was having so much fun he didn't want it to end.

With almost zero chance of me stopping Noddy in battle mode, it was hit and miss whether I could get him to turn and return to the team. Nevertheless, he was the reason our team had the occasional success. The same couldn't be said when I tried a gymkhana with Apache.

Being of a more sedentary variety and not at all supple, Apache found games boring. Under Ma's tutelage, I had several goes at loosening her up on a long lunge rein. This exercise of having her move in circles around me was intended to help her rhythm and balance. It didn't.

Disinterested in the process, she usually hauled me off towards the nearest field in a dead straight line. On the day of our only gymkhana, with no confidence in my mount's athleticism, I was picked for the Bending race.

The race began, and off we lolloped at a slo-mo canter. More by luck than judgement, we managed to negotiate the first pole. Much to the dismay of my howling teammates, that was it.

"Come on, Beth, get her to *turn!*"

"I can't. She won't!"

"You've knocked down another one, *beeeend!*"

"I'm *trying!*"

Predictably, the race was a disaster. Apache mowed down all but one pole, leaving a pile of splintered sticks on the ground. Understandably, we were banned from the speed and agility races. This left the Sack race, where every team member was involved.

We had to canter up to a hessian sack, get in it and hop back, towing our pony behind. Simple. To her credit, Apache summoned up a respectable canter to the bag. Not quite last, I flew out of the saddle and jumped into my sack. This was about the same time she discovered a patch of fresh clover.

I started hopping with one hand on my sack and the other on Apache's reins. And stopped. Head down and focused on the sweet-tasting fodder, Apache wouldn't shift. As I feverishly hauled on the rein, I realised I wasn't the only one having difficulties.

Cries of encouragement and derision came from team members and parents as several bored ponies wandered off while their riders scrambled into sacks. Others decided the bags were ghosts and had a panic attack.

"Hurry up, Sarah, fetch Patch back!"

"Hop quicker, Gareth. You're *far* too slow, dear!"

"Carys, hang on to the reins. Pixie'll stop rearing in a minute!"

It's funny how one can pick up a parental voice from a roaring crowd. Ma's voice floated above the clamour.

"Pull, Beth."

"I am, Ma, but she won't budge."

"Use both hands!"

"I can't. My sack keeps falling off!"

"Jodhpurs, *darling*, tuck the hem into your jodhpurs!"

It was a sensible idea. With both hands now free, I leant backwards, tugged on the reins, overbalanced and fell in a hessian heap on the ground. This created activity, of sorts. Apache raised her head, mildly aware that action was required.

The succulent crop of clover just beyond my head became my next downfall. So close to doing the right thing, Apache spotted the new treat and made a beeline for it, treading on my hand and foot as she went.

"*Owww*, Apache!"

"Never mind, Beth, accident. Now get up and finish the race!"

We came a dismal second last.

On the whole, Di fared much better on Ponni. Speed was their forte, stopping wasn't. Ponni didn't have any brakes. The Walk, Trot, Canter race was where they came unstuck. All competitors had to do was walk to one end of the arena, turn and trot back. And then turn around and canter to the finish line. Easy-peasy.

The idea of this race being to exemplify a rider's precision and control was lost on Ponni. They managed the walk, although, in the excitement of the *off*, Ponni crab-scuttled down the course with Di huffing and puffing on top.

Puce with exertion, Di stood in her stirrups, trying to execute a controlled trot, which turned into more of a scramble. And as they turned for the canter, Ponni turned into a derby winner and bolted.

With pigtails streaming, Di valiantly steered him along the course. And then through a mass of scattering spectators before ending up, lost, in the maze of horse boxes. These were not uncommon scenes at gymkhanas.

If we weren't being thrown off a pony somewhere, the summer holidays included beach visits. Living so close to Anglesey meant we were spoilt for choice. During the Middle Ages, the island was known as *Mam Cymru*, Mother of Wales, because its fertile fields were the breadbasket for the north. We knew it as a gently undulating, blissful place peppered with farms, colourful towns, and spectacular beaches.

Benllech on the east coast, with its golden sand and temperate waters, was always on our list. Cute houses line the headland here, looking towards the Great Orme, a lumpy limestone headland on the mainland coast. It's picture-postcard pretty.

At low tide, the sand stretches for miles. It was idyllic, except for one thing. Watching Paddy padding off on beach-users meet and greet missions caused Ma great anxiety. It took us ages to bring him back.

Swimming until our fingers and toes turned crinkly, castles in the sand, donkey rides along the flats, and ice cream cornets from musical vans tinkling their approach. These were fun days out.

Llanddwyn, on the west coast with its beautiful tidal island, was our favourite beach. Access was through the Newborough pine forest. As woodlands go, this was pretty modern. It was planted between 1947 and 1965 to protect Newborough, the adjacent village, from blowing sand while helping to stabilise the dunes.

Trudging from the car park always seemed to take ages, but it was worth it. We scrambled over dunes, dragging deckchairs and windbreakers, swimming stuff, and picnic kit to see who could reach the beach first. That first sight of the endless sandy expanses was heaven.

Since we always seemed to have most of the beach to ourselves, setting up camp in a preferred spot was never a problem. We foraged for stones to pin down towels, unfurled windbreakers and succumbed to a slathering of slippery sunscreen. And then we were released to play.

The underfoot touch of soft sand, sometimes too burny to walk on. The rippled surface that made the arches of your feet feel funny, that imperceptible slope to the sea, and warm shallows, home to fascinating shells and intriguing sea creatures. These were the ingredients of perfect beach days.

We chased around with the dogs, played ball, and paddled and swam. And then we settled down to start building sandcastles, an important business. Or at least it was until Monty joined in and demolished our creations with his shovel-sized paws.

Suddenly starving, we flopped onto towels, ready to devour whatever was offered. If Ma was catering, the picnic was beautifully prepared and presented on ceramic plates with kitchen cutlery and paper napkins for accidental mishaps. Not so if we went with our next-door neighbours.

Food appeared in a jumble, and everyone dug in. For us children, it didn't matter how it came. We were all ravenous. And there was one common denominator that bound all picnics together. Regardless of preparation, we crunched our ways through sandwiches sprinkled with grains of sand. For years, I assumed this was how the foodstuff earned its name.

Relaxing after lunch, we played spotting games. Who could name the biggest mountain across the water on the mainland? What was the name of the wading birds on the shoreline? What type of squirrel did we pass in the forest? And where is Saint Dwynwen's church? Pa told us a special myth associated with this one.

"Now, girls, did you know that the name Llanddwyn means The Church of St. Dwynwen?"

"No, but it doesn't sound very interesting."

"Ah, Di, it might when I tell you that St. Dwynwen is the Welsh patron saint of lovers."

"Fab. Di's reading soppy stuff at the moment."

"Jean Plaidy's books are *not* soppy!"

"Stop squabbling, and I'll tell you the story. There are several versions, but here's one you'll enjoy."

Pa and myths. That was enough to attract any child's attention. We sat, lips pursed, poised.

"Dwynwen was a fifth-century princess. She was the prettiest of King Brychan Brycheiniog's 24 daughters."

"Imagine having 23 sisters. Yuck!"

"Thank you, Di. Yes, he was a busy king. Dwynwen fell in love with a local youth called Maelon Dafodrill, but King Brychan had already arranged for her to marry a prince. Maelon took the news badly and threatened her.

Dwynwen was distraught, frightened. She ran away and begged God to help her, which came in an unusual form."

"Ooh."

"Dwynwen was visited by an angel who gave her a potion to help her forget Maelon, but it also turned him into a block of ice. God lent a hand by granting Dwynwen three wishes. Her first wish was that Maelon be thawed. Her second wish was for God to help all true lovers, and her third wish was that she would never marry."

"I wonder why she didn't want to marry, ever?"

"There's an old phrase, Beth, once bitten, twice shy. I'll explain that to you another day. Anyway, to thank God, Dwynwen became a nun and set up a convent on Llanddwyn Island. Her name means, 'she who leads a blessed life'."

"That's a lovely name."

"It is. Dwynwen lived as a hermit until she died in 465 AD. Her church on the island became a shrine in the Middle Ages, as did its well. It was said to predict the destiny of lovers depending upon whether a sacred fish swam in its waters. And in addition to being the Welsh patron saint of lovers, St Dwynwen is also the patron saint of sick animals."

This was a twist I found far more appealing.

"I like the sound of her. Good riddance to rotten Maelon!"

Long days on the beach always ended in the same way, a tired march back to the car with a parent at the rear fielding cast-offs. Sand was in bags, sandals, pockets, hair, ears and fur. And mouths.

As a treat, we sometimes stopped to buy an ice cream or lolly on the way home. My choice was usually a Lyons Maid Strawberry Mivvi with its thick sticky red ice coating and creamy vanilla ice cream centre. Di preferred ice cream 99 cones with a Cadbury's flake stuck in the middle. We rode out the return journeys contentedly, catching drips, batting off helpful dogs, and ending up a sticky mess by the time we got home.

Afterwards, luxuriating in baths, a big meal, and relaxing in front of the telly completed these carefree days. We always slept well after beach trips. And there were more treats to come, one of which was always a highlight of our summer.

The Wonder of Welsh Words

Traeth
Perfect for holidays, try saying 'tri-th', and you have the word for **'beach'**.

Chapter Sixteen

'Better educated than wealthy.'

Welsh Proverb

We adored our Grandma and Grandpa. A summer holiday was never complete without a week spent at their home in Devon. Their bungalow was tucked away down a leafy lane near a hamlet with thatched roof houses and a pretty village green. It was the type where one might expect Miss Marple to live. And Grandma had a similar personality.

Brought up in colonial India, there's likely to have been something of the rebel about Grandma. While her early years were focused on learning how to be a lady, drinking tea and practising her elocution, Grandma also spent much of her time outdoors with her rescued pet leopard.

Grandma was an ardent animal lover and had wonderful stories about her exotic wildlife safaris. We loved looking through her old photographs. Then a young *memsahib* attended by punkah wallahs and surrounded by beaus at socialite functions, she looked ravishing.

Her favourite pair of shoes had been made from an unsuspecting snake she had slain while it was hunting her prized birds. Nobody messed with Grandma's animals, even other animals. Grandma was feisty, a remarkable quality for someone of her stature.

Grandma was tiny. Despite being less than five

feet tall and amply endowed, she somehow seemed taller. I often wondered whether the height gain had something to do with her hair. Grandma dressed her waist-length hair in a plait, which she wound around her head like an anaconda.

Every morning, Grandma appeared, beautifully dressed with her hair in that cottage loaf shape. But it never stayed. Despite being trapped in place by dozens of pins, several were jettisoned during the day, allowing long tresses to escape. She had similar problems with her hearing aid.

Grandma had no tolerance for deafness, and even less with her new-fangled hearing machine. The contraption was fixed to her cardigan. (Grandma always wore a cardy and pearls.) From this, a sizeable cable linked to an earpiece. The problem was, it constantly whined.

Di and I tittered as Grandma tutted and tapped the control box in frustration. Eventually, Grandpa would be recruited to help. He, a tall, much quieter gentleman with a scientific bent and wicked sense of humour, would fix it in a jiffy. Only for it to start whining again soon after.

Despite these practical issues, Grandma's vivacity filled every room, as did her giggles, which tinkled merrily all day long. There was just one drawback to our visits. We were rarely allowed to bring Monty and Paddy on these holidays, but there was a good reason why.

Grandma had a passion for Pekingese dogs and Burmese cats, which allowed no room for extra canines. Schnufflling, schnorkeling, the Pekes rolled around the house with a swashbuckler's gait, their lion's manes and luxuriant coats swishing the floor. They tolerated being played with but preferred their mistress, who they adored. The cats were similar.

Raja and Beatrix were supreme beings. Sleek, chatty and indescribably beautiful, they enjoyed attention but strictly on their terms. True to their breed, they were active cats who strolled around the house and garden with us until nap time. Unsurprisingly, their favoured spot was Grandma's lap.

Picture windows in the sitting room overlooked a stepped garden and paddock at the bottom. Someone else's ponies lived there. They loved a sneaky carrot or sugar lump treat. Little pathways wound around plant borders, under archways heavy with scents of honeysuckle and roses. It always seemed sunny at Grandma and Grandpa's house.

Breakfast time was filled with wondrous aromas and sounds. But hazards lurked in that kitchen. It was Di who witnessed Ma being blown clean across the room when the ancient gas oven exploded. These piffling inconveniences didn't faze Grandma. She was a consummate cook.

Grandma produced amazing kedgerees, ever so modern cheesecakes, and made vanilla ice cream clogged with chunks of brown sugar. She covered all puddings in lashings of cream. Calories were irrelevant. No wonder she was fairly round.

Enticing whiffs had us jumping out of bed early and scampering to the warm kitchen. Rice Krispies snapped, crackled and popped in bowls as the kettle rattled and whistled its way to boiling point. Freshly browned slabs of bread pinged out of the toaster and slid into the metal toast rack, which zinged like a harp.

As we dug into our Ma-prepared first meal of the day, shrill whines from Grandma's hearing aid heralded her arrival. True to form, she appeared bursting with plans to fill another glorious day, a regular highlight of which was our annual trip to Paignton Zoo.

For us, the zoo was special. It developed from the private menagerie of millionaire Herbert Whitley and first opened to the public in 1923. Herbert believed Paignton should be a zoo of learning and conservation, not just recreation for humans. It was an inspired aspiration.

We meandered around spacious enclosures,

goggling at healthy animals, watching them go about their business. Some were eating, others pacing, playing, and a fair number were enjoying a siesta. Ma shuddered at the creepy crawlies, Di cooed at the big cats, and I was captivated by them all.

Other excursions took us through the spectacular South Devonshire countryside. Grandpa drove on these trips, thank goodness. Grandma couldn't find the third gear – never did. Whenever she drove, we cringed in sympathy for the car, which screamed in agony as it laboured up and down hills in second. It took ages to get anywhere.

We fussed over Dartmoor wild ponies, adapted to withstand their stark, wild home. We discovered lush, rolling fields and wooded valleys closer to the sea. It was all so different from our craggier Welsh landscapes. The difference in climate was evident too.

There were exotic plants in gardens, and the promenade along Torquay town's seafront was lined with palm trees. Favoured by the Victorians for its mild climate, manicured flowerbeds blushed with Mediterranean plants around an ornate water fountain. Dubbed the English Riviera, it exuded exotic flair.

But for us, a visit to the model village at Babbacombe was more exciting. The site is filled with teeny weeny houses, minute countryside, model humans and miniscule animals. Baby trains, cars and other gadgets – all in miniature. It was still being developed when we visited, nevertheless, it packed a wow factor for children of all ages.

And when the day's adventures were all but over, there were still treats to come. Sometimes we played the piano and sang, but the best fun was listening to Grandpa's stories. And there was a certain irony to this.

It was Grandma who wrote short stories, many of which were used for the BBC children's storytelling programme, Jackanory. Yet despite her success as an author, she readily gave way to Grandpa's talents as a gifted raconteur.

Di and I, ready for bed in our nighties and dressing gowns, jabbering excitedly, plonked cross-legged in front of Grandpa's armchair. Impatient. He quieted us.

And this is how every story began.

"Twas a dark and stormy night. Brigands great and brigands small were gathered around the campfire. *'Come, Antonio,'* they called to the terrible chief, *'Tell us one of your famous stories.'* And Antonio arose and said…"

"Oh please, *please* tell us, Grandpa!" we'd chorus, thrilled with anticipation.

"'twas a dark and fearsome night..."

And Grandpa continued with a created story of his own. A perfect way to end another perfect day.

As the summer holidays waned, the new school year loomed closer, a miserable proposition. Little did I know Ma had a fantastic surprise in store that would distract me for months.

"Sioux is in season, girls. She is such a fine mare we've decided that a stallion should cover her."

"That's a top idea, Ma."

"*Ahem*, yes, and I think you'll like this even better, Beth. Di is doing very well with Ponni, and your riding skills are coming on, so Pa and I have agreed that you should have her foal."

"No! *Really?*" I couldn't believe my ears.

Di poked me in the ribs.

"It'll never be as good as Ponni."

"It'll be the best ever!"

"Thank you, thank you, *thank you*, Ma. This is like having all my birthdays and Christmas presents rolled into one."

"You're welcome. Now run along, the pair of you. There are plenty of unfinished jobs that need attending to."

The hunt was on to find a suitable stallion. Ma quizzed her horsey pals and eventually found an

Anglo Arab who had the credentials to do the job. We went to the stud for a viewing. It took about three minutes to make up our minds.

Llanrwst Aga Khan Silver Fox, or 'Tomi' as he was known, was brought out of his stable. Head held high, the magnificent dapple grey stallion tossed his head and cantered around the paddock. His movements were fluid, his conformation compact. This horse was an athlete.

When he eventually stopped posturing, he trotted over to say hello. He was friendly and possessed a gentle presence. He was our boy. Ma did the deal, and we left with an appointment for Sioux to meet her beau. After that, going back to school somehow seemed less awful.

The new academic year brought changes. No longer in Junior Block, my classmates were assigned to different houses where we would live until the end of our public Ordinary Level ('O' levels) exams. We were now part of the main house system.

Each house was named after a Snowdonia mountain. Siân and I, along with a couple of dorm pals, were allocated to Hebog House. It was a remarkable building, although not for the reasons one might assume. This place plainly did not feature on the parents' visit list.

The ground floor contained two bedrooms.

Thousands of ants (which permanently infested the floor), us newbies from Junior Block, and new intake girls of the same age inhabited them. In one way, the rooms were handy, as they were a breath away from an external door. But there were challenges.

The wind screamed under the outside door, inveigling its way into our bedrooms. Our patched lino flooring almost covered the cement base, but not quite. Ancient radiators and ill-fitting windows put up a stout defence against our frigid Welsh winters, and failed. Our toes were permanently freezing, noses red and drippy, and the counterpanes were damp. It was character building stuff, or so we were told.

The older girls' dorms and House common room were on the first floor. An internal flight of steep stairs outside our bedrooms accessed them at one end and a second external entrance at the other. This was the area to be. It was built above the Domestic Science building and was always warm and cosy.

The common room was our hub. Wood-panelled walls with casement windows overlooking the quad and principal thoroughfare provided a prime position for teacher and pupil spotting. This shared space was where we chatted and relaxed. And we became proud of it.

Our house coat of arms had pride of place on the wall. Lined on either side were wooden shields displaying the names of house competition winners. Threadbare, overstuffed sofas and armchairs filled the living space. It was as close to a home environment as we could get. This, along with the rest of Hebog, was run by our housemistress, Miss Singleton.

For reasons I could guess, the poor lady had gained the unfortunate nickname of Mole. An unusual lady, she was tiny, extraordinarily short-sighted and busy. She was also good-hearted. Unlike Miss Barren, she possessed a more laissez-faire attitude towards discipline.

Miss Singleton observed lights out and the million other house rules, but took a milder approach with minor transgressions. We were even allowed to venture to the washroom during the night, which was a great personal relief. Mole patrolled the corridors after dark, but stealth wasn't her strong point.

Miss Singleton was a chain smoker with a dreadful cough. If any of us had to visit her rooms, it was with trepidation and held breath. We knew what would happen. The moment she opened her door, billows of acrid smoke instantly enveloped us. It was hard not to choke.

Mole's tiny body appeared through the fug,

hastily stubbing a cigarette into one of many overflowing ashtrays. She cleared her throat, sounding like a football rattle and peered myopically, ready to deal with the question.

Although she never smoked in the rest of the house when girls were in, the sausages of fallen ash on the floor told their own tale. Miss Singleton had been on the prowl during lessons.

If we made too much noise after lights out, Mole eventually hacked her way downstairs. She banged on our doors, issued a reprimand, and staggered back up again. I don't recall ever going to her with a pastoral problem. I daresay that wasn't her forte. But she was a good sort, and we all liked her. The same couldn't be said for several of our teachers.

Miss Roberts, aka Bogo, was our geography teacher and consummately skilled at killing a potentially interesting subject. An ex-model, she had legs like telegraph poles and a foul temper.

Miss Roberts was stick thin and miserable as sin. We sat at our desks, stifling yawns as she stalked up and down her podium, barking at the blackboard, and us. Everyone agreed that if she ate more, she might cheer up.

The lab teachers were an intense lot. Mr Roberts (no relation to Bogo, who would remain unmarried to the end of her days) scuttled around his Victorian chemistry lab wearing enormous safety glasses and making peculiar noxious concoctions in his fume cupboard. We sat at long tables with Bunsen burners fixed at intervals in front of us. Now and again, for a giggle, someone fired up a burner and stuck a pencil tip or other nearby implement over the naked flame. Locks of hair were regularly frizzled in the chemistry lab.

Other antics involved side experiments designed to break up the monotony of learning periodic tables. Probably my favourite boredom beater came from a chum who was a scientific whizz.

One day, Jane crept into the lab before the lesson began and made a concentrated concoction of potassium permanganate crystals in ethyl alcohol. She smeared the sticky goo on the end of blackboard chalk and planted it on Mr Roberts' table.

Sniggerlying aware of the prank, we sat, hanging on Mr Roberts' every word, waiting for him to write up another interminable experiment. It had to happen. It did. He picked up the treated chalk and approached his huge roller blackboard.

Fizzzzz! Pop!

A classic tiny explosion as he made contact. Poor Mr Roberts almost jumped out of his skin.

And then there was Miss Whitby, the biology

teacher. She had an odd look about her. Rather like her lab, Miss Whitby stank of formaldehyde. She had a collection of dustbins containing abnormal sea creatures, part-submerged in the stuff. I'm pretty sure one was a dogfish, or at least had been. It had taken on an ambiguous form with a tail segment at one end and a few teeth at the other. I've no idea what happened to its fin. It wasn't where it was supposed to be.

Miss Whitby delighted in pinning frogs to racks and opening the poor creatures up. She was a neat worker. Intestines were heaped in one pile, so revealing the heart and lungs. For anyone brave enough to witness the carnage, she had a poke around the remaining bits, explaining how they all functioned. The entire business was extremely grisly.

Father Paul, our divinity teacher, bucked the trend. He was lovely, soft as a brush, and always got everyone's names wrong, including Regina. He constantly called her Vagina which was somewhat awkward.

But my favourite lessons were English, taught by Mrs Williams. She looked like Grandma, except a Welsh version. Sadly, she was so ancient the poor lady died of old age halfway through our 'O' level syllabus. We missed her.

Unsurprisingly, my preferred lessons were arts-based. They might have included Classics were it not for Mr Jenkins and his suit. He wore the same one every day, throughout the entire syllabus to 'O' level exams. It reeked. We were convinced it stood up all by itself when he took it off at night.

Other highlights were art and pottery, taught by Miss Foley, our drama teacher in charge of the school Tableau performances. Miss Foley had smiley eyes. Being small, dark and fairly hairy, she looked like a paint-spattered Hobbit, bounding around enthusiastically, inspiring us with endless nutty ideas. We loved her. Predictably, though, as an outdoor type, my best lessons were sports.

Miss Bowler introduced us to many, many games. Badminton, tennis, gym disciplines and netball. Field sports, running and rounders, which, by the way, is apt to be a dangerous game, and of course, hockey. I ended up playing in most of the school teams, which said more about my lack of focus on academic studies than my prowess in the sport concerned.

Our hockey team became involved in a local league, which was fiercely competitive. We were the only private girls' boarding school in the area, the other teams were state-run day schools. The natural assumption that we would be a bunch of pushovers was ill-advised. We had unique trump cards up our sleeves.

We turned up at school venues for away games in our dilapidated charabanc, looking like a bunch of kids from St Trinian's. Calculating eyes watched as we tumbled out, listening for posh accents and girlie countenances. True, there were one or two 'plummy' twangs, but they were misleading. We were a tough lot.

Being state schools, most had modern facilities, including the new-fangled Redgra hockey pitches. These had a hard surface covered in fine pinkish-red gravel, which drained well and could withstand harsh weather conditions. I loved playing on them, although there were drawbacks. Games were vicious and fast. The ball ran true on the gritty pitch, and we rarely came away without bloody, gravel-embedded knees and elbows. Results for away games were pretty even, but all that changed when we did battle at home.

Visitor players were unused to a sloping pitch, so steep in places that on a windy day, the ball could roll by itself. Nor were they familiar with our surface condition. It was naturally lumpy with sheep poo signatures. And that wasn't all.

Charlotte came from the East End of London and was the daughter of a wealthy jeweller. A girl who bore a strong resemblance to her father, Charlotte was built like a brick potting shed. None of the other teams possessed a goalkeeper like ours.

Charlotte may not have possessed a whippet-like turn of speed, but she found her niche filling goal. She loved playing at home and determinedly defended her manor as though her life depended on it.

With our secret weapons, home games usually featured over or under hits from the opposing teams, and cusses at air shots as the ball hit a tussock and hopped over their hockey sticks. And if, perchance, they reached the mighty Charlotte, they mostly came away with a bruising.

Our matches, as with all sporting events, ended with tea. Naively expectant, our oppo assumed they would be a lavish affair. Not so. Players, officials and spectators trekked up the muddy hill and into the dining room, where a selection of ghastly sandwiches lay in wait.

Curly triangles of margarine-slapped white bread, hard around the edges, looked like they had been made days earlier. The typical fillings were spam or tasteless cheese, and a brownish fish paste if we were seriously unlucky. Everybody avoided the fish paste. It was because of our school's underwhelming catering standards I committed my first costly transgression.

The Wonder of Welsh Words

Lloegr
With that special smile combined with the blowing sound using 'h' and 'l', split this this into, 'Ll-oy-grr', to make the word for, '**England**'.

Chapter Seventeen

'In every pardon there is love.'

Welsh Proverb

Our chef was a grubby gargoyle of a man whose lair was in the oldest building. Creatures, humans, we were all terrified of him. The kitchens were dark and squalid, visible to pupils brave enough to peep through a deeply recessed hatch. The interior looked like a tomb.

Chef's countenance was perma-grim, as was his apparel. Since there wasn't an apron that could cope with his vastness, it was pretty obvious where the leftovers went. When he worked, grunted commands came from the bearlike man as he pummelled another wretched foodstuff into obscurity.

The standard of his catering was as dubious as his tarnished equipment. As we filed towards the dining rooms, we'd snatch a view. Underlings scurried around Chef like orcs, heaving enormous dented tureens from one monster burner to another.

Powdered eggs, which should have been outlawed at the end of World War 2, were served for breakfast. The unappetising scrambled pale-yellow mush languished in an opaque moat. And there was worse. We dubbed his top meat dish 'gristle burgers' for good reason. Our plates were littered with ground-up sinews and tubes after one of those meals.

Every Sunday, we were treated to a dead flat

piece of beef or lamb or a round of off-white pork. Species identification was problematic with roasts. Mashed potatoes came out of packets, the peas from tins, as did most other veg.

A surprisingly dreadful dish was the serving of plum tomatoes. They appeared in scratched stainless steel bowls, drowning in anaemic juice. Any vitamin-based values in those sad offerings had been long lost. It was strictly against the rules to use bread as a mopper-upper, so we generally left the table with pink drizzles down our fronts.

After yet another underwhelming meal, a gang of us decided to flout the school rules and search for some decent food. Our venue of choice was the Little Chef. Part of a fast-food restaurant chain gaining popularity at the time, there was one about half a mile from school. We decided it was close enough for a quick visit on Sunday afternoon.

With our audacious plan in place, we stole through the school gardens into the woods, where we faced our first challenge. The high perimeter stone wall lined with jagged shards of slate. I'm not sure whether it was designed to keep intruders out or us in. It did a reasonably good job of both.

We considered our first hurdle. Cerys wrinkled her brow.

"How about if Janice gets on all fours. We can use her as a step to reach the top of the wall?"

This seemed like a good plan to everyone, except Janice.

"Wha...what about me? After trampling me half to death, how am I expected to climb up?"

Cerys wagged her head.

"Don't you see? It has to be you 'cos you're the tallest. You'll be able to reach the first hand-holds. Anyway, if you can't, the last one up'll give you a pull from the top."

"Oh, right you are, then. Let's go."

Janice was a good sort.

We soon arrived at the restaurant. Feeling desperately intrepid, we sat down and double-counted our pocket money. There was just enough for a hamburger each and one portion of French fries. Perfect.

No doubt aided by the illicit nature of our clandestine activity, we decided our burgers were the best we had ever eaten. A debate began about the relative merits of dills in burgers. Were they a tasty addition, or a palate shocker? Partway through our discussion, Kathryn shrieked.

"Oh, *no!* Look at the time. We have to be at prep in twenty minutes."

We bolted down the last meaty morsels and pelted back to school. The distance seemed longer, the wall taller, and weeds in the woods snaggier. We made it but were woefully late.

Hastily dusting ourselves down, we dashed into prep.

Unfortunately, Bogo Roberts was on duty. Standing next to her was Dilys, our Head Girl, a doleful character who proudly polished her badge of office every day. The pair of them looked supremely self-satisfied. Bogo stalked up on her beanpole legs.

"Girls, you were seen leaving the school precincts. Where have you been?"

We had been rumbled. There was nothing for it; we had to confess. Bogo arched her pencil line brows.

"I see. You will have detention for the next two weeks. You will also be gated for a month."

It took a second for the penny to drop. Being gated meant imprisonment in the school, we would miss the exeat. There would be no going home until half term. And as if that wasn't awful enough, Bogo had another bombshell.

"After prep, you will telephone your parents and explain why you have received these punishments. You have brought disgrace to the school, and your conduct will not be tolerated. And I will deduct points from your House scores."

Utterly despondent, we gathered our books and brooded through the rest of prep, steeling ourselves for *that* phone call.

Parents' responses differed. Some laughed about the incident, others were furious, and we could almost see the telephone receiver vibrate when Janice had a tongue-lashing. She came away in tears. Finally, it was my turn. I feared the worst.

Ma answered and listened to my sorry account. Predictably, she was deeply disappointed.

"Such shameful behaviour, Beth. You must never disregard school rules. They're made for a reason, and I'm sure there was an excellent one in this case. Accept your punishment with good grace, please. I'm afraid I shall have to tell your father. Here he is."

It was the moment I was dreading. Pa, a stickler for the rules, was about to lambast me.

"Beth, I heard what your mother said to you."

"Yes, Pa. I am ever so sorry. It's just tha..."

"And I have one question."

"Um, yes?"

"Did you have mustard on your hamburger?"

"Oh. Erm, no, Pa."

"What?"

"No. I asked, but they didn't have any."

"In that case, it would have been inedible. A wasted trip. Right, let that be a lesson for you. We'll see you at half term and, well, keep your chin up."

And with that, the phone clicked.

My compatriots and I struggled through the rest of the year. There were no more cardinal sins, though detentions were not infrequent occurrences. Preparations for the summer holidays were as raucous as ever. We lugged trunks out of the storeroom and dragged them into bedrooms where clothes were stuffed in willy-nilly.

Mole scurried up and down corridors between cigarettes, attempting to oversee operations, but with so many excitable girls to deal with, her task was all but impossible. Once packed, we crowded the common room and stuck our heads out of the windows, watching parents arrive.

Old cars, new ones and posh limos with engines that purred, Charlotte's parents always had one of those. One by one, they pulled up, ready to receive their pride and joys. Whoops of delight, waving arms, mothers gushing as unions were made.

Fathers bear-hugged, then moaned about scratched paintwork as trunks were loaded. Tennis rackets, hockey sticks, violin cases, and assorted gear followed. Tearful farewells, hugs and promises to write were exchanged among friends before each girl bundled into the family vehicle. More cries and frantic waves as the car drove off.

Often, the same car reappeared five minutes later. A bashful girl dashed out to recover a vital item of clothing or equipment she had forgotten in the joyful melee. It was a thing. We all did it.

Home. It was heaven. All the animals were perky, though Hammy two was looking distinctly different. I had finally realised that Ma stealthily replaced deceased Hammys with new ones, and being a completely different colour, this little chap was a dead giveaway.

Sioux was now heavily pregnant and doing well. We left her to amble quietly around the field and rode our ponies, usually joining up with our friends. At harvest time, the farm temporarily took on an extra dimension. A playground for equestrian pursuits.

As the big Massey Ferguson combines munched crops, we used the part-cut fields as racetracks. Pretending to be jockeys, we shortened stirrups and galloped, helter-skelter, around the perimeters. Even Apache, caught in the moment, managed a decent lick for these events.

With a bit of heaving, rectangular straw bales could be arranged to form obstacles. Rows of single bales set out at intervals were ideal for hurdle races, while double and quadruple-stacked ones became our show jumps. Leaping wasn't Apache's forte, but that was no problem. A new pony had come into our care, and she jumped like a stag.

Ma had bought Strawberry, a beautiful roan. She may have been little and tubby, but she was headstrong and keen as mustard. She was going to a family after the holidays, and they asked us to give her lots of exercise. I rode Strawberry every day for almost three weeks, jumping, trekking, and messing around with the others.

Strawberry was a handful, sassy and boundlessly energetic – until the day I went into the field to saddle her. I got the surprise of my life.

"Ma, Maaaaaa, come quickly!"

"What's wrong?"

"Ma, there's a foal in the paddock with Strawberry!"

"What?"

I can get mixed up about many things in life, but a foal is not one of them. I gazed in wonder at the gangly baby. She gazed back, batting big brown eyes. Her miniature ears flickered, disturbing the stubby forelock and starter mane. Interested, she took a few wobbly steps toward me on ridiculously skinny legs.

Ma appeared, making a strange combination of tutting, gasping sounds.

"Goodness me, oh dear, I had no idea she was pregnant."

"Me neither. I just thought she was fat. Oh, no, and I was jumping her yesterday. Crikey, I hope she's alright."

Much to our astonishment, both mother and daughter seemed to be in fine fettle. Ma examined Strawberry's udders. Sure enough, there was some swelling, but very little. Concerned, she immediately called the vet.

Mr Ellis confirmed that mum and daughter were fit and healthy but that Strawberry needed a special paste to help her produce more milk. Ma's two for one purchase was offered to the intended family. She suggested that the sale be delayed until the filly was weaned from her mum. The family said no. They were enraptured and decided to have them both.

Our summer held another surprise. This time it had nothing to do with animals. Clare and Mark were given an aged Austin A40 by their parents. The idea was for the children to teach themselves how to drive on the private estate roads. It was an ironic notion, given our youth, but they decided it was safer than exposing us 'green' to public roads when we reached the legal driving age.

Di and I, totally inspired by the idea, somehow convinced our parents of the same logic. But if we wanted a car, we must pay for it ourselves. Pocket money savings were used, and extra jobs were done to add to our coffers. We eventually amassed the grand sum of fifteen pounds, enough to buy a decrepit Triumph Herald.

We had great fun in our cars, although they had quirks. 'Black Beauty', the Austin A40, had a gear lever with a cream bobble on the end fixed to the steering column. Changing gear was haphazard and felt like stirring a cake mixture. There again, it had a snazzy leather front bench seat.

The seat was slippy, but with effort, four could cram into the front. It also had quaint indicators that plinked out of the sides behind the front doors. We decided these were groovy, especially when they popped up unannounced. The front door triangular insert windows didn't close, and the main windows thunked down by themselves. All minor inconveniences until it rained.

Our car was a much newer, two-tone model. It had a folding vinyl sunroof, which gained us excellent bragging rights. Regardless that it took two of us to wrench it open, we used the sunroof on nearly every outing. One person driving, the other sticking through the roof in safari mode. Sadly, there was a practical problem with the ageing material.

The sunroof leaked and regularly jammed in the open position. Neither situation was ideal given the amount of rainfall we have in Wales. Having only one operating windscreen wiper was another drawback, especially since that was on the passenger side.

The Triumph's front doors presented a further challenge. These had a habit of opening when we drove around corners. It caused endless bickers.

"Di, slow *down*. My door opened again!"

"Stop being a baby and close it!"

"I can't. I'll fall out!"

Black Beauty had a different quirk: she had no parking brake. Consequently, she slid down slopes. On one misguided parking occasion, she ended up embedded in a tree. Fortunately, Mr Griffiths came to our rescue and hauled her out with his tractor. No harm done aside from a couple more trophy dents to join the collection.

Despite the structural anomalies with our cars, we never had a crash. And the result of our junior motoring escapades? I have no idea what happened to our jalopies, but we all passed our tests on the first attempt.

As our summer continued with beach trips, playing with friends, messing about on ponies and in old bangers, there was one exceptional event ahead. Sioux was due to foal. As the day approached, I barely slept a wink.

The Wonder of Welsh Words

Cosbedigaeth
I had plenty of these when I was growing up! This word for '**punishment**' isn't as hard to say as it looks. Pronouncing it 'cos-bedi-guyth' will get you close.

Chapter Eighteen

'To be loved by a horse, or by any animal, should fill us with awe – for we have not deserved it.'

Marion C. Garretty

The days passed agonisingly slowly. Unlike Strawberry's unnoticed pregnancy, the classic signs of imminent birth were obvious with Sioux. It finally happened on a sunny afternoon in the meadow. Ma had been watching Sioux.

"Quickly, Beth, Sioux is beginning to foal!"

It felt as though I had been waiting my whole life for this moment.

I sprinted over and stood beside Ma, watching, unsure what to expect. Sioux lay down and got up again several times. No fuss, no bother. She seemed to know exactly what to do.

"Ma, what's that whitish bag?"

"It's called the amniotic sac. The foal is inside and should appear front first in a diving position."

"I can't believe I'm watching my horse being born."

"I know, and this is a special birth as mares often foal during the night."

"That's strange."

"I believe it's an instinctive reaction for horses. They feel safer at night. Sioux is obviously relaxed. I'm surprised she didn't want to use her stable, though. Perhaps she prefers more space."

"Ooh, I wonder what colour it'll be?"

"We'll know in a moment."

"Ma, I know what I want to be when I grow up."

"What now?"

"Definitely a vet."

"Very good. In that case, you'll have to improve your marks in chemistry and physics. The sciences are essential for vets."

Mesmerised, we watched on, and finally witnessed the miracle of birth. It was a breathtaking privilege to observe. The foal lay on a mattress of fresh clover. As we watched the natural process unfold, a beautiful light bay youngster was revealed.

Sioux, snickering, turned to look at her baby. Is it possible for a horse to express rapture? Definitely. She started nuzzling and licking her foal's coat, cleaning, stimulating a reaction. Ma checked over the twitching form and smiled.

"You have a fine colt, Beth. Now you can choose a name for him."

"Wow, *exactly* what I wanted, Ma. I already have a name. Sam. Just Sam."

"Alright, but he must have a stud name. How about Ty Fawr Samuel Bach?"

I knew Ma wouldn't be able to resist giving the little mite a ridiculously long name.

"Okay, that's fine, Ma. So long as we can call him Sam."

I wanted to stay long enough to watch Sam stand, but a bellow from Pa put paid to that. It was time for my swimming lesson. I glanced adoringly at my baby colt before dragging myself away.

Going for swimming sessions with Pa was always fun. And it had nothing to do with the lesson itself. I learned to swim long ago although never particularly enjoyed it. At that time, I was working towards my Bronze Life Savers Award.

Pa, and other doting parents, watched from the viewing area. Sessions began with nonstop slogging up and down the swimming pool to improve fitness. Exercises included lifesaving without accidentally garrotting our partner. We trod water for what seemed like hours and jumped in the pool wearing clothes to practice the art of not drowning whilst wearing pyjamas.

When the lesson was over, I was always limp and starving. This was the enjoyable part. Pa bought us each a Cornish pasty at the cafe, covering his with a blizzard of salt and waves of extra-piquant Coleman's English Mustard. Of course, I copied. We wolfed our steaming snacks, washing them down with scalding hot chocolate. Unhealthy. Unspeakably delicious. Much as I loved our secret feasts, on this occasion, I was too distracted and couldn't wait to get back home.

We returned to find Sam standing. I watched, awestruck, as he tottered to his mum. Those great long legs with knobbly knees, it amazed me that he could coordinate them at all. His thicket of stubby mane and fluffball tail was black, as were his lower legs. The rest of his body was light brown.

"May I stroke him now, Ma?"

"Yes, but approach him carefully. He's likely to be nervous, and Sioux will be protective."

I approached slowly and tentatively reached out to Sam's neck. Sioux was watchful but calm as I gently stroked him. That soft baby coat, all fluffy and new. I still couldn't believe that he was all mine.

The weeks and months flew by as Sam grew. I spent every spare moment with him. I brushed him, halter trained him, and shared secrets about the adventures we would have when we could go riding. Going back to school was agony, and every time I came home, he seemed to have shot up.

Whilst all this was going on, I had horrible guilt pangs about Apache. Unfair though it was, I didn't share the same feelings for her. I'm not sure she cared much. Apache seemed just as happy with less exercise and more chill time in the field.

Sioux proved to be a natural mother. Sam was flourishing and grazing freely, so we decided to wean him at six months old. Ma opted to take things gently, and began by separating mum and son at mealtimes. They were in different fields but still able to see one another.

Gradually the period apart was extended. So far, so good, until the day Sioux lost sight of her youngster. She pounded up to the fence, neighing crazily, rearing at the tall barrier, trying to reach him. Sam was grazing at the far end of the field.

We were alerted by Sioux's frantic behaviour and rushed over to see Sam's reaction. Distressed at his mother's calls, he galloped headlong toward her and attempted to jump over the high iron fence. And floundered.

"Oh, no, *look!* Ma, look at his back leg. He kicked back. It's wedged between the rails!"

"Yes, yes, I see. Good Lord. Beth, stand back, give him a moment. He might be able to disentangle himself. Do *not* make a fuss."

I stood, wringing my hands in despair at the plight of my struggling colt. His forelegs plunged. Snorting wildly, he thrashed, writhed. Seconds seemed like hours, and yet it was over in a flash. Sam somehow wriggled his leg free of the iron bars.

He stood, shaking, confused. Sioux whinnied again, urgent, still pounding up and down the fence line. Sam gathered his wits, shook himself, and hobbled to his mum. He could not put weight through his leg.

"He's calm now, Beth. Keep an eye on him

while I call the vet. And you must prepare yourself for bad news."

I stared, distraught at the sight of his wounded leg. If it was broken, I knew he would probably be shot. In most cases, horses simply cannot bear severe leg fractures.

Heartbreaking moments passed as we watched Mr Ellis give Sam a thorough examination. I was so anxious I didn't hear his verdict. Frightened that I had misheard, I asked him to repeat his advice.

"The good news is that he has not broken his leg," he said. "But I'm afraid there is a serious soft tissue injury on his hock. He's young and could make a full recovery with proper care, but I can't guarantee it."

"Oh, Ma, what will happen if he doesn't get better?"

"One day at a time, Beth. We'll do everything Mr Ellis says and see what happens."

Sam stood quietly as Mr Ellis patched up the minor abrasion at the impact site and left us with anti-inflammatory drugs and a treatment plan. We stuck to it rigidly.

Sam spent the next ten days in the stable with a bandage on his joint and regularly applied cold compresses. And he was brilliant. For such a baby, he seemed to understand that the icky cold water and bandages were there to help reduce the swelling.

Going back to school before my boy was fully fit was torture. I fretted, wrote often, and bartered for extra telephone time so that I could ring home. Eventually, Ma had great news.

"We can relax, Beth. Mr Ellis has reviewed Sam. His hock will always be slightly swollen, but there's no lasting damage and no limp. Your Sam has made a full recovery."

"This is *fantastic* news, Ma. I wish I were home to hug him."

"*Ahem*, now you can focus on your studies, please. I dare say you've been neglecting them. We'll see you soon."

Ma was born with a stiff upper lip.

Life for a colt is apt to be event-filled. As Sam developed, the decision was made for him to be castrated. As Ma put it, he would be 'less of a nuisance' once the deed was done. Mercifully, it was a simple procedure with no traumas, aside from the obvious for our neutered youngster.

Sam's recovery coincided with a planned working holiday to Ireland. Ma wanted to look at several horses, and decided to combine the trip with some sightseeing. Pa couldn't join us, which presented a tester. Would Ma, who had no perceivable sense of direction, manage to navigate us successfully? We were about to find out.

The Wonder of Welsh Words

Genedigaeth
One of the most amazing sights I have witnessed. Pronounced 'gana-dee-guyth', this is the word for **'birth'**.

Chapter Nineteen

'Ireland has one of the world's heaviest rainfalls. If you see an Irishman with a tan, it's rust.'

Dave Allen

Holidays are exciting at the best of times, and for Di and I, this was extra special. We had never been 'overseas' before. We packed our battered old Ford escort and set off to Anglesey and the ferry from Holyhead to Dublin.

The three-hour voyage across the Irish Sea passed in a whirlwind of animated chatter, fingers pointing at 'whopping great big waves' and Ma tutting at our flourishing schoolgirl slang.

Once docked, our destination was a family friend's home in Galway in the west of the country. We rolled off the ferry, enthusiastic, giggling at the enchanting Irish lilt and enjoying brand new scenes. To curtail our dire imitations of the singsong accent, Ma launched into a story about leprechauns.

"Girls, you've heard the legends of these little men dressed in green, haven't you?"

"Beth would think they were red, Ma!"

"Would not!"

"So would. Ow! And stop pinching me."

"Now, now girls, do stop it. You're far too old for that sort of behaviour. A leprechaun is a kind of fairy. They are men with beards who wear green clothes."

"Why green?"

"I'm not sure, but it rains even more here than at home."

"Awww, I hope it doesn't rain all the time while we're here."

"Well, it isn't raining now, *is it*, Beth? Although it is getting rather foggy. Anyway, a reason for the country being remarkably beautiful is because of all the rainfall. It's often called the Emerald Isle, which is perhaps the connection with leprechauns and the colour of their clothes."

"That makes total sense."

"Thank you, Di. They say leprechauns are cobblers who repair and make shoes."

"That's an odd job."

"I suppose so. Some people think the word leprechaun comes from the old Irish word *luchorpán*, which means small body. Others say it comes from an Irish word that means shoemaker. And they say that if one is very quiet, it's possible to hear the tap-tap-tapping of his tiny hammer as he drives nails into shoes."

"I don't think anyone'd hear if leprechauns were close to us. Di never stops talking. Ouch!"

"*Ahem*. Apparently, leprechauns are mischievous and love playing tricks on people. But they are hard to catch."

"Don't they keep gold or something?"

"Yes. It's said that every leprechaun has a pot of gold hidden in the Irish countryside. He must give his treasure away to anyone who captures him. But he's a wily sprite. He can fool a person into looking away. And in that instant, he vanishes into his forest home, taking his riches with him."

"Top legend. Do they have dragons in Ireland, like ours?"

"Yes, several, Beth, and do stop using that vulgar word. You girls try to spot some leprechauns while I look for another signpost. We don't seem to have passed one for a while."

This was a worry. As well as having a terrible sense of direction, Ma was one of those people who regularly mixed up her lefts and rights. Cries of 'No, Ma, the other left' were common. It meant that trips to new places often took far longer than necessary.

Having quickly declared leprechaun spotting to be babyish and impossible in the fog anyway, we charged through several verses of *Follow the Yellow Brick Road* before resuming our favourite pastime. Sisterly bickering.

Absorbing though our squabbles were, we fizzled out when we realised we had passed the same group of mist-shrouded sheep three times. We were in the middle of what looked like a spooky moor; the visibility was almost nil.

We were lost.

"Well, girls, we haven't seen a signpost for ages now."

"You said that ages ago!"

"Don't be cheeky, Beth."

"I think we're going round in circles, Ma."

"Oh dear, possibly, Di. I'm sure we're close to the O'Driscoll's house, but it's awfully hard to work out where we are in this awful fog. Never mind, we'll stop at the next house we see."

We avoided viewing the same (now bemused) sheep for a fourth time as the car clawed through the mist in a new direction. We scanned our surroundings. There wasn't another soul on the road as clouds of thick fog rolled across the moor, obscuring the setting sun. This place was bleak.

"Sign!"

"Gracious! You scared me half to death, Di. Well done. Right, let's have a look at what it says. We're looking for a town called Clifden."

"This says something about Alcock and Brown. Is it near there?"

"Ah, no, that's the name of two brave men who made the first-ever transatlantic flight in 1919."

"Wow. They must have been heroes."

"Yes indeed. They set off from Newfoundland in Canada and landed here somewhere," replied Ma, peering into the gloaming. "They thought the land looked soft and suitable for a landing, but it turned out to be a bog."

"Crumbs, were they alright? Anyway, what's a bog?"

"Yes, they were, Beth. It's a peaty marshland, and please stop using that ghastly slang. They crashed nose-down but were unharmed. Ah, look. Lights ahead."

We stopped outside a house, and Ma rang the bell to ask for directions. As the door was flung open, bright lights and merry sounds poured out. A jovial-looking man appeared, and as he listened to Ma's pleas for help, his face creased into a broad smile.

"Ah, to be sure, I know de O'Driscoll's. Derr a fine family, ye've not a ting to worry about. Derr gaff's not far from here. It's manky weather, to be sure. Come in and join de family while I write down de instructions. I'll telephone dem to say yer on yer way."

Ma developed an instant bout of starchy Englishness.

"Oh, goodness me, thank you, but we wouldn't *dream* of interrupting you."

After several more failed attempts at encouraging us to come in, the utterly un-insulted man left the front door wide open while he made the call. He returned with his wife and a large sheet of paper containing two lines. It hadn't been necessary to write them down, we were very close.

"They'll be waiting on yer now," he said, handing over the bag of sandwiches his smiley wife had rustled up. "Be sure to tell them Ciarán O'Malley sent you. And be careful of de sheep. Derr devils for roaming on de roads. Next time you pass, you'll join us for a dram. We'll be glad to see yers anytime."

This encounter contributed to Di and I forming three primary impressions during our trip to Ireland. All the people we met were unerringly generous. They always offered us food, and everyone's name began with an O. Top folks.

Our hosts were typically kind, and better still, from my point of view, they owned Irish Wolfhounds. The immense hunting dogs seemed even bigger than Monty, and they captivated me. The first male, Logan, stood around three feet at the shoulder. He held his great shaggy head in a dignified manner, calmly allowing me to stroke his wiry fur.

The O'Driscoll's lived in a cavernous house with dark corridors; it was down one of these where I met the second wolfhound. Excusing myself from the sitting room, I set off in search of the bathroom, tramping over thick rugs along the way. I was in mid-step onto another when a voice boomed behind me.

"Don't tread on that," laughed Mr O'Driscoll, "it won't thank you. That's Finn, not a rug!"

Sure enough, an enormous head rose at the sound of his name. Finn filled the passageway.

Horsey doings were the central theme of this holiday, one of which was a visit to the Dublin Horseshow. Di and I had heard about this famous show's reputation and were incredibly excited. Would it be the same as our big county shows? Ma had all the answers.

"This show has been run since 1864, girls. Isn't that marvellous?"

"Yes, definitely. Are there any Irish Wolfhound classes?"

"It's a horse show you clot, not dogs!"

"I'm asking Ma, not you!"

"I don't believe so, Beth. There's plenty to interest you both, instead. The Irish love their horses. Over a thousand ponies and horses compete here in different classes. It's a super event. Come along now, and do *not* get lost, Beth!"

We goggled at the sights. Crowds of spectators, some purposeful, others milling about, many beautifully dressed. A melee of accents contributed to the cosmopolitan atmosphere, and not just Irish. Visitors from all over the world watched, admired, and made deals.

There were show classes, hunter classes, pony

competitions, stallion classes, coloured horse classes, event horse classes, and more. There was too much to take in. We snuck up to the collecting ring of a showjumping arena to see if we could spot some of our heroes.

Here, riders registered with the event competition steward before warming up their horses over a selection of practice fences. Proud, breathtakingly fine animals in pristine condition appeared, keen to get started. Most riders were very controlled, but a couple surprised us.

"Begorra! But it's a fine day for jumping de sticks, Séamus. Come on now, let's have dat pole up a little higher for a craic. Yer nag's barely noticin' de jump."

"Right you are, Callum, but I'll not be windin' him too early."

"Not a bit of it. A tenner on it says he can take two notches higher in his stride."

"You're on!"

Intrigued by the exchange, Di asked Ma for a translation.

"What does begorra mean?"

"It's a popular Irish word. It's rather like saying 'my word!'"

And that was that. Begorra became our new favourite word, which we plagued Ma with for the rest of the holiday.

We watched some of the world's greatest show jumpers. There were dramatic refusals and spills, but mostly, the rhythm of each rider and horse was fluid and stylish. Though we could have spectated all day, time was against us, and there was still so much more to see.

We wandered around the exhibition areas. There were craft workers and businesses from all over the country selling their wares. There was live music and street performers, food to die for, a million different scenes and sights to woo the senses. We had a wonderfully memorable day.

Parting company with the O'Driscolls was like leaving close family. Once again, the Irish bonhomie exuded from these kindly folks. Even Finn and Logan seemed sad to see us go. Would we come back soon? We'd love to!

The last part of our holiday took us on another horsey mission to Limerick – where limericks were invented. Much to Ma's despair, it gave rise to a dreadful flow of uninspired five-line stanzas. This time, we stayed with the O'Connor family, whose hospitality, if that were even possible, surpassed our previous hosts. No donkey-sized dogs this time, but they had some fine horses for us to coo over.

Once Ma's business was done, we explored the quirky town, flourishing on the River Shannon's banks. Limerick's streetscapes are blemished with the evidence of brutal sieges in the seventeenth century and decorated with grandeur from the Georgian eighteenth century. It was an interesting melange, but more exciting still was our trip to Bunratty Castle.

Despite being Welsh, where castles are as common as mushrooms, the sight of Bunratty Castle blew our socks off. The splendid fifteenth century fortification was built on the site of a Viking trading camp. It is the most complete and authentic castle in Ireland and, in its heyday, was the stronghold of the O'Brien clan. Another O. At the end of our tour, there was one more indulgence in store. The medieval banquet, and we had tickets.

We filed into the castle banqueting hall to a raucous welcome from the Earl's Butler. Serving wenches offered goblets of honeyed mead. It was sticky, strangely pleasant stuff that made my head go fuzzy. We toasted an era of Irish fortune, and then the feast began.

My eyes were out on stalks for most of the evening as we were immersed in the boisterous ambience. Madrigal singers, jesters and jugglers, all dressed in medieval garb, entertained us. Food appeared in wooden bowls and platters and was eaten with daggers or fingers. It was a brilliant way to end our holiday.

We said our goodbyes and packed our car for the last time. Heading back to Dublin, we passed a place called Neenah, a pretty town with a cylindrical castle.

"Is this where our hourse, Neenah, came from, Ma?"

"Yes, it is, Beth."

As we chattered away about our Irish adventures, Ma had a thought.

"I feel we must have some souvenirs from our holiday here in Ireland."

"Groovy idea!" we chorused, thinking about presents.

"Yes, I have the very thing we must take home. Peat!"

"Whaaaat?"

"It's marvellous for the fires and will be a fond memory of our time here. Now, let's stop at the next bog and remove one or two sods."

And that is how Di and I ended up with lumps of peat stuck under our feet all the way back home.

As soon as we unpacked I dashed out to check on Sam, with Monty in hot pursuit. My handsome colt snickered his welcome before nuzzling my pockets, hungrily searching for Polo mints. I returned to cuddle the rest of our furry and feathery family members, and was halfway through my inspection when Pa settled us down. He had some concerning animal news.

The Wonder of Welsh Words

Gwyliau
I looked forward to them all. This word for **'holidays'** is tricky, and it's pronounced 'goo-illy-I'.

Chapter Twenty

'A jump jockey has to throw his heart over the fence – and then go over and catch it.'

Dick Francis

"Did you enjoy yourselves?"

"Begorra! So we did, Pa," we chimed.

"Girls, *really*." Ma was begorra'd out.

Pa answered our interrogations about the animals. All seemed well until we got to the smaller ones.

"Unfortunately, the two Dutch rabbits escaped from their cages when I was feeding them."

"Oh, Pa, that's awful! Are they lost?"

"Don't worry, Beth. They're in the walled garden, busy creating a warren and perfectly happy. Especially Buck."

Pa was right. It wasn't long before a dynasty was established. We had bunnies coming out of our ears. Happily, the offspring were as docile as their parents, and as fast as they were produced, we gave them away.

Pa eventually got sick of seeing his lawn peppered with holes and poo. Ma was exasperated for different reasons.

"Dear me, this whole reproduction business is completely out of hand. Girls, you must catch Buck."

We dutifully trapped and returned the loving pair to new, separate hutches with palatial grounds.

Our visit to Ireland had been fruitful for Ma. She had an announcement. Despite her version of enthusiasm being a small, controlled smile, we knew she was excited.

"Girls, we are going to have two ex-racehorse broodmares."

I was amazed. Racehorses? This was unbelievably exhilarating.

Di was more interested in the transaction's economics.

"Cor, Ma, racehorses are super-expensive. You have to be loaded to buy them. Where did we find enough money to buy two?"

"Really, Di, do stop using that uncouth language. It's extremely rude to talk about money. As it happens, we're part of a syndicate. And before you ask, it means that we have part ownership of the horses, although ours is, *ahem*, admittedly an extremely small part. Uncle Jim is one of the other owners. We recently discussed the opportunity and have decided to go ahead. Christian, his son, works in the industry and has made all the arrangements."

Jim was a family friend who had been elevated to the ranks of unclehood. I'm not sure why, but we all loved him.

We still had questions. Di refocused on the horses' previous racing activities.

"Cool! Were they jumpers, Ma?"

"No. The horses were flat racers and have been

moderately successful. Nothing special, but their breed lines are excellent, so they have the potential to produce future winners."

This breed line business sounded intriguing.

"Are they the same as dog pedigrees, Ma?"

"Similar, Beth. They're precise for thoroughbred racehorses. Many stallions and mares were used to establish the thoroughbred breed, but three special stallions became the recognised founders."

"How long ago was that?"

"Goodness, centuries ago. During the seventeenth and eighteenth centuries, three important stallions were imported. The Darley Arabian, the Byerley Turk and the Godolphin Arabian were brought from the Middle East, Hungary and Africa. There are lots of different stories about their histories."

"Wow, I didn't realise bloodlines went back so far."

"Yes, they're essential for keeping breed strains pure and tracing winners' successes. I believe the Darley Arabian is the direct male line ancestor of approximately ninety per cent of all thoroughbreds. The Byerley Turk and the Godolphin Arabian make up the remaining ten per cent between them."

"But how do they know?"

"They kept records. At first, they were approximate until a man called James Weatherby started the first official racehorse bloodline book in 1791. This is a very famous register called the General Stud Book. It has been updated every four years since."

"Crikey! So, are our mares recorded in it?"

"Yes. The book records the breeding of registered thoroughbreds, and their foals will need to be registered too. There are several rules, and it is vital to prove a thoroughbred's background."

"Wow, I can't wait to see our very own racehorses!"

"Their racing days are over now, and we probably won't keep them for long. But, yes, it will be fun."

Fun? Yes, Ma was definitely thrilled.

We were set to work before they arrived, ensuring the two biggest stables were fit to receive our racers. We splashed special paint on the iron bars and mangers, the wood dividing wall was brushed, walls washed, and cobble floors disinfected. Then Ma cast an annoyingly critical eye over the stable yard.

Our next job was raking the gravel. The rockery in the middle was weeded, and for some weird reason, Ma added new plants. Then the bothy, used for saddlery, fodder and cosy winter teas by the fire, had to be spring cleaned. And it didn't stop there.

Di and I nearly went on strike when Ma said we needed to disinfect the water pails and feed buckets.

"Oh, come on, Ma. They're fine for Ponni and the others. Why do we have to give these nags all this special treatment?"

"There's no need to be grumpy, Di, and they certainly aren't nags. These horses are important and..."

"So are Sam and Apache!"

"Yes, they are, Beth, but we must do all we can to ensure that the mares have the best treatment. Now come along, girls. And those bales are in a dreadful state. They need sorting out and the floor brushing. Straw on one side and hay on the other, please."

Muttering about having the cruellest mother in Wales, Di and I slogged in sulky solidarity with the dogs in tow until we got to the lowest straw bales.

"*Argh!*"

"Stoppit, Di. You gave me a fright!"

"Rat! Didn't you see it?"

"No. Where? Cool. Did it run up your leg?"

"No way! You're blind as a bat. *Argh*, there's another one."

"Gross! Look, tons of them. Shall I go and get Hercules?"

"No, silly, they're bigger than your grotty ginger fleabag!"

"Diiii, don't be horrid!"

We were used to vermin, but not in these numbers. Di had disturbed a nest of extremely healthy rats. As we screeched in horror, small furry athletes zoomed out of bales, up walls and into corners. Paddington, nose to the ground, wasn't remotely interested, not so Monty.

Energised by the desire to protect his girls, he bounded in to hunt down the hairy demons. Ever seen a Great Dane trying to catch a rat? Gangly legs, crashing into bales and failing spectacularly, it isn't a pretty sight.

Ma was even more terrified of rats than she was of spiders.

"Don't worry, girls," she shrieked from the mounting block outside. "I'll get your father."

Inside, chaos reigned. Bales split, straw flew, and rats scattered. It was a frenzy of bloodcurdling howls, schoolgirl screams, and scuttling paws. Even Paddy raised an interested eyebrow. We eventually grabbed Monty's collar and hauled him out as Pa arrived with his 20 bore shotgun.

"Stand aside, everybody, and stop this screaming. Beth, you hold on to Monty. Di,

Paddington's wandering off again. Take them both into the house, and I'll deal with this."

Several booms later, peace was restored. Temporarily. It was country life as we knew it.

Sadly, we were back at school when the newly pregnant mares finally arrived. Desperate to see them on our first exeat, we grilled Ma on the way home. We demanded to know every single detail of their first few weeks.

It seemed that these horses were very different from our others. Ma, mistress of the understatement, laid down the ground rules.

"Both mares are rather spirited, girls, *ahem*, especially Guerlain. And Sephora is very nervous, so you must behave calmly around them."

Nodding obediently, we had more questions. Essentials first.

"Those are silly names. Can we call them something else?"

"They're their racing pedigree names, Beth. They seem to respond to them, so I think it's best if we don't alter anything."

So, Girty and Sephi they became.

After batting off the usual onslaught of furry welcomes, we joined Ma for the mares' lunchtime feed. Initially, it was impossible to tell what they looked like behind the lower wood partitions. But there was one prominent feature, and it was unnerving.

"Ooh, Ma, she has one eye bigger than the other!"

"Yes, Beth, this is Guerlain. It's an interesting feature."

"Can I feed them?"

"Not at the moment, but you may once you've learnt the routine. Now stand back, please, and watch."

Ma, armed with the feed bucket, opened Guerlain's stable door with Di and I peeping behind. She was huge. A beautiful bay with two obvious characteristics. She had a foul temper and looked mad as a box of frogs. The eye thing didn't help.

"Ma, they're rolling round in circles."

"What are?"

"Those eyes."

"Don't be ridiculous, Di. And watch."

Guerlain glared at us, stamping her hooves, lashing out at thin air.

"Over!" commanded Ma.

The mare swept to the far side wall, pawing the ground, trying to take chunks out of the cast iron manger. That horse had teeth like spades.

"This is what one must do every time we feed

her. Otherwise, she can become somewhat troublesome."

I looked at the quivering wall of muscle, wondering precisely what Ma's version of 'troublesome' might entail. On the other hand, Sephora stood fretfully while the food was poured into her manger. Her behaviour didn't surprise me. Living next door to Girty would make anyone a nervous wreck.

Despite their eccentric behaviour, both horses fascinated me, and I couldn't wait to work with them. When the holidays started, under supervision at first, I gradually took over their general care. This involved little beyond feeding, grooming, and taking them to the field each day.

To my surprise, I found that Girty's antics were all hot air. Her thrashings and gnashings were bravado designed to disguise an underlying neurosis. So long as I used confident commands, 'Over!' being the food-related one, I was at minimal risk of being booted out of the stable. The same applied with grooming, although her reaction was different again.

'Stand!' was the command to avoid being stamped on or bitten. Observing me with her special eye, she stood relatively quietly as I tied her up and started the routine. The first job was to comb her mane. I had to stand on an upturned bucket to reach. Just one kick and she'd turn the thing into a skittle.

As I was halfway through, it occurred to me that her halter rope was pretty long. This was risky. She could have taken a chunk out of my backside at any point. Being bitten by Kitty innumerable times probably had nothing on this big lass. Girty swung her head, turning me into a human pendulum, but nothing more. I'd got away with it.

Her coat came next. Still on my bucket to reach her back, I started with the blunt-toothed currycomb. I was gentle, concerned that she would object. Far from it. Girty stopped fidgeting. I followed up with the dandy brush, removing mucky bits brought to the surface from currycombing. So far, so good.

I set it aside and reached for the body brush. Using long sweeping motions, its soft bristles distributed the coat's natural oils. Girty was relaxing. Each brushstroke caused a groan of delight, or at least that was my interpretation. As I worked, she swayed gently to the motion, staring dreamily ahead.

I finished with a towelling stable rubber. This brought out a gorgeous burnished glow to her bay coat. Smiling at how easy it was to groom a racehorse, I confidently ran my hand along Girty's flank and gathered her tail from the side. *Thwack!*

Out lashed a hind leg, missing me by a bat's wing. I'd found a tickly spot.

Since the grooming session had gone well so far, I decided that a couple of straw stalks in Girty's tail wouldn't do any harm. I retreated to the relatively safe end, gave her one more buffing, and was done.

Sephi behaved similarly. I discovered she had a tickly spot too, which was under her tummy. Instead of kicking out, she bounced around, looking close to tears. I resorted to cleaning those areas with a stable rubber instead.

With both horses groomed, I stood back to admire my work. They may not have been race day ready, but they were gleaming. I imagined saddling one of them and pounding along a track. The thrill of speed, the power of the mighty animal extending beneath me, it was incredibly alluring. Sadly, with these horses, it would have to remain a dream.

My final morning job was to take the mares to their meadow. It sounded like a simple activity, but as I found on the first day, Girty made sure all interest levels were switched to the max.

Both horses had leather halters. I clipped Sephi's lead rein on first and led her out of the stable. A couple of gnashes and stamps later, I had Girty out too. Then the fun began.

With me in the middle, our walk to the field only took about eight minutes, during which Girty went through a series of antics. She bucked, reared, shied at offending leaves and baulked at branches. She decided the wheelbarrow was a ghoul and lashed out at invisible foes behind. It was like walking a demented yo-yo.

We stopped at Sam and Apache's paddock to have a chat on the way past. Mistake. These big girls fascinated Sam. He started neighing and strutting, which did Girty no good at all. She snorted and started half-rearing again, so I swiftly moved forward with her still dancing on two legs.

Amazingly, we reached the field in one piece. And then something unexpected happened.

The moment both mares touched the grass, they became even more agitated. I hastily unclipped them and watched, amazed. The pair shot off, following the perimeter fence, furlong after furlong; they galloped around the five-acre (two-hectare) field.

I stared, aghast, terrified that one of them would tumble and break a leg. There was not a single thing I could do about it. This was grass, and to them, it was a racetrack. After two laps, to my relief, they settled down and contentedly grazed for the rest of the day. It took them a long time to lose that habit.

Apache had been watching the action too. She didn't quite yawn but plainly decided they were tedious neurotics and returned to breakfast. Not Sam. Still spellbound, he forlornly hung his head over the paddock rails, neighing plaintively, dying to join in the fun.

I walked over to them, apologising for the temporary abandonment, promising a long ride for Apache and schooling for Sam. Little did I know there were big changes ahead that would affect us all during the summer holidays.

The Wonder of Welsh Words

Llygaid
There was definitely something strange about Girty's. Try saying 'hl-uuh-guide' and you'll be close to the word for **'eyes'**.

Chapter Twenty-One

'...the Swellies...once you are committed there is often no turning back.'

Beaumaris Lifeboatman

Sam was old enough to be broken in. We had done much of the work, but the practice of training him to be ridden took time and skill, the latter of which Ma decided we didn't possess. She was right.

So far, I had spent hours and hours grooming Sam. Shoeing and hoof-picking, no problem, though he had tickly hind hooves. I could lean against him, crawl under his tummy, and faff around making interesting plaits with his mane and tail.

He was fine with a halter, and I could lunge him, although we regularly ended up in knots. I had placed Kitty's old felt saddle on his back, but not a leather saddle. Nor had I attempted to fit a bridle for fear of being too rough. Having inherited his mum's docile temperament, so far so good, he hadn't batted an eyelid.

With mixed feelings, I waved off my boy. Sad, because he would be away for at least four weeks, but filled with anticipation at the thought of riding when he came home. His absence coincided with an offer I was desperate to accept.

Most holidays were taken up with boats and animals. We crewed for Pa during the racing season in his Fife, although as Di grew older, she spent more time sailing with friends. I had started to do the same. Pa was a proud member of the Royal

Anglesey Yacht Club (RAYC). Based in beautiful Beaumaris, it overlooks the Menai Strait and distant mountains of Snowdonia across the water.

Although established earlier, the RAYC was formally recognised in 1885 when Queen Victoria granted the club a Royal Warrant. It is one of those venerated old clubs, a detail which was initially wholly lost on me.

I recall the RAYC building as being a nautical version of my school; crusty around the edges. Most of the administrators seemed pretty frail, too. However, I quickly learned that looks can be deceiving.

Serving with titles such as Commodore, Vice Commodore, and Rear Commodore, the club officials mostly had double-barrel names and lengthy peerages. Not that owning a great tract of land was a prerequisite for membership. So long as applicants could demonstrate a passion for sailing, it welcomed ordinary enthusiasts like us.

Deservedly proud of their club's traditions, what the officials lacked in imaginative job titles, they made up for in other ways. Those still nimble enough to sail were fiendishly competitive. Relationships were forged and ruined in the pursuit of victory. And, feeble or fit, they partied as hard as they raced.

The yachting world is sociable. Di and I were regularly parked with a Schweppes bitter lemon in the corner of somebody's home or planted in the cockpit of an old wooden launch moored in the Strait. While we sipped pop, our parents knocked back G&Ts with their sailing buddies, regaling one another with salty tales, race by race.

Young club members were equally keen. Weapons of choice were dinghies. Some, like the newly designed Lasers, cut through the waves like daggers. Others skimmed gracefully like damselflies, barely touching the surface as they planed. And then there were the Fireballs. These challenging double-handed racers shot across the water like bullets, rewarding athleticism, punishing incompetence.

I rarely got involved and watched, green with jealousy, as daredevil sailors hooked body harnesses to the mast cable. They planted feet on the dinghy gunwale and hoisted their bodies over the watery precipice. As the wind freshened, the sailors' body weights counterbalanced the boat as it flashed through the sea. Quick and slick. Just the rush of boiling waves beneath.

It was much to my regret that being the weight of a flea, I was never heavy enough to try the trapeze. The experts were a chunky lot. Instead, my brief foray into dinghy sailing began with a Mirror dinghy. A far more sedate vessel.

The Mirror was a relatively new kid on the block. Jack Holt and TV do-it-yourself expert Barry Bucknell designed the boat in 1962. They came up with a craft that cost £63.55 in decimal money and could be built at home using copper wire stitching and glue.

They named their boat after the UK Daily Mirror, a newspaper with a primarily working-class distribution, because it was universally affordable. It quickly gained popularity and an international reputation. Despite being listed among the top 50 boats to have changed the sailing world, my first impressions were tainted.

Still hankering after having a go at flying the trapeze, the first time I saw a Mirror, I couldn't help feeling disappointed. The boat was a blunt-ended shortie. In stark contrast to the sleek racers, it was apparent that there would be no nautical heroics. Or so I thought.

Here's the thing about dinghies. Like rowing boats, they're wobbly. An advantage of the Mirror is that the crew sits *in* the boat rather than balancing *on top* as one does on several racing machines. Nonetheless, jumping from the jetty and landing on the boat's gunwale edge is inadvisable. You'll end up in the drink. I know this now.

I was paired with Rupert. He was a solid lad a couple of years older than me and lots heavier. Being a relatively experienced dinghy sailor, Rupes took the helm, and I crewed. The cheerful red main and jib sails seemed like handkerchiefs compared to Pa's Fife, but set correctly; they propelled the chubby little lass along at a great lick.

Sailing these little boats could be brilliant fun. They did all the things the bigger boats do. They were even fitted with webbing toe straps fixed to the cockpit. Whilst they didn't allow the daredevil trapeze, we could slot our feet under the bands and lean our torsos seaward to counteract the boat's heeling action in the wind.

To say that we were a competent team was pushing it, but we were managing relatively well. Sadly, that didn't last long. It was during a stiff breeze day, our sailor-speak for: *don't bother going out, you're not good enough,* when our first mishap occurred. And it was because of Belinda.

There we were, amongst a small flotilla of dinghies, scudding along happily, spray saturating us like a rainy day. With my feet jammed under the toe straps, I leaned out, focusing on not letting go of the jib sail rope, and Rupes was supposed to be steering a safe course. Little did I know, he had spotted Belinda streaking past in her sporty Laser.

With a foppish grin, Rupert promptly forgot what he was doing. Whilst turning to give the current love of his life a hearty wave, he thrust the steering arm away from the mainsail causing the boat to turn downwind. It was a swashbuckling move too far. Catching me totally unawares, the boat swung around.

"Gybe-ho!" he yelled.

"Whaaaa?"

With a rattly *flump*, the mainsail slammed over to my side, with me still hanging over the edge. Unprepared for this impromptu technical manoeuvre, I was dunked, creating a bow wave with half my body submerged. The sorry upshot was inevitable. Gravity soon took effect, and the boat capsized.

Thank goodness for life jackets.

Moments later, we popped up like a couple of corks. Thrashing around to the retractable daggerboard, we started pushing down on it to right the boat. The dinghy righted itself, and with Rupes hanging on, I scrambled into a lake of seawater in the cockpit. Now it was his turn.

"I can't get in. I'll have the boat over again," he bawled.

Half-minded to leave him there, I reluctantly motioned for Rupert to climb in at the boat's back end. The dinghy wallowed drunkenly in the choppy sea as he had another go. I offered encouraging instructions.

"Come on, Rupes, get in!"

"I can't. It's too rough. You'll have to...."

"*What?* The sail's flapping. Stop swallowing water; you're gurgling."

Wavelets were swamping Rupert.

"Hurry up, Rupes. Belinda's watching."

"*Is she?*"

Belinda swept up again, and much to his chagrin, magically slowed down to offer help. If he hadn't been half-drowned, I think Rupert would have blushed. Her appearance became the perfect impetus. With supreme effort, he clambered into the cockpit, raising a cheery wave in an attempt to look nonchalant. It didn't work.

With abilities like ours, one might have thought that we were best suited to larger (non-easily-capsizable) boats, or dry land. But no. Rupert was given a dinghy for his birthday and invited me to crew for him in the Menai Strait Regattas.

Given our dubious track record, there were inevitable mixed feelings. Were we capable of staying upsides for an entire race, let alone a series? Still, the opportunity to take part was too good to pass up. I gratefully accepted and went along to have a look at his pride and joy.

I'm not sure what I expected, but it wasn't that. The boat, and I can't recall its design, was smaller than the Mirror and even stubbier. Di, who had recently secured a crewing place in a smart GP14 dinghy, joined me.

"Hmm, you're really going to sail in that?"

"Course, why not?"

"It looks like a bathtub. Which end is the bow?"

"Very funny. I think it's fine. Just not as sleek as your snazzy boat."

"You can say that again. I've never seen one like that before. Ooh, look, and it's got a paddle. D'you know, it looks a bit like a fibreglass coracle."

Di left with that thought hanging in the air as Rupert appeared, armed with sails, ready to give his new boat her maiden voyage.

Rupert's father had assured us that Tubby, as she quickly became known, was virtually unsinkable. We would soon put that theory to the test, but the initial statement was comforting. She was rigged the same way as the Mirror and had three standard sails, including a spinnaker.

Unlike most boats I had sailed in, which had great big, ballooning spinnakers, Tubby's was like a multi-coloured hankie. We would use it to propel her faster through the water when sailing downwind. And being dinky, it was easy to furl, as were the mainsail and jib.

Our first outings were successful, but there were teething problems. Rupes, who was a bit of a lump, found it a tight squeeze, but we diplomatically decided that he was excellent ballast in a freshening sea. The other, more tricky, issue we had was the centreboard. The retractable keel regularly sprang out of its housing.

The idea of the centreboard, or any keel, is to balance the wind force on the sails. Without one, the boat cannot sail upwind and is blown sideways. It reduces the tendency for a dinghy to tip over in rougher conditions, acting as a stabilising underwater wing.

Tubby behaved nicely, chugging through the waves like a tug until, without warning, her centreboard popped up, sending us scooting sideways. This wasn't a problem in calm conditions, but it was a different matter in the wind. And unless we were prepared to sail downwind for the rest of our sailing days, she had to be fixed.

We tried many different ways to mend it ourselves, but none worked. With the prospect of navigating the notoriously dangerous Swellies becoming ever more terrifying, Tubby had to be taken to the local boatyard for repairs.

Meanwhile, Rupert and I worked out a system of moving around the boat without getting wedged like sardines. I mastered a speedy-ish technique with sail management, and Rupes promised not to drop his tiller the second he saw Kathy. She was his latest wannabe sweetheart; Belinda had been ditched after the capsizing incident.

Ridiculously for a tiny boat that didn't have much going for it, Tubby could be entered in several dinghy races under the Portsmouth yardstick handicap system. This system assigns a different rating to each boat class in a mixed fleet. In theory, the handicap system gives every boat an equal chance of winning. Some say it favours slower vessels. That being the case, it was a trump card since we were probably the slowest dinghy on the Menai Strait.

Splendidly organised by the RAYC, the Menai Strait Regattas took place over a fortnight. Many courses ran north from Beaumaris towards Puffin Island, although others required passage through the treacherous Swellies to Caernarfon. Hugely popular, sailors flocked from different clubs in the area and farther afield.

Regattas were exciting, filled with edgy moments, potential disasters and joys. And there was nothing quite like the *boom* from the cannon as the boat crossed the winning line. The festival promised its usual nautical thrillers, desperate endeavour, and celebrations on and off the water. I was hooked.

Around sixty boats were competing in the series. There were regattas for big offshore cruisers, dinghies in handicap fleets, and the classic yachts, including the One Design Fifes. With so many entrants competing on a relatively narrow patch of water, much could go wrong and often did.

The opening dawned on a fine, breezy July day, and I was due to crew for Pa. Bob, a strapping, unflappable gentleman who had sailed with my father for years, joined us. Complete opposites, they were great friends, which was just as well.

Pa was fraught with tension. He approached every race as though his life depended on winning and constantly lost his temper. None of this bothered me or the long-suffering Bob. From the moment we cast off towards the start line, Pa started.

"What the blazes, Beth? Pull that sheet [rope] in tighter. We won't get anywhere with the jib flapping like lettuce."

"Sorry."

"Bobbbbbb, strewth, man! Too slow. You're *far* too slow on the release. We'll practice going about again."

"Right-ho, Old Man!"

And so it went on. There was no point arguing. Pa was in *the zone*. As the wind freshened, waiting for the start cannon to sound, jockeying for position was tricky. Get it wrong by overshooting the invisible line, and we'd have to take a penalty. Trim the sails correctly, and the start will be successful.

We got off well. The Fife cut gracefully through the water, neck and neck with the front runners. And then we approached the first buoy. The idea is to circle the floating marker as close as possible and head for the next turning point. In a regatta with a large fleet competing, conditions can get uncomfortably tight.

"God's teeth! Jackson's taking our wind. *Bounder!* Tighten that jib, Bob. We're losing ground. Now, Bob, *now!*"

There were howls of derision as boats crowded the marker, protest calls, watery chaos, near misses and actual clashes. Classic race frenzy. We were now sailing off wind, so the spinnaker had to be hoisted. This was Bob's job. Poor Bob.

"Good Lord, man, get that bally sail *up!*"

When the spinnaker was furled, Pa developed his next fixations. Boat weight distribution. And speech.

"Centre back of the boat, everyone, and not a word. Sit, Beth, sitttt."

I never fully understood why any of this was necessary for a yacht of the Fife's size, but didn't dare question Pa. Ropes were gently tweaked. The great spinnaker sail billowed, propelling the boat ever closer towards the next marker.

For Pa, split-second timing was of the essence here. At the critical moment, Bob pulled in the spinnaker. A couple of yachts in the fleet messed up. Their sails hit the water, causing an instant drag on the boats. One was shredded as they hauled it in. Precious seconds were lost as crews struggled to recover and stow saturated material. I had a moment of sympathy for the hapless sailors, but it was only a moment. In the heat of battle, it meant fewer contenders for the win.

We rounded successfully and tacked towards the finish line. The conditions had deteriorated. Our yacht pounded through crested waves, spray flying, water cascading inboard.

"Bailing, Beth, now!"

As I madly scooped water from the cockpit with a plastic bucket, Pa steered a punishing course. The yacht responded, her sleek lines driving through whitecaps, half a boat's length from our arch-rival. Nobody said a word, not even

Pa. It was the last dash to the line. Who was going to win?

And then it was all over.

The cannon sounded and then sounded again. We had come second. Smiling broadly, Pa waved heartily at the winning boat's skipper and eased off the wind.

"Well done, everyone. Come on, take the helm, Bob. Let's take her home."

It had been another thrilling race and a fantastic start to the regattas. As always, I had learnt a little more, which would stand me in good stead for the next race. Rupert and I were due to compete in the infamous Beaumaris to Caernarfon regatta in Tubby.

The Wonder of Welsh Words

Hwylio
With varying results, I did lots of this – '**sailing**'. Pronounce the word 'hoo-lior'.

Chapter Twenty-Two

'I heard him then, for I had just
completed my design.
To keep the Menai Bridge from rust.
By boiling it in wine.'

Lewis Carroll

"Don't forget the dead bodies,"

"*What?*"

"They say lots of them float around near Menai Bridge at this time of year."

"Oh, come *on*, Di, who's they?"

"*Everyone*. And last week, a diver found one on the seabed at the lobster farm. The lobsters were eating it!"

"Eeuw, that's horrible!"

"Yeah! I'm not going to eat lobster ever again. And remember, we'll be sailing through the Swellies, so you'd better not capsize."

Di had a knack for leaving thought-provoking remarks in the air.

My sister's tendencies for the ghoulish had a grain of truth. Tragically, there were documented instances of people throwing themselves off Menai Bridge and sometimes bodies were washed up on the shore. More often, a passing boat picked them up.

The day of the regatta dawned bright and breezy, which matched Rupert's personality. There were no 'Pa tantrums', racing with Rupert was relaxed and fun, especially when we actually set the boat correctly. We loved the idea of competing, though, and hoped our favourable handicap might help.

Today was the flagship regatta. Called the

'Race Through', our class was big, and the dinghy park was a chaos of preparations. Mast halyards clattered, sails flapped and crackled, crew members bickered, laughed, and teased opposing teams. Regardless of age, everyone was excited, anticipating the battle ahead.

Launched boats zipped about like tadpoles as warm-up drills were completed ahead of the start. Most were now swooshing through the water with an air of competence, but not us. Tubby tootled along at a sedate pace while I wrestled with our equipment.

I was trying to recover an escaped sail rope when I realised the cockpit was slowly filling with water. Rupert noticed my concerned expression.

"That's no problem," he said, sploshing his foot in the puddle. "It happened last week when I was out with Dad. He says it's only a little leak."

"*Leak?*"

"Yep, no sweat. Although, it would be handy if you could find something to bail out the water when it gets too deep," he added, staring vaguely ahead.

"You might have told me earlier. We haven't got a bailer."

"Huh, hadn't thought about that. How about the sandwich box? That'll do. Come to think of it, I'm starving. How about a snack now?"

"*Rupert*, the race is about to start!"

"Course. No probs. We'll eat later."

Puffs of smoke rose from the onshore start cannons. We were off. Racing machines streaked ahead. Trapezes were connected as sailors hoisted themselves, combatting the bracing wind, quickly leaving the fleet behind.

The rest of us valiantly fought for position and clear air to fill our sails. As the dinghies spread out, we chugged along well enough. Rupert masterfully steered a course that kept us abreast of the Mirrors, an early triumph. Dead ahead was the dreaded Swellies.

The race is timed so boats pass through during slack water (when the tide is turning). And that's because the tidal flow may be too strong to sail against at other tide stages. Our dinghies would have had no chance against a racing tide here.

Di's unhelpful advice flooded my mind as we passed beneath the massive Menai Bridge. The stretch of greeny-black water looked menacing. Trees on the steep mainland banks grew in a tumbled mass, casting eerie shadows on the mercurial sea. Woody fingers scratching the surface dragged the still waters, creating claw-like hands. It was creepy.

The water was glassy here, apparently motionless, but we knew better. I noticed movement. A whirlpool. The powerful maelstrom of rotating water was produced by invisible obstacles – jagged rocks. And there were many.

I knew these whirlpools were the cause of shipwrecks. RAYC retainers tell stories of smaller race yachts getting caught in them. Spinning around. Helpless. Unable to escape, they have to be towed out by safety boats. Usually, there are no severe casualties, more often, there's superficial damage to the crafts and wounded pride.

Advice given to novice sailors wanting to pass through is clear. 'Unless it's slack water, don't bother. Passage through the Swellies is never *that* safe and must be carefully navigated, even by powerboats.'

We started heading uncomfortably close to a new surface disturbance.

"Rupert, careful, change course. Don't go anywhere near those whirlpools."

"Don't worry. I don't fancy disappearing down one of those, either. Prepare to tack!"

We passed infamous rocks, which had caused sailors grief for so many years they had been given names. North Platters, *Ynys Benlas* (Blue Top Island), a rocky islet, and the notoriously dangerous Swelly rock. We watched the sinister overfalls and shuddered. Keelboats caught aground here are in trouble.

Despite having sailed this stretch dozens of times in the past, this was the first time without Pa. I felt a new respect for his attitude toward sailing. He was knowledgeable; he sailed hard and recognised the potential dangers. Pa took no chances. We were unlikely to come unstuck with our little dinghy, but I suddenly felt pretty vulnerable.

Time stood still as the fleet crept ahead. Strangely quiet, there was none of the usual banter when we came close to another boat. Every crew member was focused on steering a safe course.

Britannia Bridge and open water beyond beckoned. Dead ahead was another rocky mass. *Ynys Gorad Goch* (Red Weir Island) is a lonely islet inhabited by a single home. How the house withstands high tides amazes me. But it is these waters that provided an opportunity for the owners.

Yny Gorad Goch has a fishery dating from 1590. They built a complex system of stone weirs near eddy currents; they looked like holes in the wall to me. As water was sucked through the holes into the weirs, the fish became trapped. It was good business with the particularly large number of fish pushed through the Strait on a fresh tide.

I watched, mesmerised, as waves swirled around the rocky promontory. I could see the fish smoking chamber. Built around 1824, it stood barely above the waterline. Would it be thrilling, or hell, living on the island during a storm? I couldn't decide.

I shifted my position with a splash.

"Fancy a sandwich, Rupes? The water in the cockpit is pretty deep now, so we could do with using the box as a bailer."

"Huh. So it is. Right you are then. By the way, those Cribbin rocks look like dinosaur bones, don't they?"

I looked at the overfalls on the rocks where so many boats had foundered.

"Yep, scary. Probably no need to get any closer, then."

"No, no, you're right again. Look at the dinghies ahead. I think the wind has picked up on the other side of the bridge, so the last part of the race'll be a tester."

"Hope we don't get much more water coming inboard. We're already up to our ankles in the cockpit."

"Don't worry. We won't sink. I filled the buoyancy bags up ages ago. Least I think I did."

As the wind freshened, we trimmed our sails and were off. We leaned out as far as possible with our feet trapped under the toe strap. Tubby bounced through the waves like an ugly duckling and started gaining on our closest rivals. This was fantastic. This was what racing was all about.

Was it that split-second loss of concentration while admiring the grandeur of Plas Newydd, or the rush of water and *fizz* of spray that overwhelmed the structural weakness? Or just our incompetence? Debatable since we were powerless to cope with what happened next.

As a powerful gust hit us, the centreboard shot out of its housing. The repair had broken. Tubby heeled over and capsized. I was chucked into the sea so quickly I didn't even have time for a, *nooo, not again*, thought.

Disorientated, I opened my eyes. And stared. Beneath me, a ghoulish white shape was gliding upwards from the depths. I knew what it was. Di was right. There was a corpse in the water, and the current was bringing it to the surface. I thrashed around to the back of the boat. Rupert was already there, coughing and spluttering.

"Sorry about that. Don't know what happened. Damn centreboard coming up didn't help. And now..."

"Rupes, *Rupert!* There's a dead body floating into the cockpit!"

"Really?"

"Yes! Come *on*. We've got to get the boat going."

"Not good! Okay, hang on, let's try and right her."

Rupert, using his considerable weight, managed to get Tubby upright. As he scrambled on board, I could hear him let out a guffaw. He peered over the gunwale, looking unreasonably chirpy.

"I've got your body. Come on, give me your hand and get in. No need to be scared."

I clambered into the cockpit to join Rupert and a man-sized white polythene horse food sack.

"Here's your body. I'm calling him Neddy!"

"Very funny!"

In our defence, we weren't the only ones to capsize that day. The wind strength had caught several other crews unawares, and great activity from the safety boats. In our case, the combination of a broken centreboard and cockpit that genuinely looked like a half-filled bathtub meant we had to retire from the race.

Tubby was patched up again, and amazingly, we went on to win a couple of races in the regatta. My dinghy racing experiences had been fantastic. We would have loved to brag about our superb boat handling skills, but I think everyone was clear that this was not the case. Our real triumph lay with that favourable handicap and lots of luck.

With the regattas over, I was just about dying with excitement in the run-up to Sam coming home. Ma, fed up with me getting under her feet, lined up lists of jobs. First, I attacked the weeds on my badly neglected veggie patch.

Hercules came on these sessions, which puzzled me at first. My puss had recently taken to going on nightly hunting missions. He'd return in the early hours, smelling decidedly mousey, and settle down on my pillow for a snuggle. Always up for a snack, he'd stretch those firebrand legs and stroll down to the kitchen with me for breakfast. After that, it was the same routine. Hercules usually found a warm snooze spot for the day.

Feeling persecuted, though grateful to have temporarily escaped another paddock ragwort removal job, I got onto my hunkers and started digging. Fat docks with their broad leaves were running riot, as was the couch grass. Its wiry underground stems had crawled all over the patch. That was seriously annoying stuff.

There was also a liberal covering of hedge bindweed. Mind you, I did like their delicate white trumpet flowers. Tempting though it was to leave them, I realised that their vine-like stems were garrotting a currently unidentifiable vegetable. They had to go, too.

Hercules, who had been supervising operations from a sleeping position, sprang up. Switching to stealth mode, he started creeping across my plot. I followed his line of sight. So *that's* why he was so keen to join me.

A handful of baby bunnies were playing in the afternoon sun. Since Hercules majored on clumsy rather than crafty, I didn't think there was much chance of him catching an early tea. Instead, I watched, enchanted, as the tawny rabbits played tag, leaping over one another on those extra-springy legs.

Adopting his catlike trance, Hercules advanced. Slitty eyes, paw by paw, he crept towards his prey. Closer, closer still, instinctively navigating weedy barriers, it was going so well until he reached Ma's brassicas.

Up fluttered a Cabbage White butterfly.

Concentration shot to bits, Hercules popped up to have a swat and missed. His movement sent the rabbits scarpering back to their burrow. Doubly foiled, my poor ginger tiger plodded back and settled down on my jumper in a fluffy huff for an emergency whisker-clean.

Much to my surprise, I discovered some edible goodies, which had refused to die despite being ignored for weeks. I proudly presented Ma with my tiny harvest of beans, beetroot and peas.

Other jobs for me and Di included helping Ma tidy up the greenhouse and pick grapes. This was loud. Those screeches and screams every time a spider volunteered to help were a horrific strain on our eardrums. Shift work was essential.

And then there were the dog walks. Our poor Paddy had developed a debilitating illness that we controlled with medication. Despite this and retiring from wandering, he found a new passion for food. Our boy consumed anything he could find. Leaving him to siesta, I took Monty on long treks.

I cleaned the chickens and rabbits out, and I rode Apache so often she started looking exhausted before we'd begun. We went on beach trips and pony treks, and picnics. Sticking to our strict hygiene routine, I groomed Girty and Sephi so often they almost calmed down. That would never happen, but they were glossy. And then the day finally came. Sam was coming home.

The horsebox arrived, and Sam clattered down the ramp, looking very proud of himself. Ma gave me a pep talk.

"Remember, Sam is still very green and inexperienced. You must handle him with great care."

"Yes, yes, of course, I will, Ma. Can I ride him now?"

"You can, and make sure you wear your riding hat. He'll be far more spirited than Apache."

Music to my ears.

Sam stood remarkably quietly as I saddled and bridled him. He fidgeted as I tightened the girth, but I assured him I probably would have done too. And then came the moment of truth. While Ma held the reins, I slid my boot into the stirrup, gently hoisting myself onto his back.

Pricking up his ears, Sam bounced around, but there were none of the Girty histrionics. He just wanted to get going. Annoyingly, Ma insisted we start with a short stint of schooling. She watched as we circled her in the paddock. With each stride, I felt the power of my young animal beneath me, settling in, becoming attuned, and relaxing with me on his back.

Once she was satisfied that I wouldn't get bucked off, she saddled up Sioux, and we went for a short ride. Some days would be schooling only, working on balance and pace, others a hack. And this formed our early training while he was building up strength and confidence.

The more I rode, the more Sam's personality and self-assurance flourished. He had the kind dependability of his mum, the spirit and stamina of his dad. If he baulked at something, it was because it frightened him or he didn't understand what I asked of him.

I could never claim to be the best rider in the world, but together, Sam and I started forging a harmonious relationship. We negotiated rattly gates, small jumps, the noisy farmyard filled with animal clamour. We played with our friends on their horses and ponies. Sam took it all in his stride, and I was so, so proud of him.

The more I rode Sam, the less time I had for Apache. We knew this would happen. Despite being racked with guilt, I accepted that it was time for her to be sold.

Ma quickly found a family who wanted a 'bomb proof' pony who didn't need much exercise. They came to visit and instantly fell in love with my piebald 'Jug Head'. It was a match made in heaven, and she left soon after.

Although I felt dreadfully disloyal, I had a sneaky feeling that Apache would be delighted with her new family. They would demand little of her. The joys of living on a farm with hee-hawing donkeys for best friends and the choice of umpteen lush fields would be equine bliss.

Going back to school at the end of summer was especially agonising. This year would end with General Certificate of Education Ordinary Level exams. These were the 'O' levels we had been working towards for what seemed like years. Or should have been.

My 'slap happy', as Pa termed it, approach toward sciences was severely lacking, and maths was still a mystery. I'd have to pull my socks up if I was going to achieve passes in those. And I was bereft at leaving Sam.

Ma promised to continue Sam's training so long as I concentrated on my studies. I think we both had more confidence in her pledge than mine. My academic struggles through the winter term were rewarded by Christmas holidays on horseback. All too soon, it was back to educational toil.

The pressure cranked up in the Easter term. It felt even more gruelling. Amidst the academic misery came a carrot. Ma had a treat in store for us. She wouldn't tell us what it was, other than it had something to do with Uncle Jim. We were intrigued.

The Wonder of Welsh Words

Peryglon
There were many of these in the Swellies. Pronounced 'perr-uh-glon', this word means **'dangers'**.

Chapter Twenty-Three

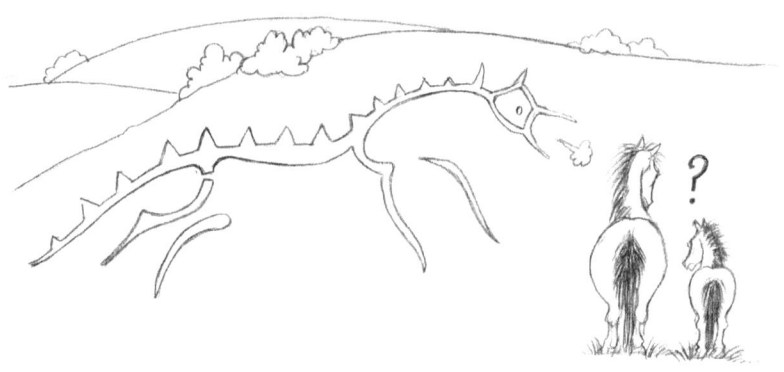

**'Do not be afraid of taking a big step –
you cannot cross a chasm in two steps.'**

David Lloyd George

We were going to the races.

This was the best news. Uncle Jim lived in the Berkshire town of Hungerford. He was a dedicated horse racing fan and invited us to stay for a few days and join him at a Newbury flat race meet.

Pa, too busy to join us, was left in charge of the animals again. Luckily for him, Uncle Jim's racehorse specialist son was in the area and offered to help with the horses while we were away. He arrived the day before we left, just as I had turned Sam out in the paddock.

"Hello, Beth, I'm here to rescue your dad!"

"Nice to see you, Christian. There's no one else about at the moment. D'you want to see the mares?"

Christian dumped his bags and followed me to the meadow.

"They're looking grand," he said. "Ridden either of them yet?"

I looked at him, stunned. Unlike his father, he always struck me as being a carefree chap, but this seemed a reckless idea, even for him.

"Definitely not. No, never. They're not for riding."

"That's odd. I thought you were the animal fanatic in the family."

"Yes, but these are racehorses, and they're pregnant. Ma would kill me if I did anything to harm them."

"Don't worry about that, they're barely showing. They could be ridden for months yet. Come on, have a go on the big bay. She looks like a pussycat."

Barking mad, crackers, total fruitcake would be more apt descriptions of Girty. I decided not to correct him.

"Are you sure it won't hurt her?"

"Certain. Do the pair gallop around the field before settling?"

"Yes, they do."

"There you are then. That's normal, they need some exercise. I'll hold her headcollar and give you a leg up."

I considered his proposal for a millisecond. Here was a supposedly responsible adult. He was giving me the chance to sit astride a proper racehorse for the first time in my life. It was too good to turn down. I agreed, although had one question.

"Racehorses need to be warmed up for ages before being ridden, don't they?"

"Cold back? We'll soon find out!"

Christian looped Sam's lead rein through the

ring in Girty's headcollar. Whispering sweet nothings, he smoothed his hand down her neck until, rolling mad eye aside, she looked almost placid. He beckoned me over.

Christian gave me a leg up onto her back with a practised hoist. I sat there for, ooh, about twenty-five seconds. Girty's head shot up. She snorted with indignation, pawed the ground, and promptly bucked me off.

"Ah well," said Christian, between belly laughs, "she was a bit skittish after all."

And that was my first experience of 'riding' a racehorse. Brief, and totally unsuccessful. I did ride racehorses in training, but that came later during my university years. And I'm ashamed to admit that I never did share this sorry episode with Ma. You'll imagine my relief when Girty eventually produced a beautiful foal.

Ma drove us to Uncle Jim's home in Hungerford. It was a long journey which improved the closer we got. We loved these visits.

"Right, girls, shout out the first one to see it."

"I'm not playing. I'm reading."

"She's not, Ma. Di's sulking."

"Am not. Stop bugging me!"

"Now stop it, both of you, and look out of the window."

"There, there it is!"

"Smarty pants."

"Well done, Di."

We gazed in awe at the vast Uffington White Horse on the hillside. The deep trenches filled with crushed white chalk 360 feet (110 metres) long possessed a huge wow factor.

"And did you know that it's the oldest white horse of its type in the country?"

"Groovy."

"*Ahem*, yes, Di. Recent excavations and new dating techniques show that the horse was created around three thousand years ago during the Bronze Age."

"Far out!"

"For goodness' sake, Beth, stop copying. I don't know why your father and I spend so much money on that school. Anyway, there's another interesting fact about a dragon in this area."

"Ooh, dragon stories, fab. Go on, Ma, tell!"

"There's a small, flat-topped mound called Dragon Hill beneath the White Horse. It is where St George is reputed to have killed *the* dragon. And the valley close to Dragon Hill is known as The Manger. This is where the legendary White Horse goes to feed."

Ma had turned into a tour guide. Mind you, as

parental stories went, these were pretty interesting.

"Aren't the Lambourn gallops here?"

"Yes, well remembered, Di. We're passing them now."

This was a place we were desperate to visit. The 550 acres (222 hectares) of racehorse training grounds looked limitless from the road. It is popular, with eight miles of turf track and seven miles of artificial surface maintained by the Jockey Club. Around 750 racehorses use the Lambourn gallops.

As usual, Ma knew all about it.

"Had you realised that anyone can watch the horses training?"

The very thought of seeing thoroughbreds in prime condition streaking over the tracks fired my imagination.

"Wow. Perhaps Girty and Sephi trained here. Can we go, please?"

"We don't have time during this visit, but one day, perhaps."

We settled back happily for the remaining minutes of our journey.

Uncle Jim's home was impeccably neat. He shared it with Honey, his beloved golden Labrador. Despite being a plump sweetheart, she had a foible. If we were in the car and her master left it unattended, Honey took it upon herself to guard the upholstery with her life. On one occasion (that I am incapable of forgetting), Uncle Jim parked outside a shop to stock up on pipe tobacco. Ma and Di joined him to buy postcards, leaving me in the car with docile, cuddly-wuddly Honey. Except she wasn't.

The second the door was closed, Honey's head loomed from the footwell with her lips curled back. Shocked, I assumed something outside had frightened her and instinctively reached toward her. Who knew that roly-poly Honey turned into an axe murdering wolverine in cars?

Staring fixedly at me, Honey snarled and slowly crept forward. Petrified, I tried sweet-talking. That had the opposite effect. Saliva dripped from her fangs as she gargled growls. I retracted my hand, which was a tragic idea.

Surviving Honey's half lunge, I sat like a statue, staring at my toes until the others returned. Back they breezed, bristling with postcards and baccy to be received with joyous licks and ecstatic yelps from Honey. I never felt the same about that dog.

The benign waterways, undulating chalky hills and rolling meadows exuded Englishness, as did Hungerford. The Kennet and Avon canal runs through the old market town adding charm to its olde worlde feel. Di indulged me on one of the canal bridges by playing Poohsticks as barges gently fared past. Regardless of age, it had to be done.

We spent ages poking around quirky antique shops, looking for bargains. Di was developing a new annoying mania for boutiques, and had to be fished out of several before she blew all her pocket money. The alternative of going to Uncle Jim's favourite pub for lunch was an ideal compromise. They even had a squashy leather armchair next to the fire reserved for him at The Bear Inn. It was a nice touch.

The day of the races dawned sunny and warm. We joined throngs of happy punters crowding through the gates, laughing, hailing one another. It was impossible not to overhear the animated banter among friends about hot favourites and the season's duds. Who would win the top race? Everyone had an opinion.

As we reached the spectator areas, Uncle Jim took us to a spot where we paused to absorb our surroundings. He handed us a race pass each. It looked like an embossed cardboard medallion with a thread.

"Loop the cord through a buttonhole so officials can see."

As I wrestled with my tag, Di started flipping

through the race programme.

"How long has the racecourse been open, Uncle Jim?"

"That's an interesting question. They raced here long before it became an official course. The first recorded race took place in 1805."

"Wow!"

"Yes, King Edward VII loved racing, and gave his support for the racecourse, which the Jockey Club eventually approved. The first *official* race meeting took place in 1905, and they have been flat and National Hunt jump racing here ever since."

"Do they have any important races?"

"Yes, several. One of the most famous, the Hennessy Cognac Gold Cup, began in 1957. It's the longest-running commercial sponsorship in horse racing. Famous winners include Mill House and Arkle. Now come along, let's get settled."

We found our seats in the stand, which offered a commanding view of the course. More and more spectators appeared, milling around on the lawn below. Trilbies, flat caps and a few toppers, some were smartly dressed, others not.

Regardless of the entry ticket bought, shooting sticks, binoculars, and programmes seemed to be the typical racing paraphernalia. Uncle Jim gave us form books and explained how the betting worked.

Studying form, he said, came in many guises.

Die-hard punters focus on a horse's lineage, health, jockey competence, and success. They'll want to know what 'the going', the turf state, is like at a racecourse. And why? Because they will know which conditions their fancied horse likes best.

"Have a look at your programmes," he said. "Here's the list for the first race. We have the runners, and information to help us decide which horses to back. The going is 'good' today, so take that into account."

Despite Uncle Jim's advice, our approach was less scientific.

"I'd like to bet on number eight, please, Uncle Jim. It's my favourite number."

"I see, Di, very sensible."

"Can I bet on Lester Piggott, please? He's my very favourite jockey."

"Erm, you can, Beth, although it'll be his horse, Jumping Jack, we bet on."

We all knew who Ma would favour.

"*Ahem*, I think I'll have a bet placed on the Queen's horse, please."

"Yes, of course."

We dashed down to the parade ring as the saddled horses appeared. Chestnuts, bays, one dapple grey; they were all magnificent. Their stable lads led them around the short circular track. In the grassy centre, owners, and jockeys wearing brightly coloured silks, stood chatting, while trainers issued last-minute instructions.

I goggled at the sleek equine athletes an arm's length away. Alert, they danced, snorted, ears pricked, eager for 'the off'. Their coats shone so brightly I could almost see my reflection as they passed.

Jumping Jack, I decided, looked exceptionally splendid and eminently bet-worthy. Uncle Jim motioned to me.

"See that slim jockey walking towards the ring now?"

"Yes."

"It's your hero, Lester Piggott."

"Wow, this is great! He looks so, sooo…"

"Wrinkly like a walnut?"

"No, Di! He looks very serious, and he's ever so thin."

Uncle Jim nodded.

"They have to keep their weights down to ride these horses. It's a hard career being a jockey. Come along now. It's time to place our bets before we're too late."

We followed him towards a long line of kiosks. I had to ask.

"Uncle Jim, how does betting work?"

"We'll use the Tote, which is a national bookmaker. Racegoers like us pick horses and put their money into a cumulative pool. Everyone with a winning ticket shares a percentage of the pot. If fewer people back your horse, you'll get a greater share if it wins."

"Cool!"

Just as we placed our bets, a hullaballoo broke out close by. Uncle Jim beckoned.

"Come and have a look at these gentlemen. Know what they are doing?"

Mystified, we shook our heads. A group of men stood next to easels with blackboards covered in names and numbers. They were surrounded by punters shouting for race information. But that wasn't what intrigued us most.

Most of the easel men wore white gloves and made weird hand signals at one another.

"These are trackside bookmakers called Tic Tac men. They use a special language to communicate with one another about race odds. They'll often wear white gloves, so their hand signals are clearly visible."

"No way!" cried Di. "That's amazing."

"It is. These men are slick operators. Their pitches are strictly hereditary, so would-be bookies often have to wait for families to die out for a chance to price the odds. Now, where would you like to watch the race? From our seats in the stand or the course rails?"

"The rails, please!"

Spectators streamed into the stands and rushed to the rails. We joined a crush close to the finish line, just in time to see the horses gathering at the metal starting gates. The atmosphere was electric, the anticipation – thrilling.

The signal was given, and they were off.

The crowd roared as runners and riders approached. It was infectious. The ground rocked as the horses thundered past. Witnessing the immense power of the galloping unit was breathtaking.

Binoculars were whipped out as horses hurtled towards the track's farthest limits. Questions were demanded. Who was in the lead? The course announcer gave a speed of sound running commentary over the tannoy. I'm not sure anyone was listening.

The horses rounded the final turn, front runners with stragglers strung out behind. Where was mine? Excitement whipped the crowd into a frenzy of renewed screams. Cries of encouragement, pleas, frustration, begging their horse to find that extra ounce of energy.

As they flew past, I caught sight of Jumping Jack's number. Lester had brought him in at second place.

"Hooray! Lester came second. Shame about your old nag, Di."

"I couldn't see properly. Where did it come?"

"Waaaay back in the field. Probably last."

"Fibber!"

"What a fun race. Girls, look at the results board. My horse has won!"

Disappointed punters groaned and hurled betting tickets in the air. Whoops of jubilance came from others as they returned to the bookies. It had been a race of mixed fortunes.

The rest of the afternoon followed the same pattern, each race as spectacular as the last. We finally left with our ears buzzing from the sounds of the roaring crowd, worn out and happy. Our betting kitty was a little higher than when we started, and we'd loved every second of this new experience.

Still inspired by what we had seen, I had a new career epiphany on our journey home. The chance to work with horses all day and then race for a job? Yep, it was crystal clear. I would be a flat racer, or a jump racer, which sounded even more exhilarating.

I consumed as many books on racing as I

could. Working with racehorses, fitness levels required, and how to join the profession, I mugged up on it all. There was only one problem. I was probably too fat. Lester Piggott was famous for his daily breakfast diet of a cuppa and cigar, which sounded pretty extreme. Since I couldn't possibly turn down Ma's excellent cooking, I decided there was a simple alternative. Long hot baths.

Turkish baths were favoured by many jockeys, as well as saunas. Easily remedied. I went through a phase of running a scalding-hot bath. With steam filling the bathroom, I'd sit in the tub for as long as I could before expiring. Ma spotted me after one such session.

"Good heavens, Beth, you're looking like a boiled shrimp. What on *earth* have you been doing?"

"I've decided to become a jockey, but I'm too podgy."

"I see. You are not too fat. You need a healthy diet to grow. Did you know that jockeys are usually short and weigh between seven and a half to eight and a half stones [49 to 54 kg]?"

"I did read something like that. I'm already about seven stones now, aren't I?"

"Yes, probably, and you are still growing. And had you considered that, despite their light weight, they must be able to control the horse when it is galloping at 40 mph [64 km/h]? That isn't easy when you haven't had a proper meal for weeks."

"Yes, but…"

"And like it or not, for lots of reasons, there are very few girls who become successful racing jockeys. The likelihood of success is, I'm afraid, tiny. So, since we're always patching up animals, why not focus on your other idea of becoming a vet? Have you given up on that?"

"No, but…"

"It's a fine one. You would work with many animals and still have time to enjoy riding. But there's just one thing we mustn't forget."

"Yes, but…"

"Sciences, Beth. If you don't pass your exams, you won't give yourself a chance to get to university. I can't think of a better reason for getting your head down and studying for next term's exams."

"I knew you were going to say that!"

Ma had done it again. She had skilfully rearranged my pipedreams and come up with an annoyingly sensible conclusion that meant I would have to work hard. Later that week, I packed my trunk. It was time. There was a sombre atmosphere back at school. Were we going to crack these dratted 'O' level exams or fail miserably?

The Wonder of Welsh Words

Rasio Ceffylau
Something we loved, though it is tricky to say in Welsh. The words mean '**horse racing**', pronounced 'rra-seeor ke-ful-I.'

Chapter Twenty-Four

Harlech:
'To live in Wales is to be conscious At dusk of the spilled blood That went to the making of the wild sky.'

R. S. Thomas

The term got off to a frantic start. Revision lessons attempted to cram our teenage heads with as much information as possible. Miss Whitby, biology, visibly disappointed at the temporary ban on gutting animals, took to drawing body parts on the blackboards instead. I don't recall being asked to draw a heap of intestines in the exam.

Mr Roberts, chemistry etc., finally remembered he had a class before him and started sharing chemical elements rather than muttering them to himself. Economic on explanations, out they came, in a muddled rush sounding like codes. It was so confusing that someone asked if he could write a couple on the board. Now there was an idea!

Dazzled by the star pupil's brilliant suggestion, Mr Roberts scribbled a long line of capital and small case letters with numbers dotted about. Most of us had no idea what any of it meant. Deeply proud of his efforts, he gravely reminded us we must never, ever get our elements mixed up with our compounds. They were entirely different. Obviously.

By the end of the lesson, my brain was a miasma of protons, atoms and chemical reactions. Which did what, and did anyone honestly understand what a nucleus was? I'm not convinced they did. On the other hand, if an exam question asked us how to turn a Bunsen burner into a blowtorch, that would be simple.

Other lessons went relatively well. Our English teacher who replaced the deceased Mrs Williams was super-keen. We wailed through Romeo and Juliet, staggered through D.H. Lawrence's dreary (I know, blasphemy) imagery in The Rainbow, and sailed through several jolly poems. These, together with the other arts subjects, were a relative breeze.

A short period of intense swotting followed while the great hall was transformed into an examination centre. Desks were spaced out, social distancing as we now know it, though for a different purpose. Any would-be cheaters would have to be a giraffe to spy on her neighbour's answers. Paper after paper was set down in front of us. Bogo Roberts was in charge. Having washed her hands of us in the Geography revision sessions, she regularly invigilated. This was her true vocation. Like a giant praying mantis, she lay in wait halfway down a row. Poised. Just waiting.

Any suspicious sleight of hand and she'd strike. Miss Roberts instantly darted to the pupil's table on her extra-long legs. Hissed challenges received whispered emphatic denials, leaving the concentration-shattered child demoralised. Another scalp for Bogo.

Sniffers were glared at and shuffled writing equipment generated disapproving looks. If anyone needed the bathroom (me), the hand stuck up requesting permission was met with furious dismay. The victim was frog marched out and supervised. It was a sure-fire method of ruining 'the moment'.

I was sitting several exams and quickly got used to the routine. As the time allowed for each one drew to a close, the adjudicator gave us a ten, then five-minute warning followed by 'Pens down, please, girls'. The hall erupted with groans and sighs as writing material was abandoned. It was the same every time. Girls flowed out of the double doors in a wave of nervous tension. There were tears, whoops, cries of 'What did you answer for number six?', 'We were never taught about Gorgo!'. 'We were Katy. That's Medusa.' 'Nooooo, I've failed!', 'You'll be okay, I bet the rest of your paper was fabbo!', and so it went on.

The tortuous process lasted for weeks. We comforted each other, let off steam and then fell on our textbooks to cram for the next exam. Some finished earlier than others. It all depended on the subject. Fraught with emotional tension, we somehow battled through. This had been the toughest challenge we had faced alone in our young lives, and it was a wake-up call.

Although my written papers were all over and done with, I still had my practical music exams. This involved grade six piano and grade eight singing. To describe my style of piano playing as workmanlike would be an understatement. I'd like to blame my early lessons with Mrs Barton, the teacher with dire bodily wind expulsions, for blighting my potential. But that would be unfair. In fact, I lacked talent. Despite this, much to my parents' surprise, I plonked my way to a pass. Next came singing, which was my 'instrument' of choice. Our parents had good voices, and in true Welsh tradition, Pa sang like a bird.

It was our Pa whose voice soared above everyone else's in church. Pa sang every day at home, and it was Pa who encouraged us all to sing. His intuitive ability to harmonise created a musical eloquence that gladdened the heart of anyone who heard.

And many years later, after suffering a catastrophic injury at sea, our Pa lost his fluidity of speech, but he could still sing. Our Pa never ever lost his Welsh voice.

Work on my Grade Eight singing exams

coincided with a special event for the school. Mr Grantham, our music teacher, was a composer and organist. He never discussed his career in school, but it was clear that he was gifted and well known within the music world. One of his singing friends was Peter Pears, at the time a celebrated classical singer. He was giving concerts in the area, and Mr Grantham invited him to take a masterclass at school. Luckily for us, he agreed.

The concept of promoting young people's musical skills was close to Peter Pears' heart. So much so that in 1947, he and his partner, Benjamin Britten, established a cultural charity based in Suffolk. Through Aldeburgh, their dream was to ensure that everyone could enjoy and experience music. Their project grew to become a phenomenal success.

The magic of some life experiences is truly unforgettable, and this was one. On the masterclass day, a small group of us sat in front of Sir Peter. He was tall with an enormous barrel chest, and for all the success he must have enjoyed, he struck me as unassuming, shy, almost.

We hung on his every word as he talked about the joy of music and different styles; opera, baroque, early music and more. He aimed to inspire, and he achieved his goal. He demonstrated several vocal techniques, each of which was spellbinding. And there was another exceptional treat to come.

When the class was over, Mr Grantham asked if I would like to have a private lesson with Peter Pears to help prepare for my singing exam. Terrified at the very thought of it, of course, I agreed.

First, Peter Pears listened to my tremulous efforts. Amazingly, he was wholly engaged. He talked to me about the history behind each piece, the emotions and passion. Then he showed ways to improve different sections. At once, so loudly the windows rattled, an instant later, whisper-soft, yet crystal clear, and all in the same, seemingly endless breath.

Peter Pears opened my eyes to vocal possibilities I had never considered. I couldn't reproduce them, but he brought the music alive. Notes danced off the score, demanding to be sung. He gave me the courage to believe I could hit that cripplingly high note and conquer the trills that had so far eluded me. And sometimes he sang with me, discovering those hidden nuances I had missed.

My lesson was over in a flash. I was exhausted, utterly inspired, and unbelievably grateful. With no room for excuses, I passed my Grade Eight exam with flying colours. After my privilege, it would have been a crime if I hadn't.

The term was almost over. Our treat for completing the exams was a trip to a place we had longed to visit. Harlech Castle, one of the 'iron ring' fortifications built by King Edward I during his second campaign in North Wales.

Each castle was a mighty fortress, from Flint around the coastal fringes to Aberystwyth, their purpose was simple. The English king's ring established awesome power over the Welsh. They were near-impregnable bastions of resistance, and from them, insurrections were swiftly dealt with.

We chattered excitedly as the coach took us along winding roads bisected by brooding Snowdonian mountains. The earthy tablecloth surround formed a jigsaw of tiny sheep-filled fields partitioned by higgledy-piggledy slate and stone walls. A familiar landscape. Finally, our destination took shape. I caught my breath. Huge, foreboding, Harlech was as immense as I had hoped.

The teachers gathered us together in the car park. Miss Williams, history, was in charge and dead keen to start imparting historical gems.

"Now, girls. We need to remind ourselves of some interesting features before we go any further. Who can tell me how long it took to build the castle?"

Belinda, aka Pigtails, stuck up her hand.

"Seven years, Miss Williams?"

"Yes, well done. Any ideas how many workers were involved?"

Pigtails knew that too.

"It was 950, Miss Willams."

"Swot!" hissed someone.

"Who said that?"

A sea of angelic faces beamed at Miss Williams.

"Excellent, Belinda. And does anyone know how much it cost to build the castle?"

"Go on, Piggy," whispered Janice, "you're bound to know."

"8,184 pounds, Miss Williams?"

"Correct, Belinda. I'm pleased *someone* read the information I gave you. Yes, Harlech was built under the guidance of Master James of St George, the King's architect."

Pigtails' hand shot up yet again.

"But I thought he was the Constable of the castle."

"Yes indeed. Harlech was far cheaper to build than Caernarfon or Conwy because it was smaller and less ornate, though remarkably secure. The King was so pleased with his work he appointed Master James Constable of the castle."

It was easy to see why King Edward would be satisfied. The towering citadel was constructed high on a rocky crag overlooking Cardigan Bay and the Irish Sea.

Bustling excitedly, we headed for the interior. The classic 'walls within walls' design took form, melding with the daunting natural defences. Cardigan Bay to the west and a rural backdrop rising to the Rhinog mountain range, it was a geographically strategic masterpiece. Yet, despite all this, Harlech did not go unchallenged.

We climbed the long flight of steps to the entrance, agog. Foundations of inner rooms, a bakery, chapel, the great hall, there was so much to explore. It was mind-boggling to be among these trappings of a thriving household.

We were herded to the seaward side and a steep stone staircase plunging below. Miss Williams told us more.

"This, girls, was known as the Way From the Sea. Those steps descend almost two hundred feet to the castle rock base."

"*Amazing!* Who used them, Miss Williams? The sea's miles away."

"Good point, Jenny. The coastline has altered over the centuries and, with it, the sea level. In its early years, water lapped the castle rocks on the turn of the tide."

"That is so hard to imagine!"

"I know. The sea helped castle occupants

withstand several uprisings because supplies were brought by ships. They sailed up a channel, offloading at a quay way down there by the rocks."

We followed her pointing hand. The thought of having to lug supplies up those steep steps was exhausting.

Kathryn, a somewhat bloodthirsty but otherwise normal girl, could always be relied on for a question about battles.

"Were there revolts, Miss Williams?"

"Yes, Kathryn, many. In the autumn of 1294, Madog ap Llywelyn led a Welsh uprising. It was in response to the English imposition of taxes. Several castles were overrun, but not Harlech. Instead, the castle was besieged."

"What happened?"

"Amazingly, only 36 people, including ten crossbowmen, a chaplain, blacksmith, carpenter and stonemason, were stationed at the castle. Can you imagine the terror they must have felt?"

We could. We really could. Hanging on Miss Williams' every word, we urged her to finish the story.

"The siege went on for months. Despite the tiny group, they held out with the help of supplies sent over by ship from Ireland. The rebellion eventually failed."

We gazed at the rocky spur and those steep

stairs with a new appreciation. Their existence truly had helped save lives.

Dying to learn more about the castle's bloody history, we nagged our teacher for other stories. Miss Williams motioned for us to sit on lumps of hand-hewn castle rock. She dispensed our vile sandwiches and told us about the fate of Owain Glyndŵr, the medieval ruler and last 'true' Welsh Prince of Wales.

"In 1404, the castle was captured by the Welsh prince, Owain Glyndŵr, during the final major rebellion against English rule. Together with nearby Machynlleth, Harlech became the centre of Glyndŵr's vision of an independent Wales."

"Hooray for Wales!"

"Yes, Jenny, quite."

"Prince Owain set up home in Harlech. He summoned his followers from all over the country to attend a great parliament. Some say it was at Harlech Castle that Owain Glyndŵr was formally crowned Prince of Wales. Sadly, his glory didn't last."

Gripped, we pleaded with her to continue.

"Harlech was besieged yet again. This time by the forces of Harry of Monmouth, who later became Henry the fifth. Although Owain's men fought bravely, the supplies ran short, and they were exhausted."

"Did they lose the battle?" demanded Kathryn.

"Eventually. But it was because of the castle's defences that they managed to hold out for so long. In the end, the constant bombardment of heavy cannons wore them down. The enemy firepower included an immense cannon called the King's Daughter. It was used so much it even exploded at one point."

"*No!*"

"Yes, though the damage to Harlech was already done. With its defenders hungry and exhausted, the castle eventually fell in 1409. Prince Owain Glyndŵr escaped, but many others were captured."

We all had questions about the riveting history surrounding us and the bravery of the Welshmen's efforts to retain the castle. I had to ask about the song we all knew. It was sung at school, in ceremonies and used in famous films.

"Was it that battle where the song *Men of Harlech* comes from, Miss Williams?"

"Some say it is, although others think it commemorated a later battle. There was another major siege of Harlech between 1461 and 1468. It is famous for being the longest siege in British history."

"Wow!"

"I know. Here, everyone, read this short leaflet

while we're eating. It'll tell you about the background to the siege."

During the Wars of the Roses, Harlech was held by the English Lancastrians and commanded by a Welshman, Dafydd ap Ieuan ap Einion. Although the siege is said to have lasted for seven years, the castle only came under intermittent attack.

The turning point came in 1468 with a political uprising. It caused the Yorkist King Edward IV to announce an invasion of France. Louis XI retaliated by funding an incursion led by the Lancastrian Earl of Pembroke. Pembroke landed close to Harlech in June 1468 and raided Wales.

Convinced that Harlech must be captured, King Edward commissioned his Lord Herbert to raise an army in the border counties. Almost nine-thousand Yorkist soldiers were gathered. Herbert split his force in two. His brother Richard commanded one half and approached Harlech from the north, while Herbert attacked from the south.

We finished reading the information, desperate to learn the next chapter in Harlech's history. Kathryn voiced our thoughts.

"Were there lots of conflicts, Miss Williams?"

"Yes, many, Kathryn. And it wasn't easy for the invaders. As you know, we are well defended by mountains here in Wales. The armies faced dangerous terrain. Yet they battled on, forging ahead on a ruthless campaign."

"What happened when they reached Harlech?"

"The Yorkist brothers joined outside the castle and began their final siege. This was a true siege, with the castle under bombardment and blockaded by land. There were no more ships in the area to supply Dafydd ap Ieuan ap Einion. They began to starve."

"Did they give up?"

"Not at first. Herbert offered terms to Harlech, but Dafydd ap Ieuan ap Einion refused. He had fought in the Hundred Years' War between England and France and had other ideas. Some say he bragged that in his youth, he held a castle in France *so* long that all the old women in Wales spoke of it. Now he would hold Harlech so long that all the women in France would speak of it!"

"I don't know whether that was brave or silly!"

"Who knows, Kathryn? And so the battle began. It was short, less than a month, but vicious, dreadful. Battered by the immense Yorkist army, the poet Hywel Dafi later told of men being 'shattered by the sound of guns' and 'seven thousand men shooting in every port, their bows made from every yew tree'.

And to answer your question, Beth, they say

this is the battle that inspired the song *Men of Harlech*. So, girls, think about what I have told you while I read part of the song's lyrics. Close your eyes and imagine what it must have been like to battle against thousands of men. The brutality. The terror."

> Men of Harlech, march to glory,
> Victory is hov'ring o'er ye,
> Bright-eyed freedom stands before ye,
> Hear ye not her call?
> At your sloth she seems to wonder;
> Rend the sluggish bonds asunder,
> Let the war-cry's deaf'ning thunder
> Every foe appall.
>
> See, they now are flying!
> Dead are heap'd with dying!
> Over might hath triumph'd right,
> Our land to foes denying;
> Upon their soil we never sought them,
> Love of conquest hither brought them,
> But this lesson we have taught them,
> "Cambria ne'er can yield!"

I hung onto every word, we all did, visualising the raging battle. Men desperately defending from the rocky battlements, firing missiles at their enemy, pouring boiling liquid through murder holes, anything to repel the onslaught. Screams, warcries. And death.

The stone I sat on and our surroundings had taken on a new, profound significance. The clamour, chaos, the ground beneath our feet, this was the very place where men had actually died. It was so hard to imagine all that bravery and suffering, yet perhaps not.

"And so," continued Miss Williams, "the castle succumbed under this furious onslaught in less than a month. Fifty prisoners were taken, including the Welsh constable Dafydd ap Ieuan ap Einion, who had kept his Harlech safe for so long."

"Was Dafydd ap Ieuan ap Einion killed, Miss Williams?"

"No, Kathryn. Eventually, he, and most of the garrison were pardoned in December 1468. Come along now, everyone. Let's have a look at the cylindrical towers. One was used as a prison dungeon in medieval times. I have a feeling you'll enjoy seeing that."

Our castle had fulfilled its promise. Unsurprisingly, we yodelled *Men of Harlech* for most of the trip back to school, with Miss Williams, having thoroughly inspired herself, pointing out battle points along the way.

It was trips like this that, much later, caused

me to question why we Welsh are so proud of our heritage. What does being Welsh truly mean?

The Wonder of Welsh Words

Brwydr
An act that has marked the history of Wales. Pronounced 'brroo-drr', this is the word for **battle**.

Chapter Twenty-Five

'Welsh is of the soil, this island, the senior language of the men of Britain; and Welsh is beautiful.'

J. R. R. Tolkien

Driving across the English border into Wales can be a mystifying experience. Signposts, usually headed by a proud red dragon, bear the words '*Croeso i Gymru*', Welcome to Wales. Yes, signposts are bilingual. They've all been that way since 1983 and many for a long time before.

Non-Welsh-speaking motorists often become confused by the linguistic riddles. Mid-translation, they'll get lost and occasionally veer off track, risking minor mishaps. Frustrating though it may be for those who come adrift, there's a reason for this observance.

There's a saying in Wales, '*Cenedl heb iaith, cenedl heb galon*', 'A nation without a language is a nation without a heart'. The Welsh language is at the heart of our culture and still nurtured today. It is a singsong tongue, especially in the south. JRR Tolkien used Welsh tones as a basis for Sindarin, one of his Elvish languages. And many believe rural Wales inspired his depiction of The Shire. Did he name the Hobbit settlement of Crickhollow after Crickhowell? Possibly.

When Di and I grew up, many people in our area spoke little or no English. These were generally older folks who worked at the docks and slate quarries. We listened to the rhythmic poeticism of the language, the lilt, inflexions, catching words here and there, looking to our bilingual father for help when we got stuck.

Although we had Welsh lessons at our primary school, the language commonly spoken at home and with our friends was English. Sadly, we never progressed, but we had fun with some of the popular misnomers.

It disappointed me to learn that *wibli wobli* didn't mean jellyfish, *slefrod môr* being the correct term. A favourite of mine is *smwddio* which sounds like smoothio. It means ironing. Classic! And much as I would have loved *popty ping* to mean microwave oven, sadly, the word is *meicrodon*. There again, it pays to be on one's linguistic toes ('*toes*', being Welsh for dough). *Moron* means carrot, *plant* means children, and *hen* means old. It can be confusing.

As you now know, pronouncing Welsh words can be a tongue-twisting experience. Visitors blow raspberries in their attempts to articulate words beginning 'Ll', as in Llanddwyn. The 'ff' words such as *ffordd* (way, or route) causes much fuffing, and the use of a 'W' pronounced 'Oo' leaves most folks flummoxed.

Being born into this linguistic maze didn't stop us from finding some place names challenging. And we weren't the only ones. In Wales, place names are often descriptive. It can lead to complicated names and none more so than the little village on Anglesey with the longest train station name in the world.

Llanfairpwllgwyngyllgogerychwyrndrobwllllantysiliogogogoch translates as Saint Mary's Church in the hollow of the white hazel near a rapid whirlpool and the Church of Saint Tysilio. It's more of a sentence, really, one with a back story.

The village's name is likely to be a marketing ruse, one that is still effective today. It was originally called Llanfairpwllgwyngwll, which was already a mouthful, though not sufficiently long enough for an enterprising local tailor. While facts are hazy, it is said that he invented the extension. And why? Some say it was as a family joke which caught on. Others believe it was to encourage people on the newly arrived trains in the midnineteenth century to stop in the village. Whatever the truth, do you think anyone uses its full name? Nope. We knew it as Llanfair PG, and the villagers called it Llanfair.

There are some Welsh words which simply don't translate into English. For me, they epitomise the Celtic passion and emotions which run deep in every Welsh soul.

Cwtch means cubby hole, but it also implies

hug, though this is no ordinary fleeting squeeze. *Cwtch* means wrapping your arms around someone to make them feel safe, sheltered, protected in the world. It's profound, unique, reserved only for a few. The equivalent is impossible to convey with one English word.

Hiraeth is loosely translated as an overpowering longing or homesickness for one's homeland. This emotion is as wistful as it is intense. There are examples where the word *hiraeth* is used in English songs and poetry. Probably the most famous is the song written by Gladys May Jones about Wales, *We'll Keep a Welcome in the Hillsides*.

The song is written in English except for one word. *Hiraeth*. This depthless yearning has no direct translation.

> Far away a voice is calling
> Bells of memory chime
> Come home again, come home again
> They call through the oceans of time
> We'll keep a welcome in the hillsides
> We'll keep a welcome in the Vales
> This land you knew will still be singing
> When you come home again to Wales
> This land of song will keep a welcome
> And with a love that never fails

> We'll kiss away each hour of *hiraeth*
> When you come home again to Wales

And then there is *Hwyl*.

I remember the first time Pa used the word. I was due to sing in a concert where we would perform Bach's *Mass in B Minor*. Pa played a recording of the opening movements on his gramophone. As we listened to the extraordinary Kyrie, I became overwhelmed with emotion. Goosebumps rose on my arms, tears welled as I struggled to control inexplicable feelings. Pa could see how moved I was.

"Can you feel it?" he said.

"I can't describe what I feel. The piece, somehow it makes me want to cry."

"Yes, that's *hwyl*. It's a sense so strong inside that it stirs your soul."

Pa was right.

This sense of *hwyl* shows itself in perhaps less obvious settings. Sport is important to most nations. In Wales, football (soccer) has a passionate fan base, and when I was growing up it was especially popular in the north. Our team may not have enjoyed resounding success then, but that didn't stop fans supporting them with heartfelt fervour through thick and thin. Known today as the Red Wall, fans earned their name during the EURO 2016 football tournament for wearing replica red shirts, just like their heroes. They became the team's twelfth man, winning such high respect that the organisers gave them a special award for their entente cordiale.

For the first time since 1958, our Welsh footballers made the nation proud by qualifying for the 2022 World Cup finals in Qatar, and did they go alone? No. Thousands of the Red Wall fans went to cheer their boys along. They were joined from afar by scores of ardent supporters back in Wales and multitudes worldwide, captivated by the team's courage, determination, and song.

Yma O Hyd (We're Still Here) was released in 1983 by Dafydd Iwan, a much-loved Welsh folk singer. The song, which talks about the strife and resilience of the Welsh, is more of an anthem. It has become the footballing ballad of the nation, which rings around stadia at international matches. With a chorus that sounds like a defiant war cry, it's difficult not to be caught up with that intense emotion: *hwyl*.

We were brought up with rugby, a sport that captures the spirit of countless Welsh folks. Supporting Wales is not simply about being a fan. It runs deeper. Rugby is part of our identity.

The game, played with a funny shaped ball, is revered in the hills and valleys, in the mountains and along coastlines. Players and all associated with rugby are idols. Just like their footballing counterparts, their successes have taken Wales to the world stage. That's no mean feat for such a little nation.

On international match days, the same thing happens in every supporters home, bar, and stadium. When 'our boys' set foot on the pitch, breaths are held, faces radiate excitement, anticipation, fear and hope. That sense of *deepest emotion* is palpable.

And, as you might guess, song is inextricably linked to these occasions. Go to any sports arena worldwide, and you'll likely hear sporadic outbursts of song. Pop music blares out of loudspeakers, toots on trumpets, skirls of bagpipes. It's fun, and it's entertaining. It's a bit different for us Welsh. Attending an international rugby match where our boys are playing can, at first, feel like going to chapel.

There's often a choir on the pitch before the match begins. Murmurs of expectancy ripple around the stadium as the Welsh rugby team lines up for the national anthem. But this is no ordinary piece about battles and kings or queens. The Welsh national anthem is a chorale about its people and the love of their country. The song talks of brave heroes, poetry, language and culture. The valleys, mountains, and the guarding sea that combine to make Wales so very precious.

As the anthem begins, so does the groundswell of emotion. Thousands upon thousands of supporters rise and break into song. They fill their lungs and sing at the tops of their voices, joining their players. They know every word. They sing in harmony. Of course they do, they're Welsh. And even when the choir has stopped, the supporters continue.

For the opposing side, just like the Red Wall, Welsh rugby supporters are a formidable force. The sound and passion is awe-inspiring, especially at home matches. It's natural. Fans are filled with that inexplicable emotion called *hwyl*.

I remember a teacher telling us where the Welsh reputation for singing came from.

"It was in the eighteenth century," said Miss Williams, "when thousands of migrant workers came to fill jobs in the southern coal and iron industries."

Did they love Wales? We wondered.

"Yes and no," she continued. "The work was hard, often dangerous and poorly paid. Families found comfort in community singing."

I found this a stirring concept.

"Where did they sing, Miss Williams?"

"Often in chapel. Their community spirit boosted the Methodist faith. Lots of new chapels were built where congregational singing took place. It was the same situation with our slate quarrying communities in the north."

Philly nodded sagely.

"Singing is the best bit about our church services."

Philly evidently attended a similar chapel to ours. She wanted to know more.

"Did they only sing in chapel, Miss Williams?"

"Ah no. Workers also sang on the way to their collieries and quarries. They sang during their breaks. And you know how proud we are of our male voice choirs?"

We nodded enthusiastically.

"This was the period where they began. Although the Welsh love of music and poetry came even earlier."

Miss Williams took us back to the Middle Ages, where Welsh bards and minstrels assembled for an eisteddfod, which initially meant a 'session' of poetry and music competition. Over time, interest in these competitions lessened, and by the seventeenth century, eisteddfod had lost its appeal. The competition was revived in the nineteenth century to showcase Wales's artistic ethos. A council was formed to organise the annual National Eisteddfod of Wales, celebrating the country's culture and language.

The event is still held each summer alternately in North or South Wales. There are awards for music, prose, drama, and art, but the coveted honour is always for poetry. It's the place to see native fluent Welsh speakers at their finest. And it is Eisteddfod that inspired a hybrid celebration.

After the Second World War, the British Council backed the people of a modest North Welsh town with a grand vision. Its name is Llangollen. They wanted to use eisteddfod to promote the concept of lasting peace. Funds were raised, and pledges made to reinvest proceeds in the event.

In June 1947, they held the first International Musical Eisteddfod. Fears that nobody would come were quickly quashed. The International Eisteddfod was a resounding success. Groups from ten countries journeyed to Llangollen, joining 40 choirs from England, Scotland and Wales.

The next few years saw many more countries taking part. In 1953, Queen Elizabeth II visited the Eisteddfod as part of her post-coronation tour of Wales. By this time, singers and dancers of 32 nationalities had competed in Llangollen. They had created a truly international festival, all run by volunteers.

I remember my first visit to the International Eisteddfod. It was another school trip and a nightmare for the teachers in charge of pupil-herding. As our ancient coach creaked over hills and ground through the valleys, Miss Foley supplied us with information.

"The Llangollen International Eisteddfod is world-famous, girls. Can anyone guess how many people have competed since it began?"

Janice, recently released from the purgatory of being gated yet again, was in a spirited mood.

"About four thousand-ish, Miss Foley?"

"No, Janice, many more. Remember, the festival started in 1947, and since then, contestants from over 100 nationalities have performed."

Karen knitted her brows.

"Then it must be about twenty, no, forty thousand people if we include the choirs, Miss Foley?"

"No, Karen, lots more. Over three hundred thousand people have taken part!"

By anyone's standards, this was an awe-inspiring number.

"And here's another interesting fact. Who can tell me which famous singer came here?"

I had this one in the bag. It had to be my latest hero. Up zoomed my hand.

"I know, Miss Foley. Sir Peter Pears?"

"No, Beth, even more famous. In 1955, Luciano Pavarotti sang in the choir from his home town of Modena. His father was the conductor. The choir won first prize in the Male Voice Choir competition. Pavarotti returned to give a spectacular concert in 1995."

"Fab!"

In an instant, sleepy Llangollen in the middle of nowhere had taken on superstar status. We poured out of our coach, chattering, hopelessly excited. With our teachers clucking like overgrown hens, we were steered through a town dressed in festival clothes.

Hundreds of spectators were already lining the street to watch a parade. There were dancers in national dress, some singing, others playing weird-looking instruments, colourful costumes from countries far and wide. The scenes were intoxicating.

As the procession passed, Miss Foley led us towards a collection of marquees in a field. Each was abuzz with art demonstrations, vocalists, and dancers.

"Come along, girls. There are lots of interesting mini-events here. We'll have our lunch and listen to the group of singers I want you to hear."

Katie groaned.

"Oh no, Miss Foley, do we have to have chef's sandwiches *again?*"

"Yes, we do, Katie. There's nothing wrong with them. I expect we have fish paste today, which is extremely nutritious."

It was an easy guess. They stank.

Settling down, we munched lank sandwiches in front of a schoolgirl choir. We listened to their expressive harmonising, dead jealous because they were so good. We loved each presentation and desperately wanted to compete, too. With fishy fingers grabbing spare seats, we nipped into other tents to watch different performers. And then we were allowed a peek of the concert hall. It seemed enormous, which was just as well. Operatic performances, pop concerts, dance troupes, and the Choir of the World competition took place on that vast, flower-decorated stage.

Our day passed in a flash. We had been immersed in oceans of colours, carried along by currents of joyful entertainment and waves of smiley faces. We left the decorated town with its carnival atmosphere worn out, in a cheerful sort of way. Little did I know that the next festival I attended would be very different.

The Wonder of Welsh Words

Gwladgarol
Etched in the soul of every true Welsh person. This word for '**patriotic**' is pronounced 'goowlad-garr-ol'.

Chapter Twenty-Six

'I grew up among heroes who went down the pit, who played rugby, told stories, sang songs of war.'

Richard Burton

Fat Dogs and Welsh Estates

Growing up in Britain during the iconic 1960s and 70s encompassed the hippy Flower Power movement and psychedelia that went with it. Not that I especially noticed. Our Welsh version was heavily diluted. It's true that many used recreational drugs, for example, though my first encounter with them was baffling.

Di was now old enough to attend local music festivals. Typical of our rustic environment, unlike Woodstock, they tended to be tame affairs. Nevertheless, they were well attended, especially by sheep. I watched, intrigued when she left with her friends, dying to know what they got up to.

When Di returned, I'd cross-examine her, pleading to be allowed to come along to the next one. For some reason I can't remember, she finally succumbed. I was still pretty young, so it took lengthy negotiations with Ma to gain permission. Finally, she gave in, but there were stipulations.

"You must stay with Di the whole time."

"I will, Ma."

"Do *not* accept food or drinks from anyone."

"I won't."

"And especially not mushrooms. You know, those magic ones."

This, even for Ma, was a strange thing to say. Di seemed to know what was going on.

"Oh *Ma*, my friends aren't like that!"

"I should hope not, Di, but one never knows what might happen at these frightful places."

"They're not! Anyway, it's only those hippies from Llanprig who eat them."

"Oh dear."

Di's hairiest group of friends duly picked us up, and we headed off to my first folk festival.

The old banger splashed through winding lanes towards the foothills of Snowdonia. It had stopped raining, which was a bonus. The buzz in the car increased as we reached a desolate area of moorland.

"Groovy!" cried someone, pointing at a small collection of tents.

Apparently we had arrived.

Walking across the wet, springy turf strongly reminded me of our weekly trudge at school. Only this time, it wasn't church we were heading for. It was a small stage and the gaudy crowd. The girls mostly had long straggly hair and headbands with flowers sticking out of the sides. Some even wore floral wreaths, which looked itchy.

"Di, what are the flowers all about?"

"It's all to do with flower power. You've seen it on telly. It's the sign of non-violence and harmony. Everyone has them here."

"Oh right. Where's yours, then?"

"I'll get one in a minute."

"Better make it ragwort then. With all the pinches you give me, you deserve a weed."

"Very funny."

The men, hairier still, mostly had bushy beards, possibly the druid coming out in them. I decided it explained why Di's friends were so unusually hirsute.

"Far out, Di, you touched down!" shouted someone, sounding like a Welsh air traffic controller.

Sheep loitered curiously on the fringes as we mingled with girls wearing floaty smock tops, the boys in T-shirts. They all wore jeans with flared hems that looked like sails. I immediately wanted a pair. And everyone was dripping with bangles and beads.

We eventually found a spot that wasn't covered in sheep poo and settled in front of a droopy-looking folk group. This generated the next phase of hippiness. Face painting. Fat flowers went on one cheek and the other, a sign I hadn't seen before.

"Di, what's that weird shape?"

"*Tsk*, don't you know anything? It's the peace symbol."

"Huh, looks like a steering wheel to me."

"You are un-real!"

Di was getting sick of me.

As the afternoon wore on, attendees chatted in small groups or wafted about aimlessly. Many were smoking, and some had started eating, which seemed like a great idea.

"Di, what have we got to eat? I'm starving."

"We had a big lunch before we left. You can't be hungry! Ma put some Polos in your pocket. Eat them."

"That's not going to help much, is it?"

"You are *such* a drag, Beth."

As I crunched my way through a tube of holey mints, I watched several little plastic bags being passed between groups. One offered to us looked like a collection of wizened pixie hats. Di, shaking her head, refused the kind gift. So *that's* what magic mushrooms were. How dull. They didn't look remotely appetising.

Inevitably, the weather changed. Down fluttered Welsh drizzle, so familiar *this* close to the mountains. It didn't stop the wailing musicians, but it did cause a slow-motion flurry of spectator activity. Out of patchwork rucksacks came several Afghan coats, the latest craze in hip hippy-wear.

The sheep or goatskin 'Afghans' were designed with the fleece on the inside. Several had embroidery patterns on the soft suede outside, but most were just grubby. They might have been warm and cosy, but there was one distinct drawback to these garments. When they get wet, they smell like a camel's armpit.

Sheep, obviously scenting some kind of herbivore community spirit, ambled over to join in. We had now reached the stage where many festival-goers probably thought the sheep were humans. Several struck up meaningful chats about nothing at all with the funky dudes, which the sheep seemed to take in good heart.

We finally left when the heavens opened, which was a mercy. Picking our ways through people strewn around with dreamy expressions, I decided that hippy festivals probably weren't my thing. But, they were a feature of the age.

This was the period when fridges were the size of Egyptian tombs. Telephones were huge, black, clunky affairs with a rotary dial and tinkly ringers. A deadly modern colour television replaced our coffin-like black and white version. Fuzzy vision, though it was, it transformed our viewing.

Westerns such as Bonanza and High Chaparral (cause of my early career choice to become a cowboy) came to life. Morecambe and Wise, adored comedians, seemed as though they were in the room, as did our favourite music hall show, The

Good Old Days, with Leonard Sachs and his elaborate sesquipedalian introductions of each performer.

Another mod con that amazed me was an installation I first saw in a drapery shop. Much as I hated shopping, I never turned down a trip to Bangor if it meant calling at Wartski. To stop me from perpetually getting lost, easy in a big store like that, Ma stood me to attention by a cash till. This was where the action took place.

When a cash machine drawer was bulging with money, the lady took out a wad of notes, rolled them, and put them in a plastic capsule. This she popped into the opening of a pipeline running up above her head. *Zoop!*, the cylinder had gone. The ceiling was a network of these magic pipes that made wind-rushing sounds. I had no idea how it worked or where they went but thought it was positively marvellous.

This was also the period of decimalisation. On 15 February 1971, the United Kingdom and Ireland decimalised their currency of pounds, shillings and pence. Our big old pennies were exchanged for little ones, and we lost favourites such as the threepenny bit. The pound was subdivided into one hundred new pence, shillings were abolished, and 'd's' (old pence) became 'p's' (new pence). Youngsters adapted reasonably quickly, but it was baffling for many older folks. During the phasing-out period, cries of 'What's that in old money?' were commonplace. It went on for years.

Aside from folk music, the period was dominated by the Beatles. Of course, Elvis Presley too. The evergreen Rolling Stones were probably only in their fifties, and while Di's taste veered towards Pink Floyd and Elton John, mine rested firmly at base level with a pop group called Slade. LPs featuring both blared out of Pa's posh record player, sending animals scampering for cover and Ma to distraction.

Pocket money bought us favourite treats, including Swizzels Lovehearts. I distinctly remember opening my first packet, desperate to read the message on the sweet.

"Ooh, Siân, guess what my one says?"

"I don't know. Tell!"

"It says 'For Ever'!"

"Aww, that's nice. Mine says 'Always'."

Powdery Sherbert Dip Dabs made you sneeze if inhaled before sucking the dipping-in lolly. There were Refreshers that pulled your fillings out and Gob Stoppers that broke your teeth.

Young fashionistas, probably a little slow to catch on in our part of Wales, favoured cheesecloth shirts and bell-bottom trousers. The brave teetering around on kitten heels and pencil skirts were relieved when drainpipe jeans and platform shoes became all the rage. Hairstyles varied, and it was something Ma was deathly serious about. She had a collection of wigs, which were the subject of several philosophical debates.

"Why have you got so many wigs?"

"You know I use them for cocktail parties and dinners, Beth."

"But you've got loads of your own hair, so what's the point?"

"They're tidy and fashionable. One must always look one's best at these functions."

"Those ones with all the grips inside look scratchy and hot. I don't think I'll bother with fashion."

"You might change your mind when you're older. Now, pass me the rollers, please. I'll use those this evening."

Ma treasured her Carmen rollers. For non-wig events, using them gave me an ideal opportunity to share my latest animal story. In return, I was on roller-passing duty. Once they had reached finger-burny temperature, I passed them over to be strapped onto her locks. Boiling though they must have been, she ended up with massive curls, the desired look. I don't recall her using much makeup, although she couldn't go anywhere without her compact. A quick dab on the nose with powder was apparently essential.

As for accoutrements, Ma believed that wearing an excess of jewellery was 'dreadfully common,' but she loved sunglasses. There was nothing minimalist about those babies. They looked like window panes.

This passion for enormous sunglasses was unfortunate in Ma's case because she had a pin head. Nevertheless, she was devoted to them and wandered around looking like a bumblebee, which was no doubt trendy.

Our parents attended many charity events, business cocktail parties and dinners during our upbringing. Ma was always impeccably dressed, Pa suitably dashing, a cravat or silk tie setting off his tailored suit. And although the sixties did swing for many, sadly for them, it didn't extend through the seventies.

Ma and Pa waited for Di to begin her career and me to finish my 'O' levels before telling us they were parting. Typical of our parents, there was no fuss, no bother.

There was great sadness, acceptance that an unsettling period would follow, and many changes. But one carried on and adapted. And we did, despite the formidable unspoken undercurrents. In truth, it was a deeply distressing, disorientating time, made even worse by what happened next.

The Wonder of Welsh Words

Tristwch
This word pronounced 'trrist-ooch' with the soft 'ch' is full of emotion. And it means '**sadness**'.

Chapter Twenty-Seven

'Better my own cottage than the palace of another.'

Welsh Proverb

The decision was made to move from Ty Fawr. Homes for humans were sought, and homes had to be found for our remaining animals. Girty and Sephi went to a stud, where they later gave birth to fine healthy foals. Girty's became a race winner.

Our beloved skewbald mare, Sioux, enjoyed a happy retirement at our riding school. We saw her regularly and rode her often. Pa bought a house close to the sea, and we based ourselves with Ma in a cottage closer to the mountains. It was never the same, but it was how things had to be.

Our new home was enchanting. The tiny slate-roofed cottage was nestled in a copse, with a stream tinkling below. We sat outside with mugs of tea, listening to the sounds of nature, spotting new woodland plants, trying to spy squirrels and birds in the leafy canopy.

Paddington flopped down next to Ma as always, bemused, as he often was these days. His thyroid illness was worsening. We could see him blinking, trying to make sense of his new surroundings through failing eyes. Ma stroked his silky head, reassuring him that there was nothing to worry about. His famous nose would stop him from losing her.

We chuckled back at the merrily gurgling brook, trying to guess the fish species and other interesting creatures we might find in its depths. Monty, now an old boy in Great Dane years, pottered about his new patch. We all had fresh discoveries ahead.

Idyllic, though it seemed, I wondered how Ma felt about the differences. We had been brought up in substantial houses. Going from eight-plus bedroom homes to a two-up-two-down cottage was quite a gear change. As usual, Ma was pragmatic.

"It's extremely convenient, Beth, and won't take a moment to clean."

This was a point I hadn't considered. When she wasn't gardening or working with the animals, Ma was cooking, clothes-mending or slogging around innumerable rooms with a mop, duster and her new-fangled hoover. It was the unseen irony of her role as an 'executive's wife'. And she had other observations.

"And don't forget how warm the house will be."

Ma was right about that, too. Much as we all loved Ty Fawr, it was leaky, draughty, and usually cold, despite having several open fires. It was why we perpetually wandered around in double-thick pullovers looking like Michelin men.

"Also, of course, you have Sam in the field. There are plenty of new places to explore with him."

"True."

"And there's space for the dogs, although they mostly snooze these days."

"You're right, Ma. I'm sure it's going to be fab."

"Fab*ulous*, Beth. Do finish your words correctly, please."

Hercules was confined to the house for a while in case he tracked back to our old home. He took this in good spirits, mainly because the cottage was riddled with mice. My little ginger ninja went on nightly missions, leaving us presents on the stairs the following day.

In the evenings, we snuggled up in the cosy parlour with Hercules curled into a croissant on my lap. Paddy lay on Ma's feet, and Monty filled the space between humans and the heat source or flung himself over Di with 'welcome home' doggy affection when she was back. And every night, it was the same routine. Hercules followed me to bed for a power nap before stalking began.

By now, Sam and I had become an inseparable duo. He had developed into a strong, reliable young horse. My boy was brave, leapt like a stag, and galloped like a racehorse, loving nothing more than a long trek. Instinctively, he seemed to know what I wanted, where we should go. And he was adjusting well to his surroundings.

Sam shared his field with a warren of chummy

rabbits, and made friends with his new bovine neighbours over the wall. As I approached for our daily ride, he trotted over, snickering, ready for action. A favourite was tracking through the woods beside the brook. Sometimes we could wade through the water, but it was mostly too rocky. Now and again, we'd stop and examine a deep pool.

Brown river trout flitted below the rippling surface. Their bronzy scales peppered with spots flashed iridescence in the sun. I'd watch, mesmerised until Sam broke the spell. Fish were okay, but a long drink of that cool water was much nicer. It was after one of our explorations that we returned to awful news.

Ma, always so self-controlled, had been crying. I was shocked.

"Wh...what's happened, Ma? Are you alright?"

"Yes, yes, although dreadfully sad. Our poor Paddy has passed away."

We knew he wouldn't be with us for much longer. We knew he was poorly, but it didn't matter. Paddington had been with us for almost as long as I could remember. He was part of our history. He was family.

As Ma daintily mopped her nose, I bawled my eyes out. Eventually, we laid Ma's devoted boy to rest in a part of the copse he loved. Ma then did what she always did during times of intense emotion. She made tea.

We sat together with Monty, one of his great paws resting on my knees, looking puzzled, upset that we were so unhappy. Sniffing, I stroked his noble head, smiling at his kind, caring eyes. It wasn't for the first time that I admired the ability of animals to accept death so much easier than humans.

We reminisced about Paddy's puppy days and what a handsome, naughty dog he was. We giggled about his incorrigible wandering spirit, at Pa being sent off to find him when he went missing on the docks. And we laughed about the grief he had given Mr Edwards, the gamekeeper who thought he was after his pheasants. He wasn't. He was just on another Paddington carefree wander.

Our English Setter had lived in blissful happiness until ill-health took over. Even then, he made the most of life and embraced his attachment to Ma. He drifted away with a full tummy, snoozing in a sun puddle. Heartbroken though we were, we knew we had to be grateful for that.

The next change in my life was transformative. The decision for me to have 'wheels'. Two. As a sixteen-year-old, I was eligible to ride a moped. After deep parental discussions, Pa and I went motorbike shopping and found an old Yamaha FS1-E 49 CC (cubic capacity).

Known as a 'Fizzy', my little yellow peril was fantastic. I could drive a car already, so learning roadcraft was relatively simple. Fizzy buzzed me over to see Pa and my friends, and was cheap to maintain, running forever on one fuel tank.

Ma seemed very impressed. The covert racing driver was revealed in her.

"Might I have a try, Beth?"

"Yes, of course, Ma. Um, you're not ever so steady on a bicycle. Are you sure you'll be okay with this?"

"Goodness, yes. It looks perfectly straightforward."

We were at Pa's house when Ma had her test drive. She stuffed tufts of recently Carmen-rollered blond curls into my helmet and mounted the bike. Looking alarmingly determined, she revved up the little two-stroke engine to screaming point. I tried pointing out that it wasn't necessary.

"Simply getting a feel for the throttle, Beth," she said, before releasing the accelerator.

It's just as well the bike was underpowered.

Skidding off, the bike covered Pa and me in a shower of gravel shrapnel. We watched, amused, as Ma cried out something indistinguishable. We assumed it was some kind of newfound lady-biker's war cry.

"You do realise your mother hasn't even ridden a bicycle for years, don't you?"

"Yes, Pa, but I couldn't say no. She seemed so keen."

Ma whizzed past us, looking thrilled, or hysterical. It was hard to say.

"See how the bike's weaving?"

"Ah, yes, I do."

"I'm afraid she has never had a good sense of balance."

"Strange that, since she's such a good horse rider. Mind you, the helmet seems to have slipped over one of her eyes, so perhaps she can't see very well."

"Possibly. Your mother does have rather a small head."

Ma zoomed past us a couple more times, less wobbly now. By the fourth-ish lap, she was looking somewhat strained. She flapped a hand as she zipped by, so we waved back. This generated a rictus grin and then a shriek.

"Any ideas what she's trying to say, Pa?"

"None at all."

"I wonder if there's a spider in the helmet?"

"The whole county would know if that were the case. Did you tell her how to operate the brakes?"

"Ooh, no, I forgot about that."

"That was an oversight, Beth."

"Sorry. It took a while to explain the gears. I didn't get around to the brakes bit."

"Is there much petrol left in the tank?"

"Actually, no. It's on the reserve tank."

"Well, in that case, we shouldn't be here all that much longer."

The bike eventually petered out halfway up the slope. Not a word was said about the brakes thing. Ma declared it was a magnificent machine and never went near it again.

The summer upheavals continued with my 'O' level results looming ever closer and the prospect of going back to boarding school for two more years. I'm not sure which I was more worried about.

I desperately wanted to spend the last two years of my school education at a day school. Naively, I thought there would still be time to switch and join the local state-run comprehensive school. With that in mind, I lobbied my parents.

Despite my attempts so far, both Ma and Pa had been absolutely against it. They were determined to return me to what they felt was the better educational establishment. Horrifically misguided.

Just as I was on the cusp of admitting defeat, an opportunity arose that I felt sure would help my negotiations. Pa had a suggestion.

The Wonder of Welsh Words

Beic modur
Possessing nearly a full set of vowels, these words for '**motorbike**' are pronounced 'beyeek-mo-dirr'.

Chapter Twenty-Eight

'Our horses know our secrets....we braid our tears into their manes & whisper our dreams into their ears.'

Anonymous

"Beth, would you like to crew on a trip to Guernsey?"

"Gosh, Pa, I'd *love* to."

Aside from the thrill of going on my first ever offshore cruise, this would give me enough time to con Pa into letting me change schools.

"Very good. I've cleared it with your mother. I have a voyage to make soon."

"Thank you. Who are we going with?"

"Mr Jenkins and his son, Gavin. He's a year or two older than you, but I expect you'll get on."

No problem there. The moment I clapped eyes on the dark-haired 'Heathcliff', I knew we would get on famously. And we did, though sadly not for the reasons my teenage heart hoped.

Mr Jenkins had bought an ocean-going yacht, but didn't feel confident about taking it offshore. That's where Pa came in. As a qualified Yachtmaster and experienced offshore sailor, he would skipper the boat and complete the chart work, teaching Mr Jenkins as he went.

We went sailing on a couple of occasions before our trip. I'm not sure which was more educational for our fellow crew members, the boat handling skills or dealing with my father. Unused to Pa's bellowing seadog self, they spent the first afternoon in mild shock. Fortunately, they took his ways in good humour.

Finally, Pa adjudged the conditions suitable for our trip. We stowed our kit in teeny weeny cabins, stuffed the galley kitchen cupboards with provisions, and cast off in the blazing sun. Perfect weather for our grand adventure. We headed south past Caernarfon with its mighty castle sitting on the water's edge, another of Kind Edward I's magnificent fortifications.

A flotilla of seagulls joined us as we unfurled the sails. The crisp jib crackled in the breeze, competing with their raucous cries. I watched as they swooped and soared, interested to see how long they would follow, what their natural range might be. Not far. Once they realised there were no free snacks on offer, they headed back towards land.

Learning the ropes, literally, was new and fun, as was getting used to the cramped conditions. I spent the first few hours trying not to bump into my crewmates. Gavin, also on his first voyage, was bumbly too. Fortunately, his easy-going nature saved him from a verbal lashing from my father.

As we sailed into Cardigan Bay on the Welsh west coast, the scenery changed gradually. Sandy beaches became pastel smudges below jagged cliffs, alive with seabirds like busy bees. Pa smiled at our wonder.

"Can you hear them?" he said.

"Those birds, Pa? No, they're too far away."

"No, the bells."

Gavin and I were puzzled, which was reasonable since there wasn't another vessel or buoy in sight.

"The legend of the lost kingdom of Cantre'r Gwaelod is based on this area, which has several shingle ridges extending out to sea."

"Ooh, do tell us more, Pa."

"As you know, most Welsh names are descriptive. Cantre'r Gwaelod broadly translates as Lowland Hundred. It referred to the administrative apportioning of land and the geographically low-lying settlements."

"Are the ridges why you set this course away from the coast, Mr Jones?"

"Yes, Gavin. It's certainly one reason."

"Anyway, Pa..." I said, impatient to get on with the story.

"Although there are several versions of this myth, they all relate to the kingdom of sixteen prosperous settlements. Steep dykes and sea walls were made to protect the lowlands from sea damage. Sluice gates were opened at low tide to drain the ground and closed again as the tide rose."

"Must have been a big job for somebody."

"Yes, it was. It was the King's knight,

Seithennin, who had the responsibility. All was well until disaster struck."

Even Mr Jenkins was interested now. We urged Pa to finish the story.

"One night during the high spring tides, there was a terrible storm."

Pa paused, pointing to the watery horizon.

"On our starboard is the Irish Sea. Study it for a moment and imagine the speed and ferocity of those tempest waves crashing against the kingdom's walls."

We nodded. We could. It was easy to picture gigantic waves out here. I involuntarily shivered. Nodding, Pa continued.

"Seithennin had attended a feast at the King's palace. Instead of closing the gates as usual, he became so drunk he forgot."

"Wow."

"A terrible dereliction of duty!"

"Terrible!"

"Mountainous breakers rolled into the kingdom, dashing over the settlements. Some escaped, including the King himself, but many perished, unable to withstand the deluge. It was a catastrophe. The sea quickly swallowed the land, leaving the kingdom forever doomed."

"What a great legend!"

"It's based on the poem *Boddi Maes Gwyddno*,

Gavin. 'The Drowning of the Land of Gwyddno'. It is recorded in the thirteenth century Black Book of Carmarthen, thought to be the earliest surviving manuscript written solely in Welsh."

"I have never heard of the book."

"Few people have. Because of this legend, some say that on a sunny day, walkers on the cliffs above Cardigan Bay can see traces of ancient buildings shimmering beneath the waves. They'll hear the distant sound of bells ringing under the sea. These are the bells of the lost kingdom."

There was a strange quietude as we absorbed the ancient myth. Its tragedy was made even more dramatic because we were passing over the kingdom's realm. Could we hear a faint pealing of bells, echoes of a tumultuous past? Or was it the yacht's song as she drove through the surf?

"And there's another interesting point you'll enjoy, Beth."

"What's that, Pa?"

"This area is rich in wildlife. If we're lucky, we might see bottlenose dolphins. There's a thriving population here."

"That would be so cool!"

We craned our necks, hoping to spot a sleek marine mammal. No luck, but that didn't matter. This whole new experience was exhilarating enough.

The boat cut through aquamarine water. As she took us farther, the jagged coastline gradually softened, and those sandy beaches gently melded with the surf. The cliffs became hills, then rises before disappearing too. With the imperceptible metamorphosis complete, we lost sight of land. We were finally out at sea.

I looked around, the sun in the west, a luminous orangey orb in a cloudless sky, the waves surging in a rhythmic pattern. The feelings of peace and serenity were indescribable. I looked at Pa's relaxed expression. No wonder he loved it so much.

Our destination was Saint Peter Port in Guernsey. So far, the cruise had run like clockwork. Pa, satisfied by our teamwork, decided we were ready for an overnight sail. This would buy us extra time in the town, where Pa said he had planned a special treat.

Mr Jenkins took the first watch. I snuggled into my bunk, cosy, weirdly excited about the prospect of taking mine later. I was equally intrigued about Pa's treat. As I was trying to guess what he had in store, my thoughts started drifting with the swell's gentle tempo. There was something indescribably soporific about those waves.

"Beth, wake up. You're on watch."

Pa's disembodied head had appeared around my cabin door.

I tumbled out of my bunk, fell over my sea-boots, and smacked my nose on a locker. Being woken up at 4.45 am is disorientating.

Determined not to let the crew down, I crept past sleeping bodies, trying not to disturb them. Despite the boat's motion, it was eerily quiet. I joined Pa on deck and a different world. Blackish grey, cold, sparkles of phosphorescence as wavelets flickered against the bow.

"Put on your lifejacket. There's a fog bank coming in."

Pa was curt. This was ominous.

"And wake up Gavin, but leave Mr Jenkins. He's had a long watch and needs to sleep."

As the dawn light crept in, our world progressively took shape and, with it, the fog bank. It looked like a titanic tsunami, smoky, dominating our horizon. The sun, a ghostly glow, radiated the gloaming, casting a pallid light on oily-calm water as it vainly tried to penetrate the murk. It was strangely menacing.

Pa was a skipper who took no chances. First, we readied the life raft pod, 'just as a precaution'. Gavin and I grabbed binoculars and took our positions on either side of the boat. Our orders were simple. Look out for approaching vessels and periodically sound the foghorn.

"And don't fall overboard!"

I checked the sails. Wraith-like misty fingers stifled the fabric, threatening to restrain our progress in the dead calm waters. Minutes dragged by as we strained our eyes, searching for danger. Perhaps a marker buoy, a promontory or another vessel.

The English Channel is a busy route for container ships. Conditions like these can play tricks on one's mind.

"Beth, have a look at this. What d'you think it is?"

I scrambled over to Gavin's side and followed his pointing hand.

"I can't see anything there. Pa? Anything on the radar?"

Pa shook his head.

"Okay, sorry, it's just me, then. I keep thinking I'm seeing things when I'm not."

I could easily relate to the difficulties Gavin was having. I was convinced I had seen the head of an ethereal sea monster breaking water a little earlier. Then again, I had recently been reading about the Kraken. Scandinavian folklore can play havoc with a teenager's imagination.

Mr Jenkins was up and making breakfast. The

smell of bacon sandwiches broke the tension. Rations were handed out. As we were about to swap positions, I had the fright of my life.

"Pa, *Pa!* There's something dead ahead. A flashing light. It's huge."

"Good. It's a navigation buoy. I expected that. Come and take the helm while I check the charts."

Relieved to have a new job, I took the metal steering wheel. Pa tapped the binnacle compass housing.

"Keep us on this course. I don't think we've drifted much, but I need to make sure."

Our passage through purgatory may have felt like an eternity, but it only lasted a few hours. Penetrating the fog bank made an instant difference. As the breeze picked up, the sun shone, warming our chilled bones. It felt incredibly liberating.

"Gavin, Beth, look to starboard."

We grabbed our binoculars and scanned the horizon. And there it was. Frighteningly close. A massive container ship, its side looked like an iron cliff face, completely dwarfing our little vessel.

"I saw it on the radar," said Pa. "It's on a different heading, so we were perfectly safe. But that shows you why risks cannot be taken in foggy weather."

During the afternoon we caught up on naps,

chatted, sunbathed, and tried to identify newcomer seabirds. Gavin, christened 'cabin boy' because of his willingness to keep everyone refreshed, was halfway out of the hatch when he hollered.

"*Land Ahoy!* Sorry to shout, but I've always wanted to say that."

Gavin had spotted Guernsey, our Channel Island destination. We had made it!

Pa navigated us past Castle Cornet, a splendid island fortification, towards Saint Peter Port and our mooring. The castle was remarkable, he said, for its defence over the island's capital for hundreds of years and as a natural breakwater for the harbour.

It was early evening by the time we secured the boat and completed our maintenance checks. Pa, a stickler for most things, including punctuality, issued his next command.

"To celebrate our first voyage together, I'm taking you to my favourite restaurant here. It's called *La Fregate*. We have thirty minutes to get ready. Best bib and tucker, everyone, please. It's a smart place."

We stared, aghast. Aside from packing for a sailing trip, not fine dining, we had been at sea for a long time. And while we were clean-ish, my hair looked like a wire wool ball. There was no point in arguing, though. And the thought of going for a posh dinner was tempting.

Precisely thirty minutes later, Pa was impatiently striding around on deck. How he had managed to store a complete evening outfit plus silk cravat in his minuscule sausage bag beat me, but there he was, looking like a mini James Bond.

Laughing at our jelly sea legs, we wobbled uphill, following Pa and the whiffs of his favourite Old Spice cologne. Despite feeling bashful about being scruffy, nobody in the restaurant seemed to care. And identifying our skipper seemed obvious, because it was Pa who the waiters addressed throughout the meal.

We toasted the triumphant first leg of our voyage, enjoyed fabulous food and teased one another with tales of mishaps aboard. We listened to Pa's salty stories and giggled at Mr Jenkins' version of what a hard taskmaster 'your father' had been with his chart work lessons. As dinner ended, he had a suggestion.

"Now that we can sail this far, how about taking the boat to France next time?"

"Cool, Dad, the same crew?"

"Of course. If it works for you, Huw? And if you'd like to come too, Beth, let's go this time next year?"

This was fantastic news. Nodding like Pavlov's dog, I instantly agreed. Luckily, Pa did too.

"Excellent idea, Robert. Would you like to sail to Saint-Malo? It has a beautiful harbour and town."

"Perfect. That's agreed, then. And next time, I'll buy dinner."

Our return cruise was blissfully uneventful. The weather was mixed, but there was none of the fog we had battled against in the Channel. As we retraced our passage through Cardigan Bay, I had an important matter to broach with Pa.

"You know we were talking about me possibly changing schools for my 'A' levels?"

"Yes, and your mother and I made ourselves clear. The answer is no."

"But Pa, it's a whole two more years, and I'm fed up with boarding. And it would be much cheaper for you and Ma."

"As it happens, the school has offered you a sports bursary. Well done, I'm proud of you. In any event, our decision would have been the same. The matter is closed."

Negotiating with my father was fruitless. As I said my goodbyes, he had another ominous gem up his sleeve.

"And I expect your exam results will have arrived by now. Don't forget to let me know."

Feeling defeated and worried, things didn't improve when I got back to the cottage. Ma had news, which she delivered carefully.

"We have cause for celebration. Well done, you have passed all your exams!"

"Wow! Thanks, Ma, what a relief!"

"Your father and I were confident you would. Now, I'm afraid there is no other way of breaking this sadness. I'm so sorry, but Monty was put down yesterday."

Exam results were instantly forgotten. I couldn't grasp what Ma was saying. Tears coursed down my cheeks as I tried to deny the truth.

"Bu..., but he was fine when I left."

"Sadly not. You know he was having difficulty standing and had that nasty cough."

"Yes, but, I thought it was just because he was old."

"On Tuesday, he collapsed and was very poorly. Mr Griffiths came over and helped me take him to the vet."

"Couldn't you have waited until I came home to say goodbye to him?"

"I am afraid not. He was far too ill. The vet said he had advanced heart disease and other complications. There was nothing he could do."

I walked away. Had to. I needed to absorb what Ma had told me. We knew Monty's health was dwindling, but losing him so soon after Paddington was heart-breaking. I bitterly regretted the timing of my sailing trip. I should have been there to help Ma, to comfort our big boy in his last hours.

Feeling horribly lost, I decided to go riding to clear my head. Sam whinnied as I approached. I hung my arms around his neck. He seemed to sense my misery, fluttering my hair with his breath, calm, waiting for the moment to take us away.

I batted back tears as we rode and rode for miles and miles, just alone together, along new tracks, revisiting recently discovered fields. We returned through the thicket surrounding the cottage and Monty's favourite walk. It was cathartic in a way, but the hurt remained.

The slate cottage seemed soulless without Paddy and Monty. Always filled with unconditional love, they had been with us for such a long time. And although life without them felt unimaginable, I tried to draw comfort in knowing that we still had a furry bundle of love in our home. My little ginger ninja.

Hercules appeared with a mouse. He dropped it on my toes, jumped onto my lap and curled up into a ball for an emergency nap. I stroked his sleek fur. In those despairing moments, I could not have loved him more if I tried.

The relief at passing my exams finally sunk in.

And though I had made my parents proud, their significance was lost in my sadness. The last week of my summer holidays was spent riding with friends and helping Ma. We had just finished weeding our tiny garden. It never took long because it truly was the size of a postage stamp.

I'd been putting it off, but it had to be done. I dragged out my school trunk and was half-packed when Ma appeared with some surprising news.

The Wonder of Welsh Words

Emosiwn
The Welsh exude this. Similar to English, this word for '**emotion**' is pronounced 'eh-mo-shoon'.

Chapter Twenty-Nine

'O, there is lovely to feel a book, a good book, firm in the hand, for its fatness holds rich promise, and you are hot inside to think of good hours to come.'

Richard Llewellyn

"I know we don't have much money, Ma, but a proper job. Really?"

"Yes, the money will be most helpful. And with Di working and you still away at school, I find that the chores here aren't taking very long. And it's so important to be productive."

"Hm, I s'pose. And you can't extend the garden. So, what kind of job?"

"I'm not sure yet, but there must be opportunities. One simply has to search for them."

"Oh, I know. What about Wartski with their funky zoop machine?"

"Dear me, no. I don't think that would suit me at all."

Despite having no formal qualifications, Ma quickly found work at a stately home near the mountains. The National Trust, a British charity dedicated to preserving places of natural beauty and historical interest, ran the estate. I had never visited the property, but it had the reputation of being large, stuffed with old furnishings, tapestries, and antique ornaments. It was exactly the working environment to suit Ma.

Within milliseconds, Ma became a brilliant tour guide, swanning around, enthralling visitors, most of whom thought she was the owner. She somehow memorised tiny details about vases, silverware, portraits and furniture. Ma had found her niche.

My successes didn't come so quickly. The upside of returning to school was being with friends who had stayed on to take Advanced, 'A' levels. Joining us were a handful of newbies who were wonderfully exotic. We had a Tongan princess, a Malaysian diplomat's daughter and a girl from Texas whose father was an oil magnate. Quite how the headmaster managed to convince their parents that our school was a worthy educational establishment beat us. We decided the ramparts had something to do with it.

Princess Angelika (call me Angel) was a delightful girl. She was large, generous with her tuck, and had no intention of doing any work. Why should she? She was booked to marry a dashing prince reasonably soon, so decided to take things easy.

Angel had special dispensations for being important. She attended lessons when she felt like it. If she did go, she'd be the one gently snoring in the back row. A big black car with blacked-out windows occasionally glided up to take her out for a meal. And when she returned, she'd share the schoolgirl's version of a doggy bag. We loved her.

While Angel cruised through the two years in a

carefree manner, the same could not be said about our Malaysian colleague. Everyone instantly wanted to become Alina's best friend, too. And why? Because Alina took being studious to a whole new level.

Alina hung on *every* teacher's *every* word. She took notes feverishly, recording *every* nugget, *every* potentially significant syllable, just in case. And when she wasn't in lessons, Alina's slim frame, heavy with textbooks, could be seen enthusiastically skipping towards the library. Alina was the go-to person in a prep crisis.

Kimberly, our Texan, was a complete contrast to the others. She was loud, naughty, and brilliant fun. But the best thing about Kim was her boils. For some reason that nobody, including Sister Jarvis (our gruesome matron with a nicotine-yellow moustache), ever managed to establish, the poor girl had lots.

One might think this would be a matter of sympathising, trips to the skin specialist and stress counselling. Not a bit of it. Kim was extra proud of them. Whenever a new one sprouted, her party trick would be to squeeze the head to find out how much gunge she could extrude. Kim was excellent entertainment value.

The downside of returning to school meant

harder academic work. We had achieved a string of 'O' levels without much effort, but it was clear that this would be very different. Standards were higher, and much more was expected of us.

Most of us were taking three or four 'A' levels (Alina pleaded to be allowed to take five), and the intensity of our studies increased. Single lessons became doubles, and instead of enjoying the freedom the advanced level studies timetable allowed, we spent most of it slogging away in our library. This, ironically, had its bonuses.

The library was special. For senior pupils, it was the best building in the school. Out of bounds to mere juniors, it was a hallowed sanctuary reserved for 'A' level students. Whilst books did not magically glide from their bookcases; the archive did have an enchanting aura.

I remember climbing the steps that very first time, turning the heavy oak door's handle, filled with expectations. Inside, I paused, absorbing the velvety quiet, filling my lungs with fusty-musty bookish odours. If there was anywhere I had a chance of learning, it was here.

The oak-panelled walls were lined with oil paintings and bookshelves. There were aisles and aisles of freestanding bookcases with decrepit ladders to remove texts that nobody could reach.

Gnarled wooden tables and chairs stood on oak floors, partially covered with threadbare rugs, their designs lost to the footfalls of yesteryear. One was instinctively quiet in the library.

As a book lover, it was easy to become distracted by the antiquarian tomes. We gently removed texts from their cosy slots and placed them on a study table. Turning pages carefully, admiring copperplate illustrations and drinking in the accompanying scripts took me to new and fascinating worlds. It was the same for my friends.

Winter evening preps were probably the best. The library was a top spot, primarily because it was properly heated. It had to be because of the valuable books it housed. We switched on flickery lamps, barely able to read in the dim light. It's probably why so many of us ended up short-sighted. Still, it was the price one paid to work in this hallowed place.

Cosy as bookworms should be, everyone slogged through the prescribed work, knowing we had a treat in store when it was done. There was always a new and as yet undiscovered literary treasure to be devoured. It might transport us to far-flung lands and introduce us to new cultures and exotic animals. It was the priceless value of books.

Di was home for a short time over the Christmas holidays. I filled her in on the usual school gossip, and she brought me up to date with her career activities, which sounded very impressive. We both agreed that Ma was blooming. Work seemed to agree with her.

Christmas Day followed the same pattern it had ever since I could remember. I woke up to a big fat stocking on my bed. How Ma crept undetected over creaky floorboards into our bedroom during the night amazed me. She should have been a spy.

Hercules and I opened my gifts, which included treats for him. Thoughtful though Ma's gesture was, as usual, my puss was far more interested in the packaging. As I carefully unwrapped each present, Hercules, slitty-eyed and wobble-bottomed, pounced. He turned into a feline shredding machine with needle claws transforming Christmas paper into confetti.

With Hercules purring on my bed, I called over to Di for the ritual Christmas stocking contents comparison session. Our plan to relax in front of the fire and read was destined for failure. By mid-morning, Ma, unable to cope with anyone 'lounging around', banished us so she could get on with lunch preparations. Grumbling about having a heartless mother, we left her trilling Christmas carols and set off to take Sam out for a ride.

The air was crisp – snatching our breath as it condensed in the morning sunlight. Freezing hands were stuffed into pockets as we crunched through bristly grass on the way to the meadow. I gazed at the frosty fields decorated with crystals refracting rainbows and sighed happily. Just for a moment, the weight of 'A' level studies lifted like the mist. It was good to be alive.

Di started laughing.

"Sam looks like a dragon!"

"Ha ha, he does. Come on, Sammy. Come and get your Christmas presents!"

Sam, energised by the winter chill, was charging around the field, leaving dragon's breath vapour trails in his wake. He pounded over, nickering for his handful of carrots and his most favoured treat, a Polo mint.

We spent the morning swapping, riding and walking. It was the first time for Di without Paddy and Monty. We reminisced about our boys, missing them terribly. As a distraction, I showed her new tracks and Sam's jumping ability. Point him at any obstacle, and he flew over. Di, suitably impressed, brought me down a peg or two by reminding me about the schooling drills I'd neglected. Even more annoyingly, she demonstrated several with unreasonable grace for someone who hadn't ridden for ages.

By the time we got back home we were starving. Alluring aromas of rosemary and thyme met us at the cottage gate, urging us to begin the festivities. It was roast goose, and our feast was almost ready.

Ma decided to cook the smaller fowl because she couldn't squash a turkey in the little oven. It seemed her experiment was going well. We pulled traditional Christmas crackers, sipped from our thimbles of sherry, toasting the chef as we prepared to eat.

Ma was, by now, thoroughly jolly and decided to have a bash at carving. This was a bad idea. The couple of 'reviver sherries' she'd snuck down were taking their toll. The crepe paper party hat had slipped over her pin head and obscured one eye. Ma was looking like a prim pirate. Di removed the brandished carving knife to save Ma from accidental self-harming and took over the carving duties. We doled out trimmings until our plates were heaving. Just as they should be. After all, it was Christmas Day.

Completely stuffed, we were ready for the ceremonial present opening. I harvested gifts from our ravaged Christmas tree. Festooned with dangly decorations, it was Hercules' winter playground, and there were regular casualties.

Age is irrelevant at Christmas. Opening a gift engenders anticipation, eagerness, gratitude and giggles. As it happens, the unwrapping is often more exciting than the contents. Just ask any cat. You'll find them deliriously happy, squeezing into empty boxes or murdering precious gift paper.

Money was short, so Ma went through a 'things' making phase. Soap was her latest fad. For such a talented person, she was remarkably unskilled at the craft. Sadly, we were presented with a box, each containing a scentless tablet of indistinguishable colour. Ma glowed with pride as we carefully opened our packages.

"This is a fab shape, Ma. Kind of blobby," said Di, examining her lump with scientific interest.

"I'm so glad you like it. It's supposed to be a Christmas tree, although I'm not sure what happened in the mould."

"Mine's groovy too, Ma. I like the bits in it. They aren't dead flies, are they?"

"They certainly are not! This was my first experiment with using lavender. Or perhaps it was sage. Anyway, the scent should come out when you use the soap."

Having gushed thanks, Di and I were looking forward to relaxing and watching a movie in the afternoon. No chance. Ma had other ideas. Off we went on a kindling foraging mission, which turned into a magical walk.

Fat snowflakes fell as we picked our way along the riverbank. Dark water traced through the white carpet, tripping over rounded river stones before plunging into deep ice-cold pools. Di and I reverted to early childhood, messing about in the stream, playing Poohsticks and getting wet through. The woodland setting inspired Di to tell another one of her gruesome stories.

"Guess what? I've been told a great legend about yew trees."

"Not them again!"

"Yes, this one's extra morbid. Listen."

"Go on then."

"There's a place near here called Llangernyw. Apparently, the villagers are told about their fate by an ancient spirit called an Angelystor."

"If this is a Welsh myth I bet he's evil."

"Good point. Anyway, each year on July 31st and Halloween, the Angelystor appears under the boughs of an old yew tree."

"Oh great. I can guess what's coming."

"Yep. The spirit declares the names of parish members who will soon die, probably in a terrible way."

"I knew it!"

"Scary, huh? And it gets better. The churchyard actually has a yew tree that botanists believe is over four thousand years old. They think it's the oldest living thing in Wales. So it must be true."

"Noooo!"

"I *knew* you'd love it."

While Di and I, giggling, exchanged gruesome tales, Ma, who had been discovering interesting fungi, pointed out useful pieces of wood to lug back for the fire. It was just as well since we were freezing by the time we returned. Finally, we did get to watch our movie and went to bed with our new books, full tummies and contented spirits.

When Di had to go back to work, it left a miserable void, until Ma came up with an inspired idea.

"Why don't we go along to watch the hunt?"

"I'd hate to watch them kill a fox."

"No, this is drag hunting. Quite different."

"I've never heard of it."

"With this form of hunting, hounds pursue a scented bag rather than an animal. One rider will set off ahead of the field. They drag a bag soaked in a smelly mixture which is irresistible to the dogs."

"That's interesting. Where are the trails laid?"

"Across farmers' land. With permission, the

hunt can choose trails with lots of gallops and jumps."

"Wow, that sounds exciting. So what happens next?"

"About twenty minutes after the trail is laid, the hounds are released, and the riders follow with the huntsman. The hunt ends when they find the bag. I believe they have three or four lines on a hunting day."

"In that case, I'd love to go. Is there any chance I could hunt with Sam?"

"Well, next year, perhaps. You'll need to earn some money to do that. It isn't a cheap day out."

"Magic!"

"Oh dear. That dreadful slang again. Anyway, that's agreed. We'll take a picnic and go with the Jacksons. And wear your riding clothes. Mrs Jackson says one rider becomes too tired to ride every line and is often looking for someone to take his horse."

This was too good to be true. We drove to Anglesey for my first drag hunt meet, which mustered outside a country pub. Several spectators were already there when we arrived. They were chatting with smartly dressed riders on beautifully turned out mounts of all shapes and sizes.

Hounds milled around scarlet-coated huntsmen with two whippers-in keeping the pack under control. Trays laden with tots of port were handed to riders, stirrup cups to sustain them for the day. It was an alternative version of traditional fox hunting, and I loved what I saw.

The master checked his watch, signalled to the huntsmen, and the hounds assembled. The hunting horn was sounded. Off they went, riders flowing, observing proper etiquette, making sure they stayed behind the pack.

Mrs Jackson pointed at a man on a massive horse at the back of the field.

"There's Mr Devlish, Beth. I've already told him you'll be happy to take his place after the second line if you'd still like a ride?"

"Yes, please!"

As predicted, Mr Devlish ambled up to us halfway through the day.

"Here you are," he said, handing me the reins. "You're welcome to take Alf for the final two lines. He's lazy, but you won't have any trouble with him."

Grinning from ear to ear, I couldn't thank Mr Devlish enough. Nodding affably, he sauntered off and disappeared up his horsebox ramp, closing it behind him. Mrs Jackson laughed at my bemused expression.

"Don't ask, Beth. Hunting is when Mr Devlish

conducts most of his private meetings. You'll find his secretary is in there, too."

Fortunately, Ma hadn't heard. It would have given her heart palpitations.

I clambered onto the vast Alf and hunted for the rest of the day, gallumping along meadows, jumping walls, gates, and brush fences. Whilst my huge mount was slow, he was docile and dependable. He also had one jumping quirk.

Alf was so big he could practically step over most of the obstacles we faced. His technique was different. For some strange reason, he tackled calf height jumps as though they were puissance fences and took the same approach with the shoulder height ones. Once I'd got used to this peculiarity, we were fine.

Mr Devlish, happy with the arrangement, invited me to ride Alf for the rest of the season. Nobody said a word about what went on in his horsebox, and I certainly didn't care.

Going back to school coincided with Ma returning to her job at the stately home. She now oversaw the guides and gift shop and was looking for recruits. I was desperate to start hunting with Sam, but I was broke. Ma suggested I come and work as a guide during the Easter holidays to see how I got on.

This was another top Ma idea, especially since

I had never clapped eyes on the place before. My expectations couldn't have been more misguided.

The Wonder of Welsh Words

Llyfrgell
It's a good one to practice your 'll's'. Put together 'hlufrr-geh-hl' and you have '**library**', one of my favourite places.

Chapter Thirty

'The best candle is understanding.'

Welsh Proverb

There I was, thinking Ma worked in a large house. Wrong. As we drove up the long winding drive, crenellations gradually emerged. A keep materialised, then a round tower, courtyards and endless gardens. I couldn't believe what I was seeing.

"I had no idea Caracraig was a castle, Ma. It's ginormous!"

"Yes. It is rather splendid."

"Is it ancient? It doesn't look as old as Harlech."

"Ah, no, it's much younger. The site originally incorporated a medieval mansion. This gothic-style castle now occupies part of the same ground."

"Cool! Does anyone live here now?"

"Yes, Robert Patterson, the Administrator. He's the gentleman who employed me."

"Ah, right. That's the chap you've talked about. He sounds nice."

"You'll find out in a moment. Come along now. We'll meet Robert, and then you can spend the day with Dilys. She's been a guide here for years and is very knowledgeable. You'll learn a great deal from her."

As we walked past cavernous kitchens, strange scampering noises filled the flagstone passage. Shouts and whistles sounded in the distance. A furry creature skidded around the corner. Then another, and more. Within seconds, several deliriously happy little dogs surrounded us.

"Aww, Ma, you didn't say there were dogs here!"

"I wanted it to be a surprise. They belong to Robert. We share an office, and they're with him all the time."

"Ha ha, they're lovely, proper little fatties. How many does he have?"

"Five at the moment, though he always seems to be on the lookout for rescues. They're Norfolk Terriers and great characters."

A man came striding down the passage.

"Ahah, there you are. Good morning, ladies. Sorry about the rabble," he said, gesturing at his furry pack. "Two minutes, and I'll be with you. If this lot doesn't have a pee soon, we'll be in trouble. Come on, you lot, out. *Out*, I say!"

I knew I was going to like this man.

Robert returned quickly and ushered us into the office. Documents flew as he swept a hand across his desk, trying to find a spot to perch. Smiling broadly, he pointed at his happy crew, absently tousling the closest shaggy head.

"First things first, Beth, allow me to introduce you to the most important household members. Here we have Crag, he's the oldest and wisest. Ben and Snow are brothers. They're constantly getting up to no good. Cori is rather shy, and Tag came from a rescue centre last month, so he's still learning the ropes."

"They're lovely, Mr Patterson. May I stroke them?"

"Yes, yes, of course. And for goodness' sake, let's dispense with the formalities. Robert, it's Robert! Now, tell me all about you."

"*Ahem*," said Ma, clearing her throat in that regal manner. "The house will be open to the public in an hour. Perhaps we could continue later?"

"Good lord, how time flies! Yes, of course. Lunch in the apartment? Right, that's organised. See you both later."

He marched out of the office with his stream of dogs in tow. I turned to Ma, shell-shocked.

"Crikey! He seems very kind, although I bet he takes a bit of keeping up with."

"Yes, indeed. Brisk, I would say, yet he has time for everyone. The staff are devoted to him."

Ma gave me a guidebook, and I was delivered to my tutor. I'm pretty sure she took a dim view of having to teach a mere schoolgirl the art of tour guiding. Still, Dilys took the responsibility exceptionally seriously. My lesson began with a whistle-stop tour of the public show rooms.

For such a tiny lady, Dilys was exceedingly speedy. We scuttled up monumental stone staircases, galloped along galleries, in and out of rooms heavy with damask wall hangings and four-poster beds. I tried desperately to keep up as she gave a top-class windmill impression, pointing out endless artefacts and important furnishings.

We returned to ground level via another staircase, next to a pair of towering stained glass windows. I was breathless. Dilys had barely warmed up.

"Here we are then," she said. "You can look after the great hall, the library and drawing room until dinnertime. Manage that, can you, *cariad?*"

Dilys was very Welsh. She called almost everyone *cariad* (love).

Library? Excellent. I was planted in my zone and left to mug up in the precious minutes before the heavy oak doors were hauled open to the public.

I began by admiring the hall, which was impressive. Flagstone floors, a colossal fireplace, and sculpted stone columns, which supported the gallery we had just thundered along. I felt sure it could take a hundred people without any bother.

I followed the red carpet into the adjoining library. It was warm, lavishly decorated with decadent burgundy reds and antique golds. It blended perfectly with the intricate oak carvings and sumptuous fittings. I could have stayed there all day.

The room, with its original furnishings, was arranged as though family members had just finished flicking through pages of a favourite book. And although guide ropes prevented visitors from touching exhibits, the antiquity of those leather-bound volumes was unmistakable.

I continued to the drawing room and a feast of opulence. Extraordinarily ornate ceiling plasterwork, William Morris wallpaper, and grand furniture made especially for the giant-sized rooms. The lavish ensemble would have welcomed honoured guests to the castle. Queen Victoria had stayed here. I'm sure she was impressed by it too.

Luckily, I only had to answer a handful of questions during the morning. Dilys bustled in to check that I hadn't broken anything and sent me off to eat. She pointed at the main staircase.

"Right you are then, *cariad*. Up two flights and take the first door you see. That's where Mr Patterson lives, it's his compartment. Tell him Mrs Davies-the-sandwedges has made his specials. Loves them, he does."

Dilys was the mistress of malapropism.

I found the door and bashfully knocked.

Luckily it was substantial, otherwise the din from the dogs inside would have alerted the entire castle.

I could hear shooing sounds as someone approached. Robert flung open the door with a smile.

"Well done, Beth, you found us. Enjoy your workout with Dilys? I'd say she has roller skates hidden under those shoes. Amazing since she's nearly as old as the building. She's eccentric, alright, a gem though. Wouldn't be without her."

"I know. She has been very helpful. Oh, and she asked me to give you a message from Mrs Davies, er, 'the-sandwiches'?"

"That'll be Mrs Davies, in charge of catering. Thank you. Already been relayed. We have another Mrs Davies who looks after the gift shop, so she's called 'gifts'. Come to think of it, one of our gardeners is a Mr Davies. Fortunately, he's the only male Davies, so he doesn't have to be called 'spades'. As you know, sharing the same surname is an occupational hazard around here."

I played with the dogs while Ma and Robert prepared our lunch, which turned out to be an excellent mixture of sandwiches, pasties and doorsteps of homemade cake.

By the end of the holiday, Dilys had knocked

me into shape. I could guide in each of the show rooms and help in the gift shop when necessary. On quiet days, she showed me secret passages, hidey holes and hidden cupboards, all the stuff the public never gets to see. We had become firm friends despite our age gap.

Dilys even allowed me special dispensation on hunting days. This allowed me to buzz over to the meet on my bike and ride Alf when Mr Devlish went off to do his unmentionables. I'm convinced Ma thought he was cleaning his horsebox.

One afternoon, we were late closing at the castle, so I offered to help Dilys lock up. It was a lengthy task. Weighed down by heavy iron keys, we closed the downstairs public rooms first. It was dusk by the time we reached the bedrooms.

The setting sun cast shadows across the four-poster bed in the Blue Room. Motes in the sunlight eddied playfully in the radiator's warm currents. I was thoroughly enjoying the peaceful ambience when Dilys grabbed my elbow.

"See it, did you?"

"Um, no. Have I missed something?"

"Her. *Her!*"

"We don't have a visitor still here, do we?"

"No, dop-ey, the Grey Lady."

"The ghost story Grey Lady?"

"Yes! She sometimes appears in these bedrooms at dusk. I'm sure I saw her reflection in that dress mirror."

"Cool, Dilys. No, I'm afraid I didn't see a thing."

Dilys looked grave.

"Ah, well, I'm septic, you see."

"Septic?"

"Yes, always have been. Seen things since I was a small child, I have. Special powers, that's what my mam said."

"Oh, I see. That's very impressive. I've never seen a ghost, I'm afraid."

"Never mind, *cariad*, you might one day."

Dilys gave my arm a reassuring pat and set off towards the Lavender wing.

"Ah, there it is again, *quick*. Here!"

I rushed over, hoping something exciting might be about to happen. Nope, nothing. I shook my head.

"Well, I can feel a pretence in this corner. I know I can. It feels all, oh, I dunno… Prick-ly, yes, that's it."

"It is a bit nippy here, Dilys. Perhaps that's why."

"Girlie, girlie, I don't know *what* I'm going to do with you. No emotions, that's your trouble.

Now hurry up before we have a full-on haunting on our hands."

I returned to school with money in my pocket and the promise of a job during the summer. A bonus had been spending lots of time playing with Robert's dogs. We had fallen into an easy routine of eating in his apartment. It seemed somehow natural, especially since Ma was so happy.

The summer term dragged on with unrelenting dollops of prep being dished out by increasingly ghastly teachers. Chef's concoctions were getting worse, and I'm sure parts of the school were starting to crumble. Not that Alina noticed. She was still nailing every piece of work and dying to get stuck into the exams in a year's time.

It must have been around two weeks before we broke up for holidays when I received a letter. It looked like Ma's handwriting. Happily, we had dispensed with the drear of Sunday afternoon writing home sessions, so it seemed odd for her to write this near the end of term. The reason soon became apparent. And it was crushing.

My precious little Hercules was dead.

Ma's decision to break the news by letter was to try and lessen the shock of finding out when I got home. She was probably right. It wouldn't have mattered how I found out. I would have been devastated, anyway.

My beautiful ginger cat had been run over on the road. Why? How? I'll never know. Just like Thomas, Hercules had been my constant. With that acute feline sixth sense, he knew whenever I was miserable and snuggled on my lap. He was cuddly when I was tired, sneaking off to hunt when I was fast asleep. Hercules' firebrand personality lit up my life with silly antics and a unique devotion.

I couldn't believe he was no more. It felt as though my world had come tumbling down, there had been too much sadness. I ran off, wanting to hide, desperate to be alone. And I sobbed my heart out for hours.

The cottage seemed empty when I got back and had become merely functional. This place was filled with painful memories of my beautiful boy. We had lost too many cherished family members here. I sensed that Ma felt the same. The charm had gone.

With her usual stiff upper lip attitude, Ma said we must bear sadness with fortitude. She reminded me how lucky I was. After all, I had the summer ahead with Sam. And I was due to go on my sailing holiday with Pa. Despite the pep talks, Ma never ever belittled the deep, overpowering emotions I felt at losing an adored animal. I'll always be grateful to her for that.

The Wonder of Welsh Words

Galar
Sadly, it affects us all at some point in our lives. This word for '**grief**' is pronounced 'gah-lahrr'.

Chapter Thirty-One

'I wanted freedom, open air and adventure. I found it on the sea.'

Alain Gerbault

An adventure to France? Yes, of course, I was incredibly lucky.

Pa was on fighting form when I arrived for our voyage. Meeting up with Mr Jenkins and Gavin was like being with family. Gavin had a rakish haircut to go with his Heathcliffian looks. Sadly, I bore no evidence of maturity other than a couple of teenage spots.

Pa took us through our refresher sailing paces before we set off. Mr Jenkins was doing very well with his Yachtmaster studies, but didn't feel ready to skipper the boat. His job on this trip would be to chart our passage to Saint-Malo.

We left our home mooring and quickly slipped into our sailing routine. Cruising across Cardigan Bay reminded us of Pa's myth. We strained our ears unsuccessfully for the sounds of ghostly bells. We could have done with Dilys on board. I'm sure she'd have heard them all.

Conditions differed from the previous summer. The wind picked up as we tacked towards the English coast. Our boat heeled over under full sail, jockeying with whitecaps, cutting through the choppy water with ease. Even though we were in the cockpit, with every new wave came a drenching. It was energising but saturating. Pa insisted that we wear harnesses. Each had a line with a clip to tether onto the rigging. If a freak wave swamped the boat and one of us was washed overboard, we would remain attached until fished out of the sea.

The weather deteriorated further as we reached the craggy Lizard peninsula off Cornwall. This is the most southerly point of mainland Britain. My heart quickened at the sight of its lighthouse. I pointed, excited about seeing this last landmark before heading across the Channel.

Pa caught my expression and smiled.

"I know," he yelled above the clattering rigging, "it's a fine sight. Sir John Killigrew built the first lighthouse at the Lizard in 1619, but it eventually became too expensive for him to maintain. It was rebuilt in 1752 and has provided a guiding light ever since, warning mariners about the hazardous waters here. Smugglers too."

"Smugglers?"

"Yes, I'll tell you some tales about them later, but now let's focus. This wind is gusting to gale force strength."

We had planned to make a night crossing, but a strong storm was blowing up, so Pa decided we should seek shelter in Salcombe Harbour. We had already been battling heavy weather for hours, so weren't disappointed with the prospect of resting in a safe haven.

Conditions were calm as we negotiated passage

to a visitor's mooring. Using the quayside showers was bliss after our dousing. Clean and dry, we discovered a cosy restaurant nearby. If Pa thought two teenagers had forgotten about his earlier cliffhanger, he was mistaken. We nagged him to tell us some yarns.

"Smuggling was rife in this area. The rugged coast is filled with coves and inlets. They were perfect hiding places for booty taken by infamous men and women. Fyn and Black Joan were good examples. They were brother and sister with a notorious reputation."

"Why *Black* Joan, Pa?"

"She was a bloodthirsty woman. Together, they smuggled goods from the Channel Islands between the seventeenth and eighteenth centuries. Black Joan is said to have murdered someone on Looe Island near here. They say her victim haunts the island to this day."

"Your Dilys would love that story, Beth."

"True, Gavin! Go on, tell us another, Pa."

"Huh, so many. Let me see. There was Hans Breton. A smuggler who was in league with the devil. He drank his brandy at the Blue Bell Inn in St. Ives. He paid duty on one barrel, which never, ever emptied. That barrel lasted for twenty years."

"I could listen to stories like this all night!"

"Not tonight, you can't, Beth. Now come on,

crew, time for bed. The storm should have passed by the morning, but it'll be a rough crossing."

Pa was right.

We set off early the following day under slate grey, rainy skies. Our boat was rigged for storm conditions. The mainsail was reefed, making it much smaller, reducing the area exposed to the wind. We hoisted a storm jib, a little version of its big sister. Our passage would be slower but safer.

The sea was choppy in the harbour. A deception. As we passed into coastal waters, a brisk wind caught our sails. The wave pattern was unsettled, lumpy, causing the boat to heel and roll. We checked the rigging, closed the hatch and sailed into open sea.

"Brace yourselves, everyone," bellowed Pa. "Make sure you're securely clipped onto the rigging."

Sky, sea, our world had become slabs of grey and dirty white. As the wind howled, the waves grew bigger and bigger. A rhythm of mammoth breakers developed, creating a vast barrel swell. With immense force, the boat was propelled up the watery face to the peak of each one. And, just for a moment, time stood still.

In those instants, we could see for miles. Foam scudding across the water, filthy spume sloughed from the crests of gigantic rollers spewed over waves. And then the boat dived. Like a thousand lost souls, the wind screamed through halyards as we plummeted, hitting the following wave's base with a shuddering *thump*.

Pa, fighting the helm, braced himself against the movement as mountainous waves smashed into the cockpit. He glanced at us.

"Everyone alright?"

Though we barely heard his shouts above the roaring gale, we nodded, huddled together in the cockpit, hanging onto the rail. Nobody was frightened with Pa in charge. Despite being thrown around like corks, the boat was balanced. Never had sailing been more thrilling.

The weather can be mischievous in the Channel. Our crazy helter-skelter voyage continued for hours, with the wind picking up before subsiding. Needle-sharp rain pricked our faces as we were drenched with spray and iron-grey maverick waves. The yacht was punished, hammered, and tossed around like a child's toy.

Eventually, the sea pattern altered again. The boat rose to the tops of smoother waves, before plunging to the base of the next trough. It was hellish, but we marvelled at the force of nature. I wouldn't have missed it for the world.

As the wind subsided and the sea became less

chaotic, Pa re-checked his instruments. Amazingly, we were still on course. I spotted specks in the sky.

"Seagulls!"

Pa laughed.

"You know what that means, crew? Beth and Gavin, on deck, please. Make sure your harnesses are correctly tethered, and watch for landfall. We're close to Saint-Malo now. It occupies a prominent position at the mouth of the River Rance. You'll see it easily enough."

"I'm so excited about this, Pa. Fancy us going to France!"

"I know. And you'll love Saint-Malo. Ironically, it was founded during the Roman era by a Welsh monk called Maclovius."

"Welsh?"

"Yes. He actually has several names. Maclovius was born during the sixth century in the monastery of Llancarfan, Glamorganshire. He was initially a ward of the abbot and performed miracles from a young age. His parents wanted him to give up monastic life, but he refused and was ordained priest by the abbot, continuing to perform miraculous acts."

"Fab. So what happened to him?"

"He eventually left Wales and sailed on a voyage to Brittany. He founded Saint-Malo and became the bishop of Aleth."

"Wow, that's amazing."

"Much of the legend surrounding him is hazy, but many churches are named after him in Brittany, and interestingly, he is the patron saint of Llanfechell on Anglesey."

"Really?"

"Yes, as a gift for his work as a healer, Maclovius was offered land in the north of the island. And you'll enjoy this. Can you guess how the land boundaries were created?"

"Tell me they were scorched by dragon's breath!"

"Hah, no! A hare was released to run free. Maclovius established a monastery which later became a celebrated centre of learning."

"We *have* to go and visit Llanfechell when we get back."

The great city constructed on a rock and guarded by ramparts gradually came into view. The buildings looked splendid. Tall and stately. I was thrilled at the thought of setting foot on French soil for the first time in my life. Despite being battered by the elements for hours, we were keen to explore. We moored, made the boat safe, and showered. We were spending several days in the port, so there was lots of time for sightseeing.

Saint-Malo oozes history. The old city with its cobbled streets, mighty battlements, archways, broad alleyways and skinny *rues*, seemed both monumental and grand. Pa said it was notorious as a den for corsairs. A bonus for us since that meant more pirate stories. It was also France's leading port for voyages of discovery to the New World, which earned it a worthier reputation.

We browsed shops, Gavin and I focusing on the chocolatiers, bullying our fathers into buying umpteen different gourmet varieties. The trade-off was hours spent in chandler stores. There seemed to be one on every street. We ate at *crêperies*, savouring each morsel of our wafer-thin pancakes, celebrating this culinary speciality of Breton culture. We relaxed in the sun at cafe tables that spilled welcomingly into the street. Nobody minded. There was a chic acceptance. *C'est la vie* in Saint-Malo.

Our last night came, and with it, Mr Jenkins' pledge to take us to dinner. He had booked us at a restaurant, which he said had a fine reputation. Anticipating a feast, we tidied ourselves as best as possible and trailed after Pa, who was looking dashing as usual. I still couldn't fathom how he packed a complete dinner outfit in that miniscule kit bag.

Our starters were excellent precursors to the much-anticipated main dish. Mr Jenkins, glass in hand, announced its arrival with pride.

"Here we are, everyone, *Fruits de Mer*, a Breton speciality and highly sought after. *Bon appétit!*"

An enormous platter on stilts arrived. Piled on a bed of seaweed was a mountain of different sea creatures; crabs, clams, oysters, winkles, sea snails, prawns, langoustines, scallops, cockles. You name it; if it had a shell on, it was there. I'd add that they were all dead, but honestly? I couldn't be sure.

I looked at the rubble of molluscs, uncertain where to start. Mr Jenkins saw me pause and decided to help.

"Here you are, Beth. Try these sea snails. They're excellent."

"Nice one, Dad. It looks like a slug, Beth. Can't wait to see what you think of it."

"Great, thanks, Gavin!"

I have always loved my food, but there was nothing I could find even slightly enticing about the lump of mucousy gristle sticking out of its shell. Mr Jenkins, eager to find out how much I loved his treat, gave me a demonstration on how to eat them.

"Just watch, Beth. All you have to do is stick the skewer into the shell and lever it out like... Oh! Oops, no idea where that went. Not to worry, I'll have another go."

I dutifully watched as number two snail was removed from its house, demo snail having been flicked to the other side of the restaurant. Mr Jenkins dipped the amorphous lump into a pot of mayonnaise and popped it into his mouth. Looking immensely satisfied, he smacked his lips and stared expectantly at me. They all did.

I carefully extracted my slimy mollusc. I swear it made a suction sound as it slid out. Feeling a bit gaggy, I stuffed it into my mouth. Round and round it went, all leathery and knobbly, I tried to swallow, but it just wasn't happening. Pa was staring fixedly at me.

"*Swallow it*," he hissed.

Slime 'n' all, down it went, and fortunately stayed there. Philistine that I am, I can honestly say that this was the most disgusting thing I have ever consumed, along with the boiled tripe Ma once made us eat. Fortunately, Mr Jenkins was quite tipsy by now and hadn't noticed that I'd turned green.

Our evening became a celebration of pirate tales and mock self-congratulation. We toasted the skipper, the boat for staying afloat and ourselves for braving the elements and managing not to fall overboard.

It was still early when we finished, so Gavin and I decided to have one last stroll, drinking in that unique atmosphere of the old city. We stopped at a bar on the way back and tried their speciality. Benedictine. We hadn't tasted it before and had no idea that it was about to blow our socks off. It was sugary, warming and after three glasses each, we'd decided it was extremely delicious stuff.

Suffocating gentle hiccups, we formally agreed that we loved every single thing about France, including its beverages. We staggered back to the boat. Giggling, we were helping one another aboard when Gavin turned to me.

"Thanks for a great holiday," he said, stealing a kiss before toppling backwards onto the cabin roof.

Laughter came from the cockpit.

"Come on, you two," chuckled Pa. "Off to bed before you fall in the harbour."

Our cruise back across the Channel was completely different. The water was glassy, and the sun shone. The only dangers facing us were cholesterol highs from gorging on the mountains of blue cheese and baguettes Pa had bought. It had been another fantastic trip, one I will always treasure.

I returned to the cottage relaxed and suntanned, ready to start my guiding job with Dilys. Ma was looking tense when I arrived. She was out of sorts as I was unpacking. Something was bothering her.

"Beth, sit down. There's something I must tell you."

The Wonder of Welsh Words

Ffrainc
A place that would become very special to me in the future. This word for '**France**' is pronounced 'Frr-ahik'.

Chapter Thirty-Two

'Wales is a land of history and mystery and to find yourself standing alone in a haunted house, castle, or even mountainside on a windswept winter's day is to feel centuries removed from the pressures of the modern age.'

Richard Jones

Ma was looking anxious. Ma never looked anxious.

"Darling, this may feel dreadfully soon for you, but I have made a decision. We are going to live at the castle with Robert."

I looked around. The cottage was a stark empty shell. No Hercules, no Paddington or Monty. What remained were sad, haunting memories filling each room.

"Ma, this is great news! I'm sure Pa has a friend too, so you're both happy."

"Oh dear me, Di said the same thing. I am tremendously relieved."

So far, I had lived in interesting houses, but never the turret of a castle. I was looking forward to the experience, especially since it would mean being around Robert's dogs.

Settling in didn't take long. I was already familiar with most rooms in the spacious apartment and loved that my bedroom had partially rounded walls. With a wistful sigh, I knew there was just one thing missing. My little Hercules curled up on the bed. I gulped back tears, refusing to start weeping again and focused on the views. The mountains looked spectacular from up here.

There was a knack for opening the sash windows, primarily because they weighed a ton.

Once I'd got the hang of pinioning myself against the bed and using all my strength to lever them up, the prize was worth the effort. I could crawl out onto the two-metre deep stone ledge and read in the sun. It was bliss.

Living with five Norfolk Terriers was wonderful. I always knew if Robert was in the apartment by the yelps and woofs.

Arph!

"Blast it, Crag, get out of the way. And you, Cori. Sorry, but you're constantly under my feet!"

Yip! Yip! Yip!

"You'll all have flat paws at this rate. Come on then, you lot, hurry up. Out for a pee. *Out*, I say!"

The best times for walks were when the castle was closed to visitors, and everyone had gone home. Having the grounds to ourselves was an indescribable honour. Ma would build one of her feasts, and we'd find a secluded spot to relax.

A secret favourite was the sunken garden. The semi-naturalised pond was fringed with fantastic dinosaur-sized gunnera. Each massive leaf with its spiky stem resembled a giant stalk of rhubarb. There were dinner plate-sized lily pads, thrones to choirs of croaky frogs. Graceful ferns and bulrushes with dark brown, cylindrical flower spikes. They looked like sausages. I watched water boatmen skating across the water's surface, amazed, trying to work out how they managed to stay afloat. And I played hide and seek with the dogs, dodging multi-coloured dragonflies and fluttering butterflies.

With Sam settled in a field nearby, we explored the estate; the meadows, oak copses and manicured avenues. Discovering the local wildlife was exciting, too. Sometimes I'd catch sight of a fox, occasionally a hare, and always rabbits. We never got lost on these pathfinding rides. The castle was an easy landmark to locate.

I returned to school for my final year with mixed feelings. I knew it was time to get my head down. Siân, Kim, Janice, and I slogged through our English texts. Forming a small but committed protest group, we decided the examining board had dealt us an unfair hand. Thomas Hardy's The Major of Casterbridge was detailed and complicated. We struggled through, chapter by chapter, dutifully underlining hidden messages, memorable prose, searching for positives. Much to the disappointment of our teacher, we couldn't find any at all. The ending, we felt, was a mercy to any sensible reader.

Shakespeare's A Midsummer Night's Dream was a redeeming feature. The enchanting Puck and silly Bottom were our favourites. We needed an uplifting play because our main text was dire. At almost one thousand pages long, it was Charles Dickens' aptly named Bleak House.

The novel is one of his finest works – a fact sadly lost on us. It was initially serialised, which could be why it was so long. There again, it might have been cunning satire by Dickens in dealing with the book's themes. We struggled through the endless London court case, precisely as Dickens intended. His point to illustrate the evils caused by drawn-out suits in the Courts of Chancery was admirably made. The imagery and ironies were as complex for us to absorb as were the miserable characters. It was interminable. Luckily, we had a trump card: our American pal, Kim.

Much to everyone's disappointment, especially her own, Kim had run out of boils. A girl of great ingenuity, she searched for other ways to entertain the troops. Kim returned, triumphant, from an exeat, and gathered her fellow English studies sufferers.

"I got something for us. It'll help with our English exams. Y'all gonna love it!"

Belinda, aka Pigtails, still loved to study, but even she was labouring.

"Go on then, tell us."

"Cheat notes! My dad bought us each a copy."

"Cool!"

"Solid!"

"You are so *rad!*"

Kim handed out pamphlets containing a synopsis of our primary texts. Descriptions of each character and simple paragraphs dedicated to the dreaded images, satire, metaphors and meanings within meanings. It was the best gift anyone could have given us. Kim was destined for great things.

Alina, our studious friend, had a sciences bent. Much to her regret, she couldn't help with the arts-based subjects. But all was not lost. For some reason, we never understood, she loved rocks. Igneous, sedimentary, metamorphic, you name it, Alina commanded encyclopaedic knowledge. For geography students, she was the go-to person for anything stony, or indeed Jurassic, for that matter. Who doesn't love a dinosaur?

Unfortunately, Alina had a problem with her chosen studies. Mr Dennis, the ageing physics teacher, eventually passed away after a long illness. We were suitably solemn when she shared the news. Gathering around to commiserate, Cerys, always practical in these situations, spoke first.

"Go down like flies here, they do, poor old chap."

We nodded. What Cerys lacked in diplomacy, she made up for with sincerity.

"So, what'll happen with your lessons?" I asked.

Alina shrugged.

"I did a fair amount of advanced reading during the holidays and have finished the syllabus, so I offered to help everyone else."

"Wow, and what did they say?"

"They said no. Mr Roberts will take over, so we'll have him for physics and chemistry now."

That was a blow. We sympathised with our clever friend about her bad luck, assuring her that her offers of help would not go unheard. Her fellow science students would definitely need extra tutoring.

We returned home for the holidays to prepare for our mock exams. We would take them at the beginning of the spring term. I knew I needed to work hard, but far more pressing matters were occupying my flibbertigibbet's brain. Drag hunting.

I had earned enough money and booked the available hunts during my holiday. On the night before our first meet, I could barely sleep. Sam and I had already competed successfully in one-day events involving dressage, cross-country and show jumping, but this was different, far, far more exciting.

I was up early and rushed over to the stable. Sam snickered softly as I approached in the chill dawn light. I slipped off his cosy, warm blanket. Ma had given him a hunter cut. Clipping his body hair in this style left a saddle shape on his back. His legs were untouched. The idea was to help him keep cool during hard riding. He stood quietly as I groomed. I wrapped rolls of thick padding around his lower legs, binding them with smart blue bandages. These would aid protection from injury as he jumped. I saddled him, gave him a final polish, and stood back to see the result. My boy was gleaming. Now it was my turn.

We arrived at the meet and were immediately surrounded by friendly faces, everyone happy to see me on my horse. Sam's ears flickered as he danced around, unused to the hounds milling among the riders. He felt like a coiled spring, filled with anticipation.

Mr Devlish ambled up on Alf and wished me well. With a wink, he reassured me that he had found another 'groom' to take my place. I looked around at the spectators. Landowners, country folk, farmers and horse lovers, and then I heard that unmistakable sound.

"*Ahem*. Beth, do check your girth before setting off."

"Good point. Thanks, Ma."

The horn bugled, another new sound for Sam. And we were off. Hounds boomed as riders streamed over the first fence. I hung back, determined to take things easy for the first few obstacles, but Sam was having none of it.

Rearing in excitement, he fought the bit and thundered, crablike, towards the jump. I gave him his head with only a couple of strides to go, hoping he would collect himself. He didn't. He refused. I ended up around his ears but managed to stay on, furious at losing control.

With both of us rattled, I schooled him in a couple of circles, calming him down before taking the fence at a controlled speed. And that was that. Sam never ever refused again. Throughout his hunting career, he was fast and dependable and instinctively knew when to keep away from a faltering horse.

I found Ma and Robert ready with a speciality snack as the first line ended. I jumped off Sam's back, loosened his girth and checked him for injuries. He was relaxed, happy and looked as though he could gallop all day, and did. It was a fantastic first day out with him.

After that, Sam gained the reputation of being a horse to follow. He knew which line to pick, the safest ground, and the best section of an obstacle to clear. There was something about the speed, the challenge and camaraderie of hunting he loved too. And the best thing of all about the sport? All we were doing was chasing a bag.

My mock exam results were, let's say, middling to poor. No surprises there. Let down by an enduring lack of flair with sciences, I had given up any erstwhile dreams of becoming a vet. But I wanted to go to university. It was Pa who was appointed to give me 'the' lecture.

"You realise how disappointing these results are, don't you?"

"Um, yes, Pa. Sorry."

"Do *not* say sorry unless you mean it!"

"S...okay, Pa."

"And you realise how lucky you are to have been given this education, don't you?"

I could have argued that point but decided against it.

"Of course. Um, thank you."

"That is not the point. Do you want to go to university and make something of yourself? Or disgrace yourself?"

"University, definitely, Pa."

"In that case, buck up before you lose the opportunity! Start working and make us all proud."

It was a weighty ultimatum.

Angel, our Tongan princess, had demurely sashayed her way through the mocks, supremely disinterested in her poor results. With her nuptials beckoning, there was no need. Her husband-to-be was getting richer. Carefree though she was, it pained her to see the rest of us so tense.

As we started cramming in the run-up to the official exams, Angel did what she did best: waft around handing out Curly Wurlys. Her recent discovery of this Cadbury's chocolate-covered caramel bar was precisely the comforter we needed. And we ate loads.

Before the exams, representatives from several universities came to interview entrants. I was offered a conditional place at the University of York. It was a renowned early music centre, a beautiful ancient city and a college with an excellent academic reputation. It was my first choice, and I was fortunate to be offered a place, but this was a deferred entry.

I was young for my academic year, so my parents decided I needed to be 'finished off'. My idea of working in a racing stable fell on deaf ears. I received a resounding 'No!' from Ma and Pa, which was frustrating. For a divorced couple, they didn't disagree on much.

They entered me for a year's course at a secretarial college for young ladies in Oxford, another exceptional centre for singing. Latterly, I grudgingly admitted that learning to touch type and take shorthand (remarkably badly) stood me in good stead. Less helpful were the elocution lessons and direction from Debrett's Etiquette.

The school great hall became a dreaded examination centre again. Bogo Roberts took up her position as head invigilator. Like a sci-fi stick insect, she stalked the rows between desks, gently slapping a wooden ruler on her palm. There was something particularly odious about that lady.

The pattern for our 'A' level exams was similar to the 'O's. Exhausted with nervous tension, girls flowed out of the hall and gathered in giggly gaggles. Some of us had misread questions, a particular anti-skill of mine. We argued over answers given; anguished cries of 'we were never taught that!' were rife.

There was only one serene face throughout the exams, apart from Angel, who couldn't care less. Alina left each exam looking calm and collected. She had amassed five straight A's for her mock exams, so there was no reason she wouldn't achieve the same stunning results in the real thing.

Eventually, it was all over. School was all over. Our core group of friends and newbie best pals had cajoled, supported, and teased one another through the final two years. We could barely believe that we had stuck it out.

Packing our trunks one last time seemed weird. We hugged one another, pledging to keep in touch, and although it might be tricky with some, we were best friends and wanted to try. We hung out of the common room windows, waiting for our parents' cars to arrive, laughing, placing bets on who would come first. Of course, it was Angel's sleek limo. We knew it was hers because of the Tongan flags on either side of the bonnet. Words were exchanged between Angel and her driver. He handed her a bag which she passed to us.

"Here you are, Curly Wurlys for everyone. Happy holidays!"

What a kind-hearted lass she was.

Alina's car came soon after. That only had one flag on the bonnet. A fleet of vehicles followed – some posh, others battered. I knew when I was about to be picked up by the racket.

Yip, yip, arf, *arooOooo!*

"Quiet, the lot of you. Stop that noise right now!"

Robert had come to pick me up with all five dogs.

Leaving school was a relief for most of us. Little did we know that it would close down shortly afterwards. It later featured in an episode of the Haunted Britain television series. I had never been aware of ghost stories in the school, although Chef's awful cooking would haunt me forever. It's a shame my pal Dilys never went there. She'd have hunted down all the spooks for sure.

Waiting for my exam results was nerve-racking when I thought about it. Happily, the summer holiday was mostly too busy to worry. If I wasn't meeting friends and riding, I worked at the castle.

My role had extended to working in the gift shop and occasionally helping in the garden, but guiding was still my main job. Dilys had a large group to look after one afternoon. It was getting late, so I offered to lock the upstairs rooms for her. Nodding gratefully, she stuffed the big keys into my hands and then pulled me close.

"Once you've locked the rooms in the east wing, *don't* go back."

"Alright, but why not?"

Dilys stared owlishly at me.

"Well, it's because you just do *not* know what's going on after you've locked up, do you now, *cariad*? It's cold down there, I tell you that much."

Mystified, I promised to do as she said.

Ma and Robert had been working on a fundraiser for months with a local charity. They had decided to hold a soiree in the great hall. Local amateur musicians would entertain guests, and I was asked to sing two solos. A businessman had sponsored the refreshments, and all proceeds would go to the charity.

I was proud to be involved, mainly for the chance to sing in the hall. The vaulted ceiling way above the gallery, gave the space a superb acoustic. Even the weakest voice sounded good in there.

In the lead up to the event, Ma and Robert went to an evening meeting to organise the final details. While they were out, I decided to practise my songs. It may have been humungous, but I was never nervous about being left alone in the castle. I grabbed my music, a torch and set off with the dogs.

With the main castle lights switched off, it was pitch black as we descended the central stone staircase leading to the great hall. Just my torchlight.

Fumbling around with the lock, I hauled open the heavy iron-studded door and walked across the cavernous space to a spot where I knew there would be a lamp. I flicked the switch. It cast a weak glow over the grand piano. Easy peasy.

The dogs settled around me as I started playing the pieces. I soon concentrated, lost in a world of my own, focusing on technique, trying to fix the tricky sections. Singing here was exhilarating. Notes came out crystal clear, filling the space with extraordinary clarity, soothing the velvety darkness with a rich timbre.

Kerbang!

Clamorous sounds split the air, echoing, piercing the darkness. A split second's eerie silence. And then a harsh clatter of rattling chains. Definitely chains. And it was all coming from the east wing.

The Wonder of Welsh Words

Edellyll
Almost as scary to say as the 'real' thing, this word for '**ghost**' is pronounced 'eh-deh-hl-i-hl'.

Chapter Thirty-Three

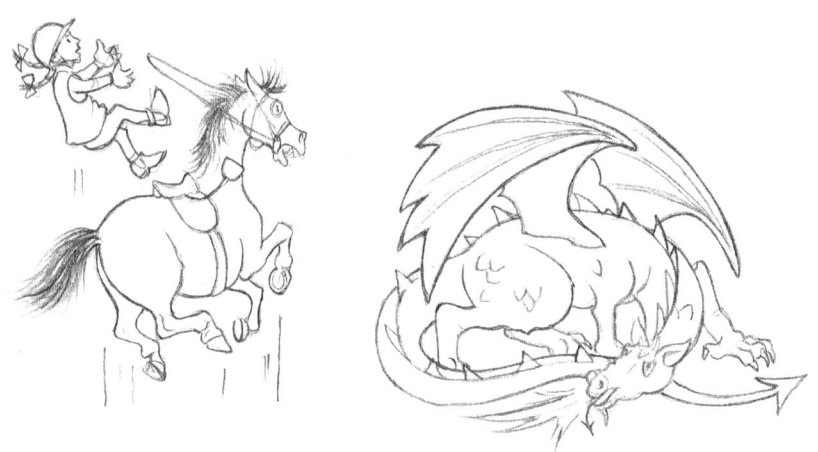

'First God made England, Ireland, and Scotland. That's when he corrected his mistakes and made Wales.'

Katharine Hepburn

I was terrified.

I grabbed my torch. The yellowish flare picked out the dogs lying next to a pillar. Strangely, they looked relaxed. Reassured, I decided that whatever was lurking up there had not come down. Yet.

There it was again. Chains. Clunking, jangling, rattling abrasively in the lofty blackness. There wasn't another soul about for miles. I was utterly alone in the castle. Or perhaps not?

I had to get back to the apartment.

The only escape was by retracing my steps. Forcing myself not to panic, I crept across the hall and flicked the switch, instantly plunging us into heavy darkness.

My torch battery started to fail. Unnerved, I shook it, reviving the yellowy glow, and called the dogs. Their skittering claws clickety-clacked over the shiny flagstone floor behind me. Horribly sinister echoes filling the void. With my senses in overdrive, I tugged the heavy door closed, turned the key and fled up the stone steps to the apartment sanctuary.

When Ma and Robert returned, I managed a polite 'How was your meeting?' before blurting out my event. Having gone over the incident repeatedly in my mind, I couldn't decide whether I'd heard things or that we really did have ghosts.

Robert came to my rescue.

"Don't worry. There's always a practical reason for these situations. Come along, grab a new torch, and we'll investigate."

We went back down the grand staircase, through the great hall and up a different flight of steps to the gallery. Robert, a few steps ahead of me, abruptly stopped.

ArrooOooo.

I nearly had a heart attack. Robert spun around.

"Good Lord, Tag, how did you sneak out? You sound like a wolf. Now get out from under my feet; otherwise, I'll tread on your paw again!"

On we continued to the east wing. Robert stopped again.

"Ahah! Here we are, Beth. No, you didn't imagine things. Come and have a look at your ghost."

The evidence was blindingly clear. A vast old portrait hung with chains had fallen off the wall and landed on a marble table. One of the chains was detached and lying on the floor. That explained the second rattle.

"Phew! I'm *so* relieved to see this."

"I can imagine. It will have made an awful racket when it came down. And before Dilys tells you all sorts of stories about ghouls tearing family portraits off the walls, have a look at the nail."

Sure enough, the old picture hook had rusted at the joint and given way. We returned to the apartment laughing about the incident. Mightily comforted, I slept like a log that night. Well, nearly. My exam results were almost due.

The soiree was a great success. Amateurs though we were, the guests enjoyed themselves, which probably had more to do with the setting than our performances. Still, they made generous donations to the charity and promised to return for future events.

The following morning, Robert brought up the post and popped it on the table. Before disappearing with the dogs, he gave me a quick squeeze on the shoulder. There it was. That official envelope. Would I have the grades I needed to go to York? There was only one way of finding out.

I *did*. I could go!

After all those years incarcerated at school, I had actually achieved a bunch of decent grades. Nobody was more surprised than I. Hollering and whooping, I charged off to tell Ma and ring Pa.

That evening, we celebrated with a bottle of champagne and more good news from Robert.

"We have a week's holiday coming up. Why don't we go to my cottage on the moors?"

This sounded like a fantastic idea. Ma nodded, so Robert continued.

"As it happens, Owen from the gardens can lend us a horse trailer, so we can take your Sam too if you'd like, Beth."

"That would be amazing, thank you."

"Good. That's all settled then. I'll arrange cover here, and we'll set off at the weekend. It's pretty basic up there, so pack your woollies. Also your walking boots, Beth. I'll take you on a couple of hikes while your Ma relaxes."

We drove for nearly two hours, all passengers in their correct places for about five minutes. Then the clambering began. A furry head appeared from the back. Cori had decided to join me in the rear seat. Giggling, I settled him beside me, which was far too much for the others to cope with. Crag, Ben, Snow and Tag started a canine assault. I ended up with a hairy panting heap on my lap. It was a hot, doggy journey.

Our route took us through woodlands to mountainous spectacular slate quarrying country and onto moorland. Robert told us more about the area.

"There are nearly eight hundred square miles of moorland here. Look to your right, and you'll see Snowdon's peak in the distance."

Ma, ever the arty one, was on a different tangent.

"Goodness, yes. And the farmland on the other side is beautiful. Those enchanting fields, they look rather like a patchwork quilt with the interlacing walls."

"They do. Enjoy them because you won't see many in a couple of minutes. What you will see is more of that heather you love."

I was more interested in the wildlife.

"What animals live up here, Robert?"

"You'll see mountain sheep, of course, but look closer, and you might spot several butterfly species. Perhaps even some black grouse."

"I'd love to see grouse."

"You'll be lucky if you have the mob with you!" he laughed, as Crag tried to join him in the driver's seat for the hundredth time.

"You're more likely to see a merlin, although they're also rare. They share the territory with peregrine falcons, hen harriers and kestrels, which prey on the smaller birds up there."

"I wish I'd brought binoculars!"

"Don't worry. I have some at the cottage. We can go fly-fishing too if you want."

"Cool, thank you. I've never tried that."

"There's a knack to it, but I'm sure you'll catch on quickly."

We drove along an unmarked ribbon road with distant mountains on one side, lakes like scattered mirrors in the heath reflecting the cornflower sky. Soon our landscape was a kaleidoscope of yellows, pinks, purples, and greens. Spiky grass, puffball heather and dark peaty patches; it was a savagely beautiful world.

"There she is!"

It was easy to tell what Robert was referring to as there wasn't a single other building to be seen. It was a tumbledown stone dwelling.

"Crawcwellt Bach, my cottage."

The dogs and I spilled out of the car. I laughed; those tubby little terriers with their tawny coats had the perfect camouflage for our surroundings. Hopelessly excited, they snuffled and yipped among the brown tussocks. They knew their home and were on a mission to reclaim personal territory. I turned, distracted by the impatient stamping coming from the trailer. Sam was keen to find out what the fuss was about. The cottage had an open lean-to barn and was surrounded by a higgledy-piggledy stone wall. It was an ideal paddock and shelter for him.

We let down the ramp. Snorting, taking in new sights and scents, Sam tossed his head with pleasure. I released him to explore the garden, chuckling as he paced up to the dogs, curious, wondering what was so intriguing. Being trodden on by one of his hooves wouldn't do them much good. Fortunately, he let them be and wandered off to examine the limits of his new domain.

I joined Ma and Robert inside. He was right, the two-bedroom cottage was basic. It didn't have heating or electricity, and it was sparsely furnished, but it had a big open fire, a roof and clattery windows. I loved it.

Ma started organising food supplies in the galley kitchen and sent me off to make the beds. I was halfway through when I heard her making unusual noises.

"Shoo, *shoo*, goodness, how naughty! Go on, *out!*"

I rushed downstairs to find Ma and Sam in the living room.

"Beth! Get your horse out of here *right now!*"

"Sorry, Ma, he's just interested in what's going on."

"I don't even know how he managed to squeeze through the door. Goodness gracious, *look* at that rug. Horseshoe imprints!"

I honestly didn't think the rug could be much more damaged than it already was, but decided not to mention the obvious. I returned Sam outside and went back to my job when I heard another gasp.

"Oh dear. I'm not at *all* sure about this."

"What's wrong now, Ma? Sam's not in again, is he?"

"No, it's the lavatory. I fear there's something very wrong here."

Robert appeared with an armful of wood and joined me to rescue Ma. I'll admit the water was pungent. And blue. Trying hard not to laugh at Ma's disapproving expression, he explained.

"Don't worry. It's a portable chemical toilet. We don't have much plumbing here, so I'll empty it regularly. I assure you, it's perfectly safe to use."

"I see."

Ma could be extremely starchy.

During the afternoon, Robert took us on a favourite stroll. I rode alongside with the dogs, who cast around, chasing enticing smells and unlucky butterflies. We reached two hillocks, which concealed a stunning scene. A secret lake. The peaty ground gave the waters a dark, fathomless appearance. I tethered Sam and ambled to the far side. From here, the calm surface reflected images of the two knolls, seamlessly symmetrical. Utterly exquisite. It reminded me of a favourite myth. Maybe *this* was the lake where Sir Bedwyr cast Excalibur.

That evening followed a pattern for the week. It was like camping. While Ma rustled up a meal on the tiny gas cooker, Robert started the generator, which had enough juice to power a couple of lightbulbs. But not for long. After eating, we snuggled in front of a roaring log fire with the dogs. Paraffin lamps and candles were lit, and we read, chatted and listened to Robert's battered old radio. It was a refreshing novelty.

We went to bed with hot water bottles. Despite being summertime, those moorland breezes whispering through the holey cottage walls made it decidedly chilly. Although not for long. Snuffles, pitter-patters, hot breath and scrambles. Cori had found me. That was cosy. I awoke the next morning covered in dogs and very hot.

Still half asleep, I ambled down to the kitchen with the dogs eager to check the garden. I opened the half stable kitchen door, and in popped Sam's head. It was fun having him so close. After breakfast, I saddled him up for our long-awaited trek.

"Don't worry, Ma. I'll be back in time for lunch."

"Be careful, Beth. The conditions can be treacherous."

The infinity of multi-coloured moorland begged to be galloped over. Although sorely tempted to let Sam have his head, I dutifully started picking our way, following sheep trods made by nimble mountain sheep walking in single file. If any animals knew what they were doing, it would be them.

One can plod only so far before a fresh horse gets fed up. And me. I eased Sam into a brisk trot. He pulled at the bit, keen to go faster. The turf felt firm, ideal. The trail had run out, but the way ahead looked identical, so I released him into a canter. Clear fresh air, endless brand new views, it was exhilarating.

Without warning, Sam skidded. Half-rearing, he came to a shuddering halt.

Unprepared for this gait change, I was thrown hard across his shoulder. As I grappled to stay on, Sam backed away, snorting. Astonished at how he had stopped so quickly, I patted his neck, trying to calm him down. I studied the ground ahead. There didn't seem to be a single thing wrong. I wondered whether he had been spooked by a snake, an adder, perhaps. Whatever it was, I couldn't see anything now. Assuming it was a freak incident, I urged him forward, but it was no good. Sam wouldn't budge.

Goading, grumping, sweet-talking. Nothing was working on Sam. He just stared with wild eyes. If only they could talk. The words were written all over his face.

"You idiot, Mum! Don't you realise what's going on here?"

It's a shame I didn't heed them.

In a fit of frustration, I decided to get off and lead him for a few paces until he regained his confidence. I looped the reins over his head and started walking. I reached the place where he had stopped. Clever animals, horses.

As I stepped forward, the ground immediately gave way. With a sickening *squelch*, my boot was swallowed. I lurched forward, disappearing up to my knees in a quagmire. Petrified of sinking, I thrashed around, still hanging onto Sam's reins for support. He backed away in alarm, dragging me as the malevolent muck sucked my legs with an iron invisible force. Panting with effort and fear, I eventually clambered out.

Shaking like a leaf, I looked at my filthy legs and back at the evil, brackish water oozing from the bog. The horror of what might have happened to Sam if he had plunged in at full stretch hit me. It was shocking.

I searched in vain for the way we had come, but there were no easily visible signs. Much of the moorland looks samey. Samier still if you're on the verge of tears. The lane was closer than trying to retrace our steps. At least the tarmac would be safe.

I didn't dare risk remounting Sam in case the same thing happened again. Instead, we gingerly walked side by side towards the road. Every time he stopped, I stopped, and we took a detour. Every time he flinched at something on one side, we changed direction. Within minutes, we had safely reached the hard surface. It felt like an eternity.

I hugged, stroked, and patted Sam, searching my pockets for an elusive Polo mint. Shaking my head, I looked at him with renewed respect. I have no idea how he knew that imminent danger lay in his path. It may have been a distinct smell or colour alteration I hadn't detected. Whatever it was, he knew we were in peril. Horses genuinely do possess a sixth sense.

Shaken, stinky, but not quite undaunted, I related our sorry tale when we got back. I could tell Ma was concerned. The practical reply was her standard reaction to dire situations.

"Never mind. At least you're both home safely. While I make tea, you groom and feed Sam, and then we'll have to get you cleaned up somehow. And do leave those ghastly boots outside. They reek!"

Robert's take on our misadventure was a little different.

"I'm afraid you came across blanket bog. It's ecologically important but bloody awful stuff and hard to see. Excellent horse. Well done, Sam."

Our next few days were pleasantly calm. Well, aside from the epic trek I took with Robert up a mountain. Forgetting to bring gloves, hat and arctic conditions jacket, I returned with frozen fingers and mild exposure. I was plonked in the bath with a brandy to warm up. And Robert? He was just wearing a jumper and jeans, and looked cosy the whole way there and back. His Special Forces career had obviously stood him in good stead.

Sam and I had gentle hacks over tracks and stony surfaces but no more intrepid rides across the moors. I wasn't going to risk that again. Robert's promise to teach me how to fly fish came at the end of the week.

It was a gorgeous day, so Ma packed a feast. She and Robert drove to the river with the dogs, and I followed on Sam. Ma started building lunch, chuntering tetchily at Sam, who decided that sandwiches were nicer than grass. I left them to it and went fish spotting.

The setting was spectacular. Water rushed over a stepped waterfall. Fresh, sparkling wavelets vaulted over rocks, cascading in frothy bubbles to the pristine river below. There were shallows and pools. It was in these depths where brown trout were skulking.

Robert produced a spindly rod and hooks,

which looked like a smaller version of the tackle we used for pollock and mackerel fishing.

"Today, we are dry fly-fishing, Beth. It means using an artificial fly which floats on the surface rather than sinks."

"That hopefully means I won't get my hook caught on any underwater obstructions."

"Quite. Now, the technique for casting is simple but can be tricky. Let me demonstrate."

Robert pulled a goodly length of line off his reel and fed it into the water through the tip of his rod. Standing square to the river, he rapidly pulled the rod up and backwards. He completed a looped, flicking manoeuvre which allowed the fly to settle delicately back on the water. Robert made it look easy.

"So, Beth, it's all about a few precise, fluid movements and releasing the energy into the line to propel it forward. I'll show you a couple more times, and then you can catch our supper."

"I'll try!"

I stood confidently and started unravelling the fishing line. Feeling like this was going to be easy, I gave Ma a cocky smile. It took me, ooh, about two minutes before I came unstuck.

The first innumerable tries saw me getting loops of fishing line trapped around boulders, tufts of grass, and Ben, who had padded over to join in.

And I hadn't even tried a cast. Robert stuck me in a different position with less foliage. I had another go.

Chuffed at getting the basics right, I tried my first cast. This time I fed the line out in a reasonably straight line. I yanked the rod up, which wrenched the line off the water, embedding the hook in my jacket. There was a sympathetic '*Ahem*' from the picnic rug.

"Never mind, Beth. I'm sure you'll get the hang of it soon."

"Yep, no problem. Just a tiny tweak needed."

The other difficulty I hadn't anticipated being that my wrist was about to drop off. I was rapidly developing a repetitive strain injury. Try as I might, I could not create the loopy shape behind me. Robert tried to help.

"Don't worry. I did say there was a knack to it. All you have to do is transfer the energy to propel the line forward at the top of the cast. Rather like serving in tennis."

Excellent analogy. Finally, this was an image I could wrap my brain around. Nodding enthusiastically, I fed out long line lengths, paused, and zipped my rod back energetically.

I ignored the shrieks behind me. Sam was obviously on another sandwich hunt. Gritting my teeth, I thrust my rod forward. Oddly enough, the rod started bending. I was about to give it a hearty yank when there was another screech.

"Napkin, Beth, you've hooked a *napkin!* Now please stop before you fasten that thing onto another dog."

It was a crushing rebuke for a wannabe expert fly fisherwoman. Mortified by my failure, I dutifully gathered Ma's punctured napkin and returned the unused rod to Robert. He gave me a reassuring smile.

"Never mind. You can have another go after lunch."

I couldn't. My wrist had stopped working.

Ma's banquet-style meal made up for my sporting disaster. After a short siesta, I took Sam for one last ride, leaving Ma and Robert to relax in the sun. We followed an old trail up above the waterfall. The views over the moor were breathtaking.

Heaving a contented sigh, my thoughts drifted to the next stages in my education. I reflected on what I might end up doing as a career. I had started determined to be a cowboy. I rejected this in favour of becoming a farmer, later scrapped when I realised that being a champion jockey was in my stars. Ma talked me out of that, which created the aspiration to nurse sick animals as a vet. But there was a problem.

With my sciences deficiencies, I couldn't pursue veterinary medicine. So what on earth would I end up doing? And where? The next four years of my life were already planned, and I would spend them in England. More education, yuck! But actually, it all sounded pretty exciting. There again, for the first time in my life, I would leave my beloved homeland.

I looked below to where Ma and Robert were sitting – relaxed, reading their books with five shaggy dots lounging beside them. I leaned forward and hugged Sam. Gosh, I would miss him. Still, I'd be home as usual for the holidays.

I thought about how lucky I was. Spoiled? Yes, though in an unconventional way. The beloved pets who had enriched my life taught me so much. I still badly missed my precious Hercules, Monty and Paddington and knew that I could never live without animals.

I considered the blessed irony of growing up in such remarkable homes, none of which we owned. And school. Boarding wasn't for me, though I had made many fantastic friends. I acknowledged our parents' sacrifices to ensure we had the best education they could afford. But above all else, there was one privilege that money could not buy.

Wherever I ended up in the future, I knew Wales would always be in my heart. This extraordinarily beautiful country filled with legend and song. That feeling of *hwyl* beat within me as strongly as ever. As Sir Anthony Hopkins once said, 'You can take the boy out of Wales, but you cannot take Wales out of the boy.' Well, the same applies to this girl too.

The Wonder of Welsh Words

Cartref
Simple, yet full of meaning. Say 'carr-trrev' and you have the word '**home**'.

Traditional Welsh Recipes

In *Fat Dogs and Welsh Estates*, I talk about the delicious meals we were given as children. Generally home-grown or locally sourced, Ma's ingredients were gathered from the kitchen garden, land and sea. We ate like royalty, although that perhaps doesn't describe the origins of Welsh cuisine accurately. It wasn't until later that I learned more about the essence of traditional Welsh cooking.

Welsh recipes passed down the generations among country folk were intended to sustain quarrymen, coalmen, farm labourers and their families. Mindful of our climate and the long working hours people endured, meals were simple and hearty, though not lacking in variety or flavour.

As for my favourites? It's impossible to say. Instead, I offer you a selection of sweets and savouries I loved as a child, together with some Welsh culinary heroes. I have included links generously shared by contributors, including *Halen Môn* and *Just a Pinch*, for each recipe on my website, but don't stop there. Many provide details on several other dishes and snippets about our gastronomic history, so they're worth exploring.

1. Mentioned in chapter 12, this Welsh staple sticks to your tummy, leaving a comfy feeling of fullness. It's **Bara Brith,** and here is a super version contributed by *The Daring Gourmet.* Visit my website for the recipe. bethhaslam.com/fat-dogs-welsh-recipes/

2. Contrary to misguided belief, there are no bunnies in this versatile savoury snack. It was a regular addition to high teas and our dining table after school. It's simple and seriously yummy. Try the **Welsh Rarebit** recipe shared by *Visit Wales.*

Visit my website for the recipe.
bethhaslam.com/fat-dogs-welsh-recipes/

3. A component of the Welsh Rarebit dish I share is called **Laverbread**. And, no, it has nothing to do with bread. Here's a recipe for this tangy seaside delicacy from *Welsh Food & Drink*. And as a tribute to this very Welsh foodstuff, the *Pembrokeshire Beach Company* has registered a **National Laverbread Day**.
Visit my website for the recipe and Laverbread Day celebration information. bethhaslam.com/fat-dogs-welsh-recipes/

4. Like all countries, different Welsh regions have prized gastronomic specialities. If you love sausage, why not try the **Glamorgan** variety? As you'll see, they're a hit with vegetarians. The team at *Great British Chefs* share a recipe from the chef, writer and MasterChef presenter *John Torode*.
Visit my website for the recipe.
bethhaslam.com/fat-dogs-welsh-recipes/

5. In chapter three, I mention Ma's 'legendary roasts', and they were just that. As you might expect, lamb joints often starred at our table. There's something inexplicably special about this Welsh-produced meat. Is it due to being reared in rain-cleansed fresh air or

the succulent grass that contributes to their unique flavour? It's hard to say. The flocks raised on the Gower and Harlech salt marshes certainly receive rave reviews. Here is a recipe for **Roast Lamb** from *Dairy Diary* you might want to try.
Visit my website for the recipe.
bethhaslam.com/fat-dogs-welsh-recipes/

6. *Cawl*, the Welsh word for soup or broth, is another sustaining family regular. In North Wales, we call it **Lobscaws**. Here's a recipe to try from chef *Ceri Jones*. Ma always added pearl barley to hers, which I had difficulty with as a child. That stuff can be slippery to fish out of the bowl.
Visit my website for the recipe.
bethhaslam.com/fat-dogs-welsh-recipes/

7. Ma let Di and I loose in the kitchen, creating this flour-based favourite. I can't admit to our efforts being ever so successful, but correctly cooked, it's hard to beat a **Welsh Cake**. Try this version from chef *Ceri Jones*.
Visit my website for the recipe.
bethhaslam.com/fat-dogs-welsh-recipes/

8. In chapter four, I recount the tale of a fishing trip on the Menai Strait. In addition to our regular

catches, we were occasionally treated to unbelievably sweet locally-sourced lobster. Ma prepared it several different ways, but never in a roll. This recipe for **Lobster Roll with Welsh Seaweed Black Butter** from the team at *Pembrokeshire Beach Food* makes my mouth water. Take note. You'll need to come to Wales if you want the best seafood!
Visit my website for the recipe.
bethhaslam.com/fat-dogs-welsh-recipes/

9. I first introduce you to Anglesey in chapter three, the island that plays a central part in my story. It boasts many taste bud-tantalising dishes, **Anglesey Eggs** being one. Here is chef and food writer *Elaine Lemm's* version.
Visit my website for the recipe.
bethhaslam.com/fat-dogs-welsh-recipes/

10. In chapter four, I describe the butcher's shop we frequented in the village. As a child, the sawdust-covered floor seemed weird, and those humungous carcasses hanging off hooks gave me the creeps. Stranger still were Ma's buying habits, including the bag of bones she regularly purchased. Mind you, the meal she produced later was sensational. Here's a recipe for **Welsh Oxtail**

Stew from *Hybu Cig Cymru* – Ma always added tomatoes to hers.
Visit my website for the recipe.
bethhaslam.com/fat-dogs-welsh-recipes/

11. No introduction to Welsh cuisine would be complete without a mention of leeks. Actually, you'll find they have already sneaked into a couple of the dishes above. Before I offer a recipe, let me share the significance of this venerable legume. Wales being Wales, its history is rooted in myths.
https://www.historic-uk.com/HistoryUK/HistoryofWales/The-Leek-National-emblem-of-the-Welsh/
And here is my tribute to the humble legume.
Welsh Leek Soup presented by chef *Sylvie* at *Roaming Taste* is scrummy.
Visit my website for the recipe.
bethhaslam.com/fat-dogs-welsh-recipes/

12. If there is a foodstuff almost universally loved, it is cheese, and it's no different in Wales. One of our famed cheeses is the classic **Caerffili**, and the one produced by the renowned *Caws Cenarth* team is extra special. Feast your eyes on their complete range – it's mouthwatering!
Visit my website for the recipe.
bethhaslam.com/fat-dogs-welsh-recipes/

13. This meaty dish is named after Merthyr Tydfil, a town in South Wales with a history steeped in the iron and steel industry. Called **Merthyr Pie**, this version is offered by the acclaimed Welsh chef Stephen Terry. Featured by *delicious. magazine*, it sounds delectable.
Visit my website for the recipe.
bethhaslam.com/fat-dogs-welsh-recipes/

14. If you thought it was the Cornish who cornered the market on the pasty, think again. Here's a foodstuff that kept colliers going down the mines. It's called **Welsh Oggie**, and *Elaine Lemm*, chef and food writer, shares her 'Giant' version.
Visit my website for the recipe.
bethhaslam.com/fat-dogs-welsh-recipes/

15. If you love cheese, you're in for a treat. Try your hand at this **Leek and Caerphilly Cheese Tart** recipe from *Village Dairy*. This recipe, which pays homage to two Welsh favourites, is easy to make and delicious.
Visit my website for the recipe.
bethhaslam.com/fat-dogs-welsh-recipes/

With the kind help of my contributors, I hope I've inspired you to try some mouth-watering Welsh dishes. And if you have a Welsh recipe you're dying to share, I'd love to hear from you. Feel free to get in touch by using this link: bethhaslam.com/fat-dogs-welsh-recipes/

A Request

If you enjoyed *Fat Dogs and Welsh Estates*
I would be extremely grateful if you could consider leaving an Amazon review.

Thank you very much!

References

Throughout, I have tried to give you a flavour of Wales, its people and their passions. Each chapter begins with an idiom or quote, and several refer to significant occurrences or famous pieces of music that have shaped my homeland. Despite this, I know I have barely scratched the surface.
In this section, I offer you a set of notes to dip into. I hope you enjoy the further reading as much as I did.

Chapter 1
'To be born Welsh is to be born privileged. Not with a silver spoon in your mouth, but with music in your blood and poetry in your soul.'
Brian Harris – educator and poet.
This quote is taken from his poem '*In Passing*': https://waleslandofmyfathers.tumblr.com/post/55125867739/welsh-poetry-in-passing-by-brian-harris

Chapter 2
'The Mabinogion and specifically the Four Branches, they have had quite an impact on Welsh literature and culture just as Shakespeare and Chaucer have on English literature.'

Sioned Davies – Professor emeritus at Cardiff University.

This quote from Professor Davies, an acclaimed expert on the Mabinogion, was made during an interview about the book. Here is the full context:

https://www.walesonline.co.uk/whats-on/arts-culture-news/story-mabinogion-impact-welsh-literature-18040842

And as you can tell from this Cardiff University piece, Professor Davies is the go-to person on Welsh myths:

https://www.cardiff.ac.uk/research/impact-and-innovation/research-impact/past-case-studies/transforming-the-mabinogion

Chapter 3
'A Man without prudence is a ship without an anchor.'

Welsh Proverb – author unknown.

Chapter 4
'Tell a gelding, ask a mare and discuss with a stallion. Pray if it is a pony.'
Unknown.
Kitty, our beloved, naughty Shetland pony, was a classic example. Here's a link to tell you more about this characterful breed:
https://www.globetrotting.com.au/horse-breed-shetland-pony/

Chapter 5
*'…As I breathe the mountain air,
And gaze with deepest awe upon
This land beyond compare.'*
Andrew Blakemore – poet.
The quote is taken from Andrew Blakemore's poem, *Snowdonia*. This evocative Youtube video includes a narration of the complete poem against the backdrop of Snowdonia. There are glimpses of the quarries I talk about and, I believe, Lake Ogwen.
https://www.youtube.com/watch?v=CoKSKTbYsSg
Snowdonia National Park has now been renamed using its Welsh name, Eryri National Park. This link will tell you more about this wild, extraordinarily beautiful area:
https://snowdonia.gov.wales/
Of the myths Pa told, we loved the ones associated

with the Lake Ogwen area. These links will tell you more:
https://www.mountain-walks.co.uk/devils-kitchen-snowdonia/
https://www.cicerone.co.uk/walking-with-heroes-myths-and-legends-along-the-snowdonia-way
And if you enjoy Welsh mythology, you might like to dip into this work, which is bursting with folklore:
https://dev.gutenberg.org/files/20096/20096-h/20096-h.htm

Chapter 6
Bodnant Garden.
'I have no doubt at all that this is the richest garden I have ever seen.'
Sir Harold George Nicolson – a British diplomat, author, diarist and politician.
This link gives you an idea of why Sir Harold was so taken by Bodnant:
https://www.nationaltrust.org.uk/bodnant-garden

Chapter 7
'Wales has more than its fair share of ghostly goings-on.'
Amy Pay – freelance journalist and content creator living in Cardiff.

Chapter 8
Beaumaris *'The greatest castle never built.'*
Anon.
This was the scene of my infamous moat dunking accident. Find out more about the history of this extraordinary fortification here:
https://cadw.gov.wales/visit/places-to-visit/beaumaris-castle

Chapter 9
'Cats are the best people'
Jeni Rizio – American musician with a passion for the Welsh language.

Chapter 10
'In riding a horse, we borrow freedom.'
Helen Thomson – author.

Chapter 11
'The slate quarries – the most Welsh of Welsh industries.'
Dr David Gwyn – slate industry expert.
This link will tell you more about the Welsh quarrying heritage:
https://www.bbc.com/news/uk-wales-57973511
During our visit, Pa tells the story of a gentleman involved in a dreadful accident at the quarry. The account is taken from this link:

http://www.penmorfa.com/Slate/Hospital%20accident.jpg

The Investiture was a profoundly significant event at the time. Here is some footage from the ceremony:

https://www.townandcountrymag.com/society/tradition/a26576659/prince-charles-prince-wales-investiture-1969-true-story/

I tried to include as many true accounts as possible in this chapter. Here is the source of one quote I used:

https://www.flickr.com/photos/pentlandpirate/22740214810

Chapter 12
'Three things give us hardy strength: sleeping on hairy mattresses, breathing cold air, and eating dry food.'
Welsh Proverb – author unknown.

Chapter 13
'Teg yw edrych tuag adref.' **('It is good to look homewards.')**
Old Welsh Saying – author unknown.

Chapter 14
'Tyfid maban, ni thyf ei gadachan.' ('The child will grow, his clothes will not.')
Welsh Saying – author unknown.
This chapter tells you about my chat with a 'kind gentleman'. His name was Jimmy Chipperfield, and this is a synopsis of his life:
https://www.bigredbook.info/james_chipperfield.html

Chapter 15
'Llanddwyn beach. Longer Than Childhood Summers.'
William Gerwyn – author.

A fan of Llanddwyn like our family and friends, here is William Gerwyn's piece, which eloquently describes this gorgeous beach:
https://www.anglesey-hidden-gem.com/Llanddwyn-Beach.html

Chapter 16
'Better educated than wealthy.'
Welsh Proverb – author unknown.

Chapter 17
'In every pardon there is love.'
Welsh Proverb – origin unknown.

Chapter 18
'To be loved by a horse, or by any animal, should fill us with awe – for we have not deserved it.'
Marion C. Garretty – author.

Chapter 19
'Ireland has one of the world's heaviest rainfalls. If you see an Irishman with a tan, it's rust.'
Dave Allen – Irish comedian. (Ma's favourite comedian.)
That famed Irish charm affected us all, and we had a wonderful holiday in Ireland. Here's a link for you to learn more about the splendid Bunratty Castle:
https://www.bunrattycastle.ie/bunratty-castle/

Chapter 20
'A jump jockey has to throw his heart over the fence - and then go over and catch it.'
Dick Francis – champion jockey and author.
Adding to my existing knowledge of the General Stud Book was fascinating. Here's some more information about its history:
https://www.weatherbys.co.uk/general-stud-book/bloodstock-studbook

Chapter 21
'…the Swellies…once you are committed there is often no turning back.'
Beaumaris Lifeboatman.
The Swellies, it needs to be treated with respect. These two links help to explain why:
https://www.caernarfonharbour.org.uk/passage-through-the-swellies/
https://wikishire.co.uk/wiki/Menai_Strait

Chapter 22
White Knight says to Alice,
'I heard him then, for I had just completed my design.
To keep the Menai Bridge from rust.
By boiling it in wine.'
Lewis Carroll – author.
Here is Lewis Carroll's complete poem:
https://www.poemhunter.com/poem/alice-and-the-white-knight/
And this is the story behind the creation of Menai Bridge:
https://menaibridges.co.uk/history/menai-suspension-bridge/

Chapter 23
'Do not be afraid of taking a big step – you cannot cross a chasm in two steps.'
David Lloyd George – Welsh politician.
Newbury racecourse, we had many happy outings here:
https://newburyracecourse.co.uk/

Chapter 24
'To live in Wales is to be conscious At dusk of the spilled blood That went to the making of the wild sky.'
R. S. Thomas – Welsh poet.
This quote is an extract from his sombre poem *A Welsh Landscape*. Here is the full version:
https://www.youtube.com/watch?v=Jb8mK3Ccslo
Our visit to Harlech had a profound impact on my friends and me. Here is a link about the extraordinary castle:
https://cadw.gov.wales/visit/places-to-visit/harlech-castle
I also talk about the famous battle song *Men of Harlech*. The lyrics I used came from the website Castles of Wales:
http://www.castlewales.com/menhar.html
Here's a version of the song that gave me goosebumps:

https://www.youtube.com/watch?v=DRtnWVvDX6k

Chapter 25
'Welsh is of the soil, this island, the senior language of the men of Britain; and Welsh is beautiful.'

J. R. R. Tolkien – author.

At the end of each chapter, I share a Welsh word with guidance on pronunciation. Still, wrapping your tongue around some of those letters is awfully difficult. This light-hearted guide might be of some help:

https://cuhwc.org.uk/book/export/html/199

The first song I talk about in this chapter mentions that special word, *Hiraeth*. Here is *We'll Keep a Welcome in the Hillsides*, prefaced by scenes featuring the Welsh rugby team:

https://www.youtube.com/watch?v=Y6TXz_shw_M

And as for those deep emotions felt by the Welsh, well, just listen to these two anthems. The first is *Yma O Hyd* (We're Still Here). The ballad, released in 1983 by Dafydd Iwan, a much-loved Welsh folk singer, has been adopted by the Welsh National football team. You'll perhaps understand why:

https://www.youtube.com/watch?v=LiAbB-6KWSM

For rugby fixtures, it is the National Anthem sung at a Welsh international match. It's stirring stuff: https://www.youtube.com/watch?v=ABo2hmj__Mw

I finish by telling you a story about my visit to Llangollen, the little town with a world famous festival: https://international-eisteddfod.co.uk/

Chapter 26
'I grew up among heroes who went down the pit, who played rugby, told stories, sang songs of war.'
Richard Burton – Welsh actor.

Chapter 27
'Better my own cottage than the palace of another.'
Welsh Proverb – origin unknown.

Chapter 28
'Our horses know our secrets….we braid our tears into their manes & whisper our dreams into their ears.'
Anonymous.

In this chapter, Pa tells a story from the *Black Book of Carmarthen*, a significant text in Welsh literature. This link tells you more:

https://www.historyofinformation.com/detail.php?id=4342

During our voyage, we encountered a fog bank. This Youtube video gives you an idea of how eerie the conditions were:
https://www.youtube.com/watch?v=1GaDFuYwVvk

Chapter 29
'O, there is lovely to feel a book, a good book, firm in the hand, for its fatness holds rich promise, and you are hot inside to think of good hours to come.'
Richard Llewellyn – Welsh novelist and playwright. Di tells me the spinechilling story about Angelystor during a woodland walk. Here is some more information about the extraordinary yew tree:
https://thehazeltree.co.uk/2014/10/26/the-darkness-of-the-yew/

Chapter 30
'The best candle is understanding.'
Welsh Proverb – origin unknown.

Chapter 31
'I wanted freedom, open air and adventure. I found it on the sea.'
Alain Gerbault – French Sailor.

Here, I recount our eventful voyage to France. Pa tells us about the Lizard lighthouse, a famous landmark in England. This link gives you some background. Scroll down to see our route across the Channel:
https://www.trinityhouse.co.uk/lighthouse-visitor-centres/lizard-lighthouse-visitor-centre
As we approach Saint-Malo, Pa tells me a legend about Saint Maclovius. These two links will give you more background about his life and miraculous work:
https://biography.wales/article/s-MALO-SAN-0550
https://www.nationalchurchestrust.org/church/st-mechell-llanfechell
Our destination was Saint-Malo, a place which began my love affair with France. Follow this link, and see if you fall in love too:
https://www.brittanytourism.com/destinations/the-10-destinations/cap-frehel-saint-malo-mont-saint-michel-bay/saint-malo/

Chapter 32
'Wales is a land of history and mystery and to find yourself standing alone in a haunted house, castle, or even mountainside on a windswept winter's day is to feel centuries removed from the pressures of the modern age.'
Richard Jones – Author.

Chapter 33

'First God made England, Ireland, and Scotland. That's when he corrected his mistakes and made Wales.'

Katharine Hepburn – American actress.

I leave you with a song close to my heart that encapsulates the best of Welsh male voice choirs: https://www.youtube.com/watch?v=eAPmmZmZAJg

Acknowledgements

Writing a book about my childhood was challenging. Why? Because the events took place such a long time ago. Recalling scenes, situations and emotions were fun, but I needed help with some details. I researched extensively and sought advice from several people in Wales whose generosity in offering their time and support has been extraordinary.

Of particular note, my heartfelt thanks go to Ray for her help and hugs to other close school friends I haven't seen for years, though I hope to soon. For my nautical adventures, I want to thank Tim Knowles, Secretary of the Royal Anglesey Yacht Club, for his advice on the sailing elements in the book. Also, thanks to Mr Ray Beer, who kindly gave me a copy of his excellent publication on the History of the Menai Strait Regatta.

For the expert advice I received on Harlech Castle,

I am indebted to Kerry Smith, Head Custodian of the castle. Also, Siân Roberts, Blue Badge Tourist Guide for Wales, whose help on historical detail, Welsh culture and language has been invaluable. And I'm deeply grateful to Professor Sioned Davies, Professor emeritus at Cardiff University, for her encouragement and support.

In response to popular request, I included an introduction to Welsh Recipes. I am deeply grateful to all those contributors whose names I mention in the Recipes section and on my website Welsh Recipes page. Their support and generosity in sharing fabulous dishes has been extraordinary. And I am deeply grateful to Elle Draper, my website designer, for sticking with me and creating such a wonderful online home for my Fat Dogs, which now includes Welsh food. Elle is patient, professional and an absolute star.

Special thanks must go to my American friend, Liz Moore Kraus, who helped with our quirkily different interpretations of the English language on either side of the pond. Other stars included David Springett for kindly assisting me with sailing technicalities, Alison Moore and Gill Gregory for being fantastic sounding boards and brilliant with ideas. Thanks also to my amazing beta readers, Pat Ellis, Julie Haigh, Sandy Mckenna, Lisa Rose Wright and Alyson Sheldrake, who generously gave their time to scrutinise the book before publication. Their advice and comments have been invaluable.

As always, I'm hugely grateful to Maggie Raynor (www.equestrianprints.co.uk), my illustrator, who has been with me for each episode in the series. Her work is superb; my Fat Dogs wouldn't be the same without her artistry, and she has found a new passion in this prequel. Drawing dragons!

And as for my Facebook friends, what gems they are. Every time I've appealed to them with a problem word or tricky meaning, they've helped out. They're full of ideas, too. Their suggestions resulted in my sharing a map, recipe links and research information. I'm immensely grateful for their support and input.

As for my mentor and editor, I couldn't be luckier. Despite being an incredibly successful New York Times bestselling author, busy with her work, Victoria Twead at Ant Press (www.antpress.org) has given me all the help, advice and time I needed to prepare this episode. She's a close friend who laughs, loves life and animals as much as me, and I am forever indebted to her.

I must also include my favourite Facebook group: We Love Memoirs. It's a place I go to chat about books and other stuff with like-minded folks, many of who have become lifelong friends. I recommend membership in WLM to anyone (reader or author) who loves reading and writing memoirs as much as I do.
https://www.facebook.com/groups/welovememoirs/

Finally, I want to thank my sis, Di, for allowing me to share our story. I wouldn't be without her for the world!

I sincerely thank you for reading this book. I hope you enjoyed it, and if so, do join me for my Fat Dogs adventures in France with my husband, Jack, and our menagerie of animals.

About the Author

Beth Haslam was brought up on a country estate in Wales. Deep in the countryside, her childhood was spent either on horseback, helping the gamekeepers raise pheasants, or out sailing. A serious car crash in 1991 ended Beth's full time career in Personnel management, so she set up her own Human Resources consultancy business.

As semi-retirement beckoned, Beth and her husband, Jack, decided to buy a second home in France. This has become a life-changing event where computers and mobile phones have swapped places with understanding the foibles of the French, and tackling the language. Beth is now occupied as never before. Raising and saving animals, writing, and embracing everything rural France has to offer; she's loving it!

Contacts and Links

Website: bethhaslam.com
Books - Blog - Newsletter - Photos

Email: fatdogsfrance@gmail.com

Chat with me and other memoir authors and readers in our Facebook group,

WE LOVE MEMOIRS:
https://www.facebook.com/groups/welovememoirs/

facebook.com/bethhaslam

twitter.com/fatdogsfrance

instagram.com/fatdogsandfrenchestates

Ant Press Books

AWESOME AUTHORS ~ AWESOME BOOKS

If you enjoyed this book, you may also enjoy these Ant Press titles:

MEMOIRS

Fat Dogs and French Estates - Part I by Beth Haslam

Fat Dogs and French Estates - Part II by Beth Haslam

Fat Dogs and French Estates - Part III by Beth Haslam

Fat Dogs and French Estates - Part IV by Beth Haslam

Fat Dogs and French Estates - Part V by Beth Haslam

Fat Dogs and French Estates - Boxset, Parts 1-3 by Beth Haslam

Dear Fran, Love Dulcie: Life and Death in the Hills and Hollows of Bygone Australia collated by Victoria Twead

Chickens, Mules and Two Old Fools by Victoria Twead (Wall Street Journal Top 10 bestseller)
Two Old Fools ~ Olé! by Victoria Twead
Two Old Fools on a Camel by Victoria Twead (thrice New York Times bestseller)
Two Old Fools in Spain Again by Victoria Twead
Two Old Fools in Turmoil by Victoria Twead
Two Old Fools Down Under by Victoria Twead
One Young Fool in Dorset (Prequel) by Victoria Twead
One Young Fool in South Africa (Prequel) by Joe and Victoria Twead
Two Old Fools Boxset, Books 1-3 by Victoria Twead

Butting Heads in Spain: Lady Goatherder 1 by Diane Elliott

From Moulin Rouge to Gaudi's City by EJ Bauer
From Gaudi's City to Granada's Red Palace by EJ Bauer

Heartprints of Africa: A Family's Story of Faith,

Love, Adventure, and Turmoil by Cinda Adams Brooks

How not to be a Soldier: My Antics in the British Army by Lorna McCann

Moment of Surrender: My Journey Through Prescription Drug Addiction to Hope and Renewal by Pj Laube

One of its Legs are Both the Same by Mike Cavanagh

A Pocket Full of Days, Part 1 by Mike Cavanagh

A Pocket Full of Days, Part 2 by Mike Cavanagh

Horizon Fever 1: Explorer A E Filby's own account of his extraordinary expedition through Africa, 1931-1935 by A E Filby

Horizon Fever 2: Explorer AE Filby's own account of his extraordinary Australasian Adventures, 1921-1931 by A E Filby

Completely Cats - Stories with Cattitude by Beth Haslam and Zoe Marr

Fresh Eggs and Dog Beds: Living the Dream in Rural Ireland by Nick Albert

Fresh Eggs and Dog Beds 2: Still Living the Dream in Rural Ireland by Nick Albert

Fresh Eggs and Dog Beds 3: More Living the

Dream in Rural Ireland by Nick Albert
Fresh Eggs and Dog Beds 4: More Living the Dream in Rural Ireland by Nick Albert

Don't Do It Like This: How NOT to move to Spain by Joe Cawley, Victoria Twead and Alan Parks

Longing for Africa: Journeys Inspired by the Life of Jane Goodall. Part One: Ethiopia by Annie Schrank
Longing for Africa: Journeys Inspired by the Life of Jane Goodall. Part Two: Kenya by Annie Schrank

A Kiss Behind the Castanets: My Love Affair with Spain by Jean Roberts
Life Beyond the Castanets: My Love Affair with Spain by Jean Roberts

The Sunny Side of the Alps: From Scotland to Slovenia on a Shoestring by Roy Clark

FICTION

A is for Abigail by Victoria Twead (Sixpenny Cross 1)
B is for Bella by Victoria Twead (Sixpenny Cross 2)

C is for the Captain by Victoria Twead (Sixpenny Cross 3)
D is for Dexter by Victoria Twead
The Sixpenny Cross Collection, Vols 1-3 by Victoria Twead

NON FICTION

How to Write a Bestselling Memoir by Victoria Twead
Two Old Fools in the Kitchen, Part 1 by Victoria Twead

LARGE PRINT BOOKS

Chickens, Mules and Two Old Fools by Victoria Twead (Wall Street Journal Top 10 bestseller)
Two Old Fools - Olé! by Victoria Twead
Two Old Fools on a Camel by Victoria Twead (thrice New York Times bestseller)
Two Old Fools in Spain Again by Victoria Twead
Two Old Fools in Turmoil by Victoria Twead
Two Old Fools Down Under by Victoria Twead
One Young Fool in Dorset (The Prequel) by Victoria Twead
One Young Fool in South Africa (The Prequel) by Joe and Victoria Twead

Fat Dogs and French Estates - Part I by Beth Haslam

Fat Dogs and French Estates - Part II by Beth Haslam

Fat Dogs and French Estates - Part III by Beth Haslam

Fat Dogs and French Estates - Part IV by Beth Haslam

Fat Dogs and French Estates - Part V by Beth Haslam

Fat Dogs and Welsh Estates - Series Prequel by Beth Haslam

A Kiss Behind the Castanets: My Love Affair with Spain by Jean Roberts

Horizon Fever 1: Explorer A E Filby's own account of his extraordinary expedition through Africa, 1931-1935 by A E Filby

Horizon Fever 2: Explorer AE Filby's own account of his extraordinary Australasian Adventures, 1921-1931 by A E Filby

A is for Abigail by Victoria Twead (Sixpenny Cross 1)

B is for Bella by Victoria Twead (Sixpenny Cross 2)

C is for the Captain by Victoria Twead (Sixpenny Cross 3)

How to Write a Bestselling Memoir by Victoria Twead

Publish with Ant Press

AWESOME AUTHORS - AWESOME BOOKS

This book was formatted, produced and published by Ant Press.

Can we help you publish your book?

Website: www.antpress.org
Email: admin@antpress.com

Facebook: www.facebook.com/AntPress

Instagram:
www.instagram.com/publishwithantpress
Twitter: www.twitter.com/Ant_Press

We publish beautiful, bestselling books.

www.ingramcontent.com/pod-product-compliance
Lightning Source LLC
Chambersburg PA
CBHW070454120526
44590CB00013B/645